70407

Dagg, Anne
Giraffe: its biology,
behavior, and ecology

DATE DUE			
~~MAY 5 1982~~			
~~AUG 1 6 1983~~			
~~MAR 2 6 1984~~			
JUN 1 6 1987			
MAY 1 4 1991			

The Giraffe

ITS BIOLOGY, BEHAVIOR, AND ECOLOGY

The Giraffe
ITS BIOLOGY, BEHAVIOR, AND ECOLOGY

Anne Innis Dagg
J. Bristol Foster

VNR VAN NOSTRAND REINHOLD COMPANY
NEW YORK   CINCINNATI   ATLANTA   DALLAS   SAN FRANCISCO

Van Nostrand Reinhold Company Regional Offices:
New York   Cincinnati   Atlanta   Dallas   San Francisco

Van Nostrand Reinhold Company International Offices:
London   Toronto   Melbourne

Manufactured in the United States of America

Published by Van Nostrand Reinhold Company
450 West 33rd Street, New York, N.Y. 10001

Published simultaneously in Canada by Van Nostrand Reinhold Ltd.

15 14 13 12 11 10 9 8 7 6 5 4 3 2 1

Library of Congress Cataloging in Publication Data

Dagg, Anne Innis.
   The giraffe : its biology, behavior, and ecology.

   Bibliography: p.
   Includes index.
   1. Giraffes.   I. Foster, J. Bristol, joint author.
II. Title.   [DNLM: 1. Artiodactyla.   2. Behavior,
Animal.   QL737.U56 D125g]
√ QL737.U56D3   599'.7357   75-33181
   ISBN 0-442-22431-1

THE GIRAFFE

Some writers have discovered ugliness and a want of grace in the giraffe, but I consider that he is one of the most strikingly beautiful animals in the Creation; and when a herd is seen scattered through a grove of the picturesque parasol-topped acacias which adorn their native plain, and on whose uppermost shoots they are enabled to browse through the colossal height with which nature has so admirably endowed them, he must indeed be slow of conception who fails to discover both grace and dignity in all their movements.

GORDON CUMMING, 1850

Preface

Because of its unique size and shape, the giraffe has stirred men down through the ages. In Europe giraffe were first glimpsed in Roman times and later when they were imported as curios to enhance triumphal occasions or private menageries. In the past two centuries foreigners have invaded the realm of the giraffe itself, often to shoot them for trophies or hides, or more recently to admire them. The giraffe as a species has been relatively unaffected by such contacts with human beings, but it has been drastically undermined by man's "development" of Africa; with an increase in human population and in agricultural production, most of the wild lands where giraffe lived have been tamed. This book brings together information that has been written about the giraffe because of man's interest in it. The authors draw upon their own research of many years in the wild, in museums, and in zoos throughout the world, as well as that of other workers.

Our treatment of the giraffe has been divided into two broad subject areas—ecology and behavior. The first section interprets ecology in its broadest sense, discussing first the giraffe's relationships with man and delineating how the once vast range of this species has recently been fragmented and restricted largely by man's activities in Africa (Chapters 1 and 2). Soon giraffe will probably be confined to national parks and nature reserves. More specifically we discuss the place of the giraffe in its environment, including both the ways in which giraffe have adapted to their habitat and to other species which live in it, and the ways in which they have recently changed because of the encroachment of man and man-made structures (Chapter 3). When early giraffids moved south into Africa from Asia many millions of years ago, they spread over much of the continent, various populations becoming isolated and evolving into new forms (Chapters 4 and 5). Today we have the fossil evidence of many extinct giraffids and two living species, the giraffe and the okapi. Isolated groups of these giraffe have evolved into nine subspecies. A discussion of the distinctive features of the giraffe that distinguish it from every other ungulate, and why these features probably evolved, concludes this part of the book (Chapter 6).

The part of the book devoted to the behavior of the giraffe can be more closely integrated than that on the ecology. We begin with the activities of individuals, first in their natural environment and then in their locomotion and movements (Chapters 7 and 8). It continues by studying the behavior of groups of giraffe—how they interact in the wild and how this interaction affects their reproduction and population structure (Chapters 9 and 10). It concludes with a glimpse of captive giraffe and how they behave towards each other in zoos (Chapter 11).

The text of this book ends with four appendixes which contain reference material not gathered together elsewhere in the literature. The races of giraffe (Appendix A) will be of use to zoo curators and to taxonomists. The form and function of the giraffe (Appendixes B, C, and D) will be valuable to anatomists and physiologists who are studying giraffe or who wish to compare data on other animals with data on this species.

ANNE INNIS DAGG
J. BRISTOL FOSTER

Introduction

The authors have spent a total of four years observing wild giraffe in Africa and have written, in all, twenty scientific papers on various aspects of this animal. Although this book deals primarily with the behavior and ecology of the giraffe, the authors have also searched both *Biological Abstracts* and *Zoological Records* for all references to this species. These references are included in the bibliography to give a comprehensive survey of what scientific research has been done.

Anne Innis Dagg studied giraffe behavior and ecology during 1956–57 on Fleur de Lys farm, Klaserie, in the eastern Transvaal of South Africa (Innis, 1958). This ranch was 50 km west of the Kruger National Park. It had an area of about 80 sq km which was divided into 11 camps, each of which was supplied by water either from a dam, a trough, or the Klaserie River. About 1500 head of cattle were run on the ranch during the research, but there was no indication that these animals, or small herds of sable, kudu, wildebeest, tsessebe, and zebra, interfered with the giraffe. The average rainfall was about 65 cm per year, and the vegetation was broadly the "large-leaved deciduous bush" type of Codd (1951). At Fleur de Lys the area was largely bush veld, but some parkland, thorn bush, and grassland areas were also present.

In addition to this field work in South Africa, Dagg spent eight months during 1967–68 studying heredity and behavior in the herd of 18 giraffe at the Taronga Zoo in Sydney, Australia (Dagg, 1968, 1970a, 1970b; Dagg and Taub, 1971).

Bristol Foster worked from 1965 to 1968 in the Nairobi National Park, an area of 122 sq km on the south side of Nairobi city and open to the north end of the Athi-Kapiti Plains. The park has a large permanent water supply as a result of man-made dams and is consequently a concentration area for the game of the plains in the dry season. A forest (1092 ha) broken by patches of grass and bush lies at the western end of the park, while most of the rest of the area consists of plains divided into either short grass on reddish brown soil, or whistling thorns on black cotton soil (Foster and Coe, 1968). The plains are dominated by acacia shrubs and are occasionally traversed by narrow strips of riverine forest. Larger trees are scattered on the better-drained open sites. Foster's work was based particularly on the data that could be obtained when each individual in a population was recognizable—individual movements, herd structure, maternal behavior, birth rates, growth rates, death rates.

We have referred in the text to the works of the following five zoologists who have also studied the giraffe in the wild. John Wyatt observed giraffe in the Nairobi National Park, especially in the plains area. His master's thesis (Wyatt, 1969) concentrated on the feeding ecology of the giraffe and the effect of browsing on their main food plants.

Raimund Apfelbach observed giraffe from June until August 1969 in the Serengeti National Park, Tanzania, where Foster had also studied giraffe earlier. Here the vegetation is largely open savannah with mixed acacia woodlands. Apfelbach's data were collected in a 12-page typescript article (ca. 1970).

Carlos Mejia continued studying giraffe in the Serengeti, completing his field work in 1971. He concentrated on giraffe behavior, especially the dominance hierarchy in males and mother-calf relationships (1971–72).

Backhaus (1961) studied giraffe in the 4,800-km² Garamba National Park, which lies in the northeast corner of Zaire bordering Sudan. The park is traversed by many small streams and valleys. The vegetation ranges from densely forested areas to grass steppeland.

Finally, Berry's observations from 1963 to 1969 of the giraffe in the Luangwa Valley, Zambia, were published in 1973. These animals frequented the open woodlands and riparian forests in small herds, seldom venturing into more open country.

Other studies of specific facets of wild giraffe, such as lists of food plants they have been seen eating, are discussed also under the appropriate headings.

Dagg is especially grateful to the people who enabled her to go to Africa—Dr. C. S. Churcher; Dr. and Mrs. (Dr.) D. W. Ewer; her mother, Mary Quayle Innis, who made the year financially possible; and Mr. Alexander Matthew, who provided the giraffe to be watched and herself with room and board. She must thank also those who have given her help since that time, either in person or in letters, particularly her husband, Ian R. Dagg.

Foster also has been able to complete his research only by the kindness of many people. He extends his gratitude to the CanadianInternational Development Agency, which financed his appointment at the University College, Nairobi; to Professor D. S. Kettle, who provided all help possible; and to Mr. Perez Olindo, Director, Kenya National Parks, who permitted the research. He also owes his thanks to his wife, Dr. R. M. Sadleir, Mr. D. Kearney, Dr. M. J. Coe, Professor R. R. Hoffman, Dr. and Mrs. R. M. Bradley, Mr. R. McLaughlin, Dr. M. Gosling, Mr. A. Duff-MacKay, his graduate students, and the many people who supplied old photographs of giraffe taken in Nairobi Park.

Dr. George Schaller and Dr. L. Harrison Matthews made many valuable comments on earlier versions of the manuscript as did Dr. C. S. Churcher on an earlier version of Chapter 5. Both he and T. Monod graciously gave us permission to reprint figures from their works. Mrs. Elizabeth Steven, Provincial Museum of British Columbia, prepared the illustrations, while Mrs. Jean Spowart typed the manuscript. Mr. C. A. Campbell kindly edited the final version of this book.

Contents

1 *Giraffe and Men*

The giraffe has never been common in the civilized world, and was only represented by a few captives on and off for many centuries (Mongez, 1827; Phipson, 1883; Dawson, 1927; Jennison, 1928; Laufer, 1928; Cansdale, 1952; Wendt, 1956; Liddell, 1956; Dembeck, 1965; Spinage, 1968a,c). The giraffe was imported into Egypt as early as 2500 B.C., at which time it no longer occurred there naturally. It was known as *ser* or *mimi,* two translations of the Egyptian hieroglyphics signifying the giraffe. These animals were captured near the tributaries of the Nile and floated down the river in barges constructed with flat sterns suitable for the loading and unloading of exotic animals. Queen Hatshepsut received a giraffe this way that was sent as a gift to her zoological gardens in Alexandria from the land of Punt, since she had decided to conquer this region of gold and spice by kindness rather than by force.

A giraffe also crowned a royal procession given by Ptolemy II in honor of Dionysus. This procession, which took all day to pass through the stadium at Alexandria, included 24 chariots each drawn by four elephants, seven smaller chariots drawn by seven pairs of saiga antelope, 12 camels loaded with spices, 2,400 hounds led by slaves, 30 hartebeest, 24 oryx, 24 lion, 16 cheetahs, four lynxes with their cubs, and a single giraffe.

It is probable that the head of a giraffe on the body of a man was used in Egyptian times to depict Set, the god of evil who, like the giraffe, was thought to live in desert regions. Set was always drawn with square ears which made

1

identification of the head difficult. In the past, Egyptologists had identified Set as part sphinx, griffin, degenerate ass, oryx, greyhound, donkey, fennec, jerboa, camel, okapi, long-snouted mouse, aardvark, wart hog, jackal, and tapir. However, it is now generally agreed that the square ears are really horns, the horns of a giraffe whose ears are hidden by the wig worn by most Egyptians to keep off the sun (Jensen, 1934).

The zoo at Alexandria provided the first giraffe seen in Rome, an individual that Julius Caesar imported in 46 B.C. The animal was called a "cameleopard" in the advance publicity because it was as big as a camel with spots like a leopard. The Romans were delighted at the thought of seeing this strange beast. They imagined it would be as large as a camel but as fierce as a leopard—a hopeful combination to people bored with the minor bloodbaths provided by lions and gladiators. They were disappointed. Pliny wrote cryptically, "It was as quiet as a sheep." Even so, Caesar included giraffe in the mass slaughter of 400 lions and 40 elephants that was held to consecrate his forum.

Giraffe were also noted for the part, not always useful, that they played in Roman religion. In one religious ceremony at the altars of the Sun and Moon, the sacrificial animals were confronted with their first giraffe. Four white horses and a pair of bulls were so terrified by the apparition that, ignoring religious protocol, they stampeded wildly off.

With the decline of the Roman empire, giraffe largely died out and were forgotten in Europe. In 636 A.D. the writer Origines confused the giraffe or cameleopard with the chameleon. Even in Egypt giraffe were uncommon. When the Egyptians defeated the Nubians in the seventh century, the annual tribute demanded by Egypt from the defeated country was 360 human slaves and one giraffe. The relative value of a man and a giraffe could hardly be compared.

Arab scholars were as interested in the giraffe as the Egyptians and Romans had been, but their interest was entirely academic since few of them had seen one of these creatures which they called *xirapha,* an Arabic word meaning "one that walks swiftly." One Arab geographer wrote in 1022 that the father of the giraffe was a leopard, the mother a camel. He scorned those who believed that a stallion could father a giraffe. "It is well known," he insisted, "that horses do not mate with camels any more than camels mate with cows." Another Arab scholar disagreed with the geographer's simple explanation of the giraffe's parentage. He asserted that the offspring of a cross between a male hyena and a female Abyssinian camel had to be crossed in turn with a wild cow to produce a giraffe.

The Persians were as shaky on giraffe behavior as the Arabs had been on their reproductive habits. About the year 1300 they believed that, although a giraffe female bore giraffe young, as soon as the young was born it fled from its mother, since her tongue was known to be so rough that if she licked her young its skin and flesh came off. The young only dared approach its mother after three or four days.

The meaning of a giraffe that appeared in a dream was considered by one Arab. In general, to dream of a giraffe meant that a financial calamity was imminent. However a giraffe might also signify a respectable or beautiful woman, or the receipt of strange (and bad) news, which would come from the direction in which the giraffe was seen. If the giraffe entered a country or town, disaster would befall the dreamer's property and there would be no guarantee of safety for anyone visiting the property. Subsequently, if none of these events occurred, the giraffe represented a wife who had been unfaithful to her husband. It must have been rare that none of these conditions was fulfilled after the dream.

The giraffe was reintroduced into Europe in 1215 when the Sultan of Egypt gave a giraffe to Frederick II, the Holy Roman emperor, in exchange for a polar bear. Frederick sent this or a second giraffe abroad later to tour various European cities and towns. From that time until just over a hundred years ago, the few giraffe that reached Europe were all presents from Eastern rulers. When one was sent to Italy in the fifteenth century, everyone knew what a cameleopard was, but few had read Pliny to determine its temperament. Cosimo de Medici of Florence engineered an experiment to see if his rare "Mameluke monster" were indeed more like a camel than a leopard. In honor of a visit paid to Florence by Pope Pius II, Cosimo put a giraffe, several lion, some bloodhounds and a number of fighting bulls together in a pen set up in front of the government buildings. The pope, Cosimo and a variety of hangers-on then waited to see which animal was the fiercest. The lions and dogs lay down to sleep, the bulls chewed their cuds, and the giraffe pressed itself against the fence, trembling with terror. It was undoubtedly more like a camel than a leopard.

About the same time Lorenzo the Magnificent also received a giraffe, but he appreciated its pacific temperament and left it in peace. This giraffe became the pet of the city of Florence. When it strolled through the streets with its keeper, the ladies crowded onto their balconies to feed it apples. Although Lorenzo had promised Anne, daughter of Louis XI of France and heiress to his menagerie, that he would send her this giraffe for her collection, he did not keep his promise. Florence's reputation was at stake in the rivalry between the Italian zoos, and Lorenzo could not rest until he had acquired still another giraffe for his collection. This addition gave Florence the advantage over Naples, whose zoo had previously been considered the best in Italy because of the presence of a zebra there as well as a giraffe.

Because of Lorenzo's appreciation of the giraffe, his friend Constanzo wrote him an epigram in Latin in which the giraffe is speaking to Lorenzo and complaining at having been deprived of its horns by the writers of the past—Diodorus, Pliny, Solinus, Strabo, Varro, and Albertus Magnus. Diodorus, for example, had described the giraffe as "a mixture of camel and pard, long-necked and with a hump on its back like a camel, but the shape of the head, the form of the eyes, the color, hair and length of the tail are just like the pard."

Giraffe were again largely forgotten in Europe during the next few hundred years, but individual giraffe remained in the Near East. In 1597 a Scotsman, Fynes Moryson, described a captive giraffe he saw while visiting Constantinople. This animal was "called *surnapa* by the people of Asia, *astanapa* by others, and *giraffa* by the Italians. . . . He many times put his nose in my necke, when I thought myselfe furthest distant from him, which familiarity of his I liked not; and howsoever the keepers assured me he would not hurt me, yet I avoided these his familiar kisses as much as I could." John Sanderson, a London merchant in Constantinople, reported of it, "Two Turkes, the keepers of him, would make him kneele, but not before any Christian for any money"; and Melchior Lorch, a traveler from Flensburg who painted a watercolor of it, wrote under the picture, "A strange and marvelous beast, the like of which we had never seen before."

Soon after 1600 the first giraffe were imported into China by sea. The Chinese were as impressed by these animals as the Europeans had been, regarding them as an auspicious omen presaging a prosperous government, good harvest, and a peaceful reign. The Jesuit Ferdinand Verbiest wrote, "When any come to see them, they willingly and of their own accorde, turn themselves round as it were of purpose to shewe their soft haires and beautifull coulour, being as it were proud to ravish the eies of the beholders."

In 1805 the giraffe was brought for the first time to England by George Wombwell, an animal dealer on Commercial Road, London. This individual, which had cost £1,000, died within three weeks of its arrival. George Eliot, the novelist, echoed public amazement at this exotic animal in her description of her character Mr. Pink: "The existence of the Revising Barrister was like the existence of the young giraffe which Wombwell had brought into those parts— it was to be contemplated, and not criticised."

Soon after this, the giraffe was reintroduced more generally into Europe. Several giraffe housed at Cairo had been greatly admired by European merchants, officials, and officers, to the pleasure of the Pasha of Egypt. He arranged for the consuls of various countries to draw lots for the giraffe, and in 1826 two young giraffe were sent as gifts to the winners, Great Britain and France.

France's giraffe had been captured by Arabs in Senaar when she was two years old and eleven feet tall (see St. Hilaire, 1827; Mongez, 1827; Anon., 1832; Biers, 1923; Paulus, 1943; Guillaumin, 1946; Dagg, 1963). She was shipped to France from Alexandria with a strip of parchment around her neck inscribed with several passages from the Koran, to act as an amulet for her safe voyage. The giraffe was accompanied by a French consul, four Arabs, and three cows, the latter to supply her with her customary 20 liters of milk a day. She arrived safely in Marseilles in October, but before she could be settled there for the winter, she was towed by barge to the quarantine station outside the city. She stayed there for 15 days while the prefect of Marseilles supervised the construction of a wooden pen in the prefecture so the giraffe could live under his watchful eye.

For security, the giraffe was sent back to Marseilles from the quarantine station at night. Led by the Egyptian keepers, she walked only as far as the gates of the city. There she stopped abruptly, upsetting the keepers who were walking ahead, leading her by reins. No amount of coaxing could persuade the giraffe to follow the men into the city; no urging could persuade her to retrace her steps either. After much fruitless entreaty, she finally followed a horse through the gate. Except for occasional pauses to munch at the leaves of overhanging trees, the giraffe hounded the horse all the way to the new stable.

The prefect, who was very jealous of his new prize, sent detailed instructions for her care to the director of sanitation and every fine day from noon until two o'clock he himself walked the giraffe through the streets of Marseilles, to prepare her for her march to Paris. The prefect ordered a body cloth designed and embroidered with the arms of France for his charge to wear on these trips. The giraffe was preceded by the three cows and accompanied by six guards and policemen who protected her from the curious populace, although the giraffe was not the least upset by the noise, the crowds, or her harness. She behaved admirably, except in one small skirmish with a mule and cart, when settlement for the damages amounted to 64 francs.

Despite all this attention, the officials at the museum in Paris still worried about the health of the giraffe. They asked the prefect to keep a record of her habits and to make careful drawings of her body and head, front and side views, in case the animal should die before reaching Paris. In this eventuality they also sent instructions for the preservation of the skin and skeleton. Cuvier wrote from Paris suggesting that another keeper besides the Negro care for the giraffe, so that if the Negro should fall sick, the other could take over his tasks without the giraffe's being upset by the proximity of a person she did not know.

The anxiety about transporting the giraffe safely to Paris was also great. Should she be sent by sea, by the Rhône River, or by road? Polito, the manager of a traveling menagerie, offered to deliver the animal to Paris, but the officials feared that he would take advantage of the occasion to exhibit the giraffe en route. Exhibition would have been unsuitable, since the giraffe was a gift for the king. St. Hilaire, a professor of zoology who was sent from Paris to arrange the transportation in person, decided that the journey would be most successful by road. After arranging for an escort of police from each district to escort the procession through that territory, the giraffe and retinue set out on May 20, 1827.

Besides the police, the party included St. Hilaire and the prefect of Marseilles in a carriage, a Darfour Negro, Hassan an Arab, a mulatto interpreter, and a Marseilles groom. The giraffe, led by two keepers, was preceded by the three milch cows. Behind her followed a cart carrying husked beans, barley, and wheat to supplement the giraffe's diet of milk; behind this cart walked several other rare animals also bound for the Paris museum. Each night the expedition stayed at inns identified by signs bearing the picture of a giraffe, which proclaimed the distinction of the inns in accommodating the party.

After several days of travel, the animals showed signs of tiring. The giraffe had stepped on a nail which had been extracted from her foot before any harm was done, but one of the cows was decidedly lame. Besides, the French people along the dusty route to Paris were tiresomely enthusiastic. Rarely content with only one glimpse of the giraffe, they clustered around the inn that served as her resting place and applauded wildly on both the arrival and the departure of the animal.

Leaving a worthy doctor in charge of the giraffe at one halting place, St. Hilaire rode ahead of the group to Lyons to ensure that there would be no such demonstration there. He informed the inhabitants of the city of the care that the giraffe required lest she be upset by noise and confusion. St. Hilaire, who was particularly nervous about his charge at this point in the trip, wrote long memos to Paris, suggesting that the giraffe be taken by boat part of the way up the Rhône to guard her against fatigue. Then, instead of marching the giraffe right into Paris through crowds of eager Parisians, he advised that she be kept for a while at Fountainbleau, so that she could recuperate from the rigors of the journey.

However, everyone in Paris was anxious to see the wonderful animal, so the party continued on foot, arriving in Paris on June 30. The first of her species ever seen in France, the giraffe provoked such acclaim that troops were ordered out to keep back the crowds. Colored tickets were issued to keep in order the thousands of people who came every day to see the giraffe exercising in the parks with her African attendants. At this time, natural history enjoyed a popularity such as that now given to rockets and satellites. "A la giraffe" was the fashion from towering bonnets to dappled gloves; gowns, necklaces, and waistcoats were fashioned in the color of her spots; giraffe in palmy groves were painted on dinner services and woven into materials. "Dame Giraffe's" least movement was reported in the newspapers; she was imitated in vaudeville acts and pictured in cartoons. At the height of her glory a bronze medal was cast depicting a giraffe addressing the following words to the country, "There is nothing that has changed in France, there is only another beast here."

In July the giraffe, crowned with flowers for the occasion and wearing a ceremonial mantle, was escorted by all the professors at the Paris Museum to Saint-Cloud, where the king was living. The king, greatly pleased with his gift, allowed the giraffe to eat some rose petals out of his hand. There was no place for the giraffe to stay at the royal residence, so she returned to her home in the Grand Rotunda in Paris after this reception. The press described the meeting of the two "Grands" in detail. When the giraffe died many years later, her body was stuffed with tow and presented to the Verdun Museum. When this museum was destroyed during the World War I, only the giraffe remained intact, her head sticking up among the rubble.

The giraffe given to Great Britain also received enthusiastic royal patronage. It was kept at Windsor where George IV could visit it regularly (see Scherren, 1905, 1908; Anon., 1908a; Sitwell, 1954). The king was thrilled with his gift, so much so that Wellington complained that during one of their conferences the king would talk of nothing else. But the animal did not flourish despite the king's attention, partly because its legs had been deformed during its capture and trip through Africa. R. B. Davis, who was commissioned to paint the giraffe for the king, wrote of its journey, "It was occasionally confined on the back of a camel, and when they [the Arabs] huddled it together for this purpose they were not nice in the choice of cords or the mode of applying them." This giraffe was also painted by Agasse.[1] In two years the giraffe could no longer stand. When the king came to greet it, it was hoisted to its feet by ropes and pulleys. When it died shortly afterward, it too was stuffed with tow.

The Zoological Society of London, sad at the loss of the English giraffe and envious of the healthy French animal, sent out an expedition in 1836 to capture more giraffe. Thibaut of the Society led the party, which included an Arab and three Nubian attendants. With the aid of Arab sword hunters, they managed to kill a female giraffe and capture her calf in the Kordofan Desert. This young giraffe was fastened to an Arab for four days until it was tame enough to lope along behind the caravan. It lived without food for several days until the Arabs had taught it to suck by putting their fingers in its mouth. From then on it was nourished by the milk of female camels. After Thibaut had captured three more young giraffe, the animals were transported down the Nile and shipped to Malta, where they were accommodated in Her Majesty's dockyard. "Providence alone enabled me to surmount . . . [the] difficulties," wrote Thibaut who was paid £700 for his efforts.

The Lords of the Admiralty delegated one of the first steam vessels to transport the giraffe from Malta to London, where they were to be exhibited at the Zoological Gardens. It was some miles from the docks to the zoo, but each giraffe marched across London between two keepers who held the long reins fastened to the giraffe's head. Besides the Nubian and Maltese attendants, the escort included Thibaut in Arabian dress and a number of metropolitan police-men. As the giraffe were startled by the slightest noise, the cabs and vehicles on their route were moved to adjacent streets while the animals passed by. A cow grazing on Commercial Road alarmed the giraffe slightly, but without serious consequences. The animals walked quickly, dragging their keepers after them. Their speed increased when, on reaching the Regent's Park, they saw their first green trees in weeks. Full of excitement, they jerked their reins and waved their heads from side to side, occasionally kicking with their hind legs to the

[1]His portrait is owned by Queen Elizabeth II, who has lent it to the Zoological Society of London where it hangs in the entrance hall of the main offices. Despite the giraffe's disability, it looks in splendid condition (Harrison Matthews, personal communication).

distress of the keepers. With great effort Thibaut finally coaxed them into the elephant house with bits of sugar. The giraffe moved into the newly built giraffe house in the following year. These animals and their progeny lived in the zoo for many years, their last descendant dying in 1892.

Man has of course coexisted with giraffe far longer in Africa than in Europe. Indeed, in the past man has been one of the most important enemies of the giraffe. The Arabs have hunted them for centuries on camels or on horses, often using fresh relays during the chase because the giraffe are fast enough to outrun many of the small horses. The highest recommendation that an Arab can give a horse is to say that it can overtake a giraffe. Even then the horse has to be pressed forward at top speed as soon as the giraffe is sighted; if the prey is allowed any leisure, it can set up a steady pace which it can continue for hours (Grzimek, 1956b). Nor is the chase without danger. As it gallops over stony ground, the giraffe's hooves send showers of pebbles flying backward, a phenomenon which gave rise to the early belief that the giraffe purposely pelted its pursuers with stones. When the hunter is very close behind, the giraffe might kick. One individual pursued on horseback suddenly reared and struck the horse on the shoulder with his right foreleg, knocking both horse and rider down (Farini, 1886).

The long legs of the giraffe enable it to give substantial kicks, but they also allow a mounted Arab to sever the hamstring of the animal's hind leg with a sweep of his sword. One Arab is reported to have cut off the hind leg of a giraffe above the hock with a single blow, but this seems incredible (Aflalo, n.d.). When crippled, the giraffe is easily cut down by the swordsmen. Some horsemen drive the exhausted animal among trees where the rider can dismount and stab it with a long spear (Simon, 1962).

Other Africans have killed giraffe in different ways. In Ethiopia and Sudan, men encircled a herd of giraffe with fire and drove them up the gentle slopes of nearby hills whose far sides fell off as precipices. As many as 12 giraffe were trapped by the Africans at one time in this way, their bodies crushed at the foot of the cliffs (Philipps, 1956). Ndorobo caught giraffe in camouflaged pitfalls, a particularly effective trap for giraffe, which usually use their sight rather than their sense of smell in sensing danger (Fife, 1927); conversely the Ndorobo were less successful in killing giraffe with poisoned arrows because of the keen sight of the giraffe and their general wariness (Bryden, 1899). Many Africans used, and still use, snares to catch giraffe; others such as the Wakamba surrounded entire herds, killing a few of the giraffe as they broke away (Bryden, 1899).

Giraffe, once killed, were generally not wasted. The meat, especially that of the young and of the females, was relatively edible and certainly abundant; one large male supplied Stanley (1890) with 452 kg of fresh meat. Even when the meat was dried, it could be eaten as biltong or ground into an edible powder. The 1.2-meter-long leg bones contained much marrow, the bone itself later serving as fertilizer. The milk from the killed females was quite palatable. The hide of the giraffe furnished pots and buckets for some Africans (Cranworth, 1912) and tom-tom coverings for others (Fortie, 1938). More often it was fashioned into shields, sandals, whips, or amulets used as charms against lions (Bourgoin, 1958; Percival, 1924). The shields made from giraffe hides were especially prized because they were lighter than those made of buffalo or rhino hides but still tough enough to resist both lance and sword. The leg tendons were sometimes fashioned as guitar or bow strings or into thread for sewing (Tjader, 1910).

Perhaps the most highly valued part of the giraffe was the long tail, used for fly switches and ornaments; when settlers in Kenya drove 20 giraffe into a swamp from which the animals were unable to extricate themselves, Africans had cut off all the tails of the defenceless giraffe by the following morning, leaving the animals, still alive, to die of starvation (Johnson, 1928). Masai women used tail hairs as threads to sew beads onto their clothes (Laufer, 1928), and other Africans made necklaces, good luck amulets, and bracelets from these hairs (Baker, 1888; Johnson, 1928; Bourgoin, 1958). In the Sultanates of Tchad a chief's power was proportional to the number of giraffe tails he possessed, as these proved the value of the horses which had hunted the animals down.

Although Africans killed as many giraffe as they needed with snares, arrows, swords, and spears, the giraffe was well enough adapted to survive this predation. With the arrival of the white men and guns in Africa, the balance swung dangerously close to the complete extermination of the giraffe. The white men killed as many giraffe as they could, and their methods were so effective that thousands of giraffe were slaughtered senselessly by settlers, explorers, and hunters alike.

The Boers in South Africa were especially destructive. They ran down and killed whole herds of giraffe from horseback, often 300 or more animals dying in one year (Schillings, 1905). The giraffe flesh became biltong and the hide sjamboks—6-meter-long oxen whips cut in one piece from the giraffe's lip to the heel of his hind foot (Carrington, 1892). In 1800 the giraffe population of South Africa was described as high. In 1865 giraffe were still fairly plentiful, although Fritsch had then written, "The death-knell of the giraffe has tolled. This wonderful and harmless animal is being completely annihilated!" (Schillings, 1907). By 1900 few giraffe remained. What is now the Kruger National Park was littered with whitened giraffe bones (Stevenson-Hamilton, 1947). The Boers were forced to import giraffe hides from East Africa for as much as $25 each in order to make their sjamboks (Schillings, 1905).

In East Africa white game hunters helped to slaughter the giraffe herds. It is astonishing that the head of a giraffe with its 25-cm horns could rank as a trophy, but hundreds of such heads were mounted. Some game heads may represent an exciting African encounter, but as Stott (1950) writes, "walking up to a giraffe in the field and dropping it in its tracks must involve all the excitement and danger of bagging a Jersey heifer in a dairy yard."

It must be admitted that at the turn of the century giraffe were more wary than they are now. Most white hunters considered the chase of the giraffe on horseback to be the sport "par excellence" of the country (Selous, 1907). One, who thought that such a chase offered "a sufficiency of sport to satisfy the most ambitious hunter," shot four giraffe in 15 minutes (Bryden, 1893). Another declared that "every European hankers after the killing of at least one if not several specimens of giraffe," although he admitted that the elephant was more difficult and the rhinoceros more dangerous to shoot (Schillings, 1905). Baldwin and Selous, two other hunters, shot 17 (Baldwin, 1894) and 18 (Selous, 1907) giraffe respectively in one year, often abandoning the carcasses. The excitement of the hunt seemed to be in keeping one's coat from being torn off by the thorns and in wondering if the horse would trip during the chase (Baker, 1888). To kill, one had only to dismount and shoot the retreating giraffe above the base of the tail (Selous, 1908). Most of these European hunters enjoyed the bone marrow and the meat of the cows, which resembles veal or venison, but the flesh of the adult bulls was usually too strong to eat. Perhaps this was what Puxley (1929) had tasted when he described giraffe meat as "entirely beastly" and only less revolting than waterbuck steaks.

With such industry by white hunters, the giraffe in East Africa were nearly wiped out early in this century. One hunter wanted to shoot and stuff a collection of bull giraffe in order to preserve some specimens of this soon-to-be extinct animal which he was helping to exterminate (Schillings, 1905). Erlanger wrote that "the day cannot be far distant when the beautiful eyes of the last 'Twigga'[1] will close for ever in the desert" (Schillings, 1907). Their numbers were further depleted about that time by a plague of rinderpest, a disease to which giraffe are particularly vulnerable, which swept southward through Africa.

The giraffe would certainly be extinct today if there had not been a change both in sentiment and law toward them. With the example of the passenger pigeon and the American bison before them—animals that had been so numerous that no one had believed it possible that they would be virtually eliminated in such short periods of time—men realized that there was no purpose in slaughtering animals that did them no harm, that the world would be the poorer for each species that was wiped out. Countries began issuing licenses for the privilege of shooting game, so that the bags would be limited and the country would benefit from this use of what was to become an important natural resource. In 1913 the parliament of England was discussing the preservation of wild animals in Africa (England, 1913), but few game reserves were set aside until 1933, when the first Conference for the Protection of the Fauna and Flora of Africa was held in London.

Today most of the countries in Africa protect their giraffe by laws which punish all poachers. Occasionally a giraffe may be shot if a special license is first

---

[1] *Twiga* is the Swahili word for giraffe.

obtained from the government, but the price of such a license (£25 in Kenya) is so expensive and a giraffe-head trophy so poorly regarded that only museums that want to mount the skin generally do so. Only seven giraffe were shot on special licenses in Kenya in 1966, compared with 936 buffalo, 343 leopard, 334 elephant, 336 lesser kudu, 246 lion, 42 rhino, and 338 gerenuk. It is obvious that the giraffe is now one of the least-favored trophies.

Most giraffe live out their lives in the wilds of Africa, but with the encroachment of man and his works into what were originally the habitats of the giraffe, these animals have come increasingly into contact with civilization. Most of such contact has been amiable, giving pleasure to the people who watch this animal and, at least very recently, little fear to the giraffe. Some giraffe have become genuinely attached to people. Shorty of Hluhluwe Reserve allowed children to put hats on his head or to sit on him when he lay down. One young giraffe let itself be saddled and ridden 400 km through Africa by a Capt. Rimmington (Huxley, 1963); another developed an affection for the biologist Brehm, strolling daily up to his barge on the Blue Nile to be fed and petted (Backhaus, 1961); and giraffe in Kenya have become so accustomed to suburban life that Col. Mervyn Cowie, who lives on the edge of the Nairobi National Park, was forced to install a cattle grid under the gate of his garden to keep them out (Huxley, 1963).

Giraffe sometimes find disfavor with man. Rarely they have damaged crops by browsing on them and walking through them. They occasionally stampede through fences and telegraph wires, breaking both wires and posts and occasionally strangling themselves in the process (Johnson, 1909; Roosevelt, 1910); 1000 km of telegraph wires in Kenya were raised to 9 meters above the ground after the line was broken by giraffe one hour after the official inauguration of the system (Lane, 1948), while so many unraised telegraph wires in Africa were broken by giraffe during both World Wars that soldiers were ordered to shoot the saboteurs on sight (La Monte and Welch, 1949; Simon, 1962). Railway engines have collided with and been derailed by incautious giraffe (Roosevelt, 1910; Percival, 1924; Pitman, 1942). In 1908 a train was stopped by two of these inquisitive animals, one of which then poked its nose across the engine and broke off the headlight lanterns (MacQueen, 1910). They are sometimes a hazard at night on the roads in Africa since their eyes are generally too high to reflect a car's headlights, thereby giving the driver no warning of an animal ahead. These misadventures provide anecdotes to be related on a relaxed evening; no one would advocate retaliation against giraffe for the small amounts of damage they have caused. Eventually, because of human population pressures, giraffe will likely be restricted to National Parks and Game Reserves in Africa. Here they should be able to survive well, thrilling visitors to these parks and possibly serving as a source of meat too when they are old.

2 *The Distribution of the Giraffe*

Giraffe only live where there are trees or bushes on which they can browse. Occasionally giraffe are found on grass plains, as are those that are sometimes encountered on the flats near Lake Manyara several kilometers from the nearest bushes or trees. Such animals either may be enjoying a brief respite from insects or are merely crossing from one bush area to another. Otherwise the habitat of the giraffe extends from semiarid regions where the food leaves are growing on small thorn bushes, to areas where the vegetation is dense, as in bush veld areas of South Africa. Their range does not include the deserts or rain forests of Africa, although rarely giraffe have lived in heavily forested areas (Schillings, 1905; Roosevelt, 1910).

The kinds of trees or bushes present are also important. For example, giraffe eat most types of acacia leaves, so that giraffe will frequently be found in acacia savannahs of Africa wherever they are. But giraffe rarely eat mopane leaves (*Colophospermum mopane*) if there are alternative foods, which probably explains the limited range of the giraffe in the Kruger National Park; thousands of giraffe live south of the Letaba River where the knobthorn acacia (*Acacia nigrescens*) is abundant, but very few have ventured into the mopani-veld to the north, even though there has been nothing to prevent such an expansion for decades.

The type of vegetation depends in part on the temperature and the rainfall, physical factors that do not usually affect the giraffe directly. An exception may occur at the edge of the giraffe's range; for example, in South Africa in 1957 apparently temperatures approaching freezing coupled with wind and rain killed a large number of animals already weakened by a low-quality diet. Similar conditions caused death to many giraffe and other animals in Rhodesia in 1968 (Jubb, 1970).

Historically there is no reason to believe that the giraffe have not had time to inhabit all parts of Africa in which they can live. Probably the ancestors of the present giraffe migrated into Africa from the northeast and spread southward and westward until they occupied most of the open forest and bush areas of the continent. There are no impassable rivers cutting completely across Africa to impede such a migration, although the rain forests of west-central Africa and the largest rivers will have affected the migration routes.

The climate, vegetation, and history determine the maximum distribution of the giraffe on a broad scale; other factors are important on a local level. For example, the rinderpest epidemic at the turn of the century wiped out giraffe on such a wide front that even yet surrounding populations may not have had time to repopulate severely stricken regions. In other areas giraffe have been wiped out by poachers, by shooting, or by the advance of civilization where wild lands have been tamed into farms so that there is no longer a place for giraffe.

In prehistoric times the climate and vegetation in Africa were often different from those of today (see Moreau, 1966). Even two thousand years ago the Romans were able to grow crops in what is now part of the Sahara Desert, building up a great civilization south of the Mediterranean Sea in what is now an ocean of sand. Before that time Africans kept sheep, cows, goats, and dogs, and before that hunters lived off rhinoceros, elephant, antelope, ostrich, and giraffe. We know this because many of the early inhabitants of this area drew pictures of contemporary life on the rocks and caves among which they lived. Engravings and stone etchings drawn so naturally that there is little doubt that they were done from direct observation included all these animals. Giraffe were drawn as early as ten thousand years ago in places as far north as the Libyan Desert, as the map in Fig. 2–1 shows. This map also shows that giraffe at one time inhabited most of North Africa now covered by the Sahara Desert.

North Africa today is too poorly vegetated or too heavily settled to support giraffe. The lack of vegetation was caused in part by the agricultural practices of the early farmers there—as trees and shrubs were cut down to make room for crops the soil lost much of its ability to retain the little rain that did fall—and less rain has fallen recently. Monod (1963) emphasized the difference that even a few millimeters annually could make in the Sahara—"one has the impression that a slight increase in rainfall would return the giraffe to Adrar or Tibesti" in the heart of the Sahara. In the ancient Neolithic, giraffe apparently inhabited the high Barbary plateaus; in the recent Neolithic, with a change to a hot, dry climate and therefore a decrease in the vegetation, the giraffe were forced back into the interior of Barbary; in historic times the giraffe have been pushed south of

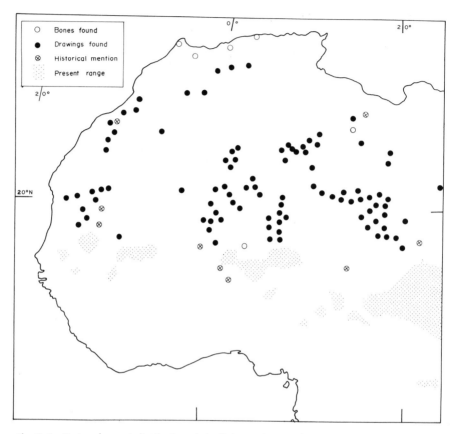

Fig. 2–1 Past and recent distribution of giraffe in northwest Africa. (After Monod, 1963)

Morocco and Mauritania by the encroaching desert, although giraffe lived in Morocco as recently as 600 A.D. (Schomber and Kock, 1961). In Egypt, where the vegetation also suffered from the decreasing rain, the giraffe disappeared between 2850 and 2600 B.C. (Monod, 1963).

The advance of the desert has not only been hearsay. A striking climatic change in the vicinity of Aïr, the semidesert Saharan region of northwest Africa, has been documented within the last hundred years (Buchanan, 1926). Formerly Aïr and the region to the north were fertile with tropical vegetation and adequate supplies of water. In 1850 Barth saw ostriches, giraffe, and lions in Aïr (Barth, 1858); in 1909 ostrich and giraffe no longer inhabited the mountainland of Aïr, and sand had flooded over the fertile area to the north; by 1922 the lions were also gone, the last two having been killed in 1915 and in 1918. Many small animals survive in Aïr, but the sand is still advancing, killing the vegetation in its route (Lhote, 1946).

During the pluvial periods of the Pleistocene, when conditions in North Africa were far easier than they are today, emigrating giraffe would have had no trouble spreading throughout North Africa as far west as Dakar, near where a few giraffe still survive, and east throughout most of East Africa. The route on which giraffe migrated south was circumscribed by the forest vegetation of the Congo basin and by the Zambezi River. Even in the dry season the Zambezi is at present too wide and deep for giraffe to cross. But by migrating east of the Congo rain forest and west above the headwaters of the Zambezi the giraffe could range into Africa south of this river, occupying the areas in which it is still found today (see Fig. 2–2 which updates the maps of Dagg, 1962a, and Sidney, 1965.)

0 500 1000 1500
KILOMETERS

Fig. 2–2 Current range of the giraffe in Africa.

As in the north, the southern giraffe do not occupy as large an area as they once did. Again this is partly a result of civilization encroaching on their range, but decreased rainfall is also partly responsible; for example, at present Lake Ngami, once a large body of water in Botswana, may on successive dry years contain no water at all. To illustrate the recession of the range of giraffe in southwestern Africa, one can examine historical records of the animal. In 1663 giraffe were encountered in Namaqualand at about 30° south latitude, south of the Orange River (Mossop, 1931, 1947; Bigalke, 1951). They may have existed even farther south, as excellent Bushmen drawings of giraffe have been found near Queenstown (Stokes, 1942), in the Tarka area (Barrow, 1801), near Graaff Reinet (Grzimek, 1956b), and on the Tsomo River (Laufer, 1928). On the other hand, Bushmen were more widespread in the past than they are today, and they can travel great distances, so that these works may have been done by artists who remembered the giraffe from journeys farther north. One hundred years later explorers traveling north first met giraffe north of the Orange River, at about 29° south. By 1890 Bryden (1891) found giraffe rare as far south as 26° south, and today few if any giraffe range south of 22° south latitude. In a period of three hundred years giraffe have withdrawn their range a distance of nearly 880 km.

The present distribution of the giraffe is mapped in Fig. 2–2 and discussed briefly here.

SOUTH AFRICA

At present giraffe only occur naturally in the lowveld of the eastern Transvaal, that area 600 meters above sea level that lies between Mocambique and the Drakensburg Range. Fossil records of giraffe from Potgietersrust (Cooke and Wells, 1947) and possibly the cave drawings from southeast Cape Province indicate that these animals were once more widely distributed. The giraffe are most numerous in the Kruger National Park, although some still live on farms and cattle ranches west of this park.

At present there are about 3,300 giraffe in the Kruger National Park (Pienaar, 1970), but there were not always this many. When much of this area was designated as the Sabi Game Reserve in 1898, fewer than 30 giraffe survived to be protected (Pienaar, 1963). Up until that time giraffe had been indiscriminately slaughtered by both Europeans and Africans to supply tails for fly switches, hides for whips, and bones for fertilizer. By 1918 there were 150 giraffe in the Sabi Reserve, and 20 years later this number had increased to 200. Most of the giraffe now range between the Oliphants and the Sabi rivers, but some have wandered farther north recently.

With an increased interest in the wild animals of Africa, giraffe are being introduced into parks outside the lowveld. The four giraffe exported into the Loskop Dam Nature Reserve in 1961 did not live long (Loskop, 1962), but giraffe introductions to the Willem Pretorius Game Reserve in the Orange Free State (Griesel, 1961) and to Hluhluwe Reserve in Natal have been successful. Shorty, one of the giraffe in Hluhluwe, learned to stick his head in car windows to accept biscuits. He had been raised by men from such an early age that he had no fear of them, but indeed kept well away from the other giraffe in the reserve. Shorty finally became too used to people because he knocked over a tourist in the rest camp. He was then excluded from this area and later from the reserve (Huxley, 1963).

Two giraffe captured near the western boundary of the Kruger National Park were transported to Swaziland, an area where they were probably never found before. They settled into the Mlilwane Sanctuary after it was officially opened in 1964 (Kirk, 1966).

NAMIBIA

Except in the coastal deserts where no rain may fall for several successive years, giraffe have ranged over the entire country in the past, although at present they are restricted to the wild drier northern region. Giraffe are numerous throughout the Kaokoveld except in the coastal desert, and many are found as far north as the Okavango River and eastward into the Caprivi Strip, where tourists can admire them from the air on a plane flying from Victoria Falls. Bigalke (1958) reported that giraffe were recently recorded from 64% of the farms in the Tsumeb district, from 17% of the farms in the Grootfontein district, and from 25% of those in the Outjo area, as well as from a single farm in the eastern Gobabis district and from the large tracts of land to the north.

BOTSWANA

Giraffe are present in the northern part of Botswana, including most of the Central Kalahari Game Reserve, but rare to the point of extinction in the south, where the last giraffe was seen in Nossob in 1882 and the few Kalahari giraffe were killed soon afterwards by Bushmen. Giraffe had always been protected near Lake Ngami in Khama's country by order of the African chief of Bechuanaland, who kept this region for his private hunting ground, judiciously only killing from 12 to 20 giraffe each year (Bryden, 1891). However, between 1942 and 1955 giraffe and other game animals were systematically destroyed in a campaign against the tsetse fly in northern Botswana (Graham, 1967). At present the giraffe population is increasing its numbers so that a herd of 54 animals has been seen in the Mababe Depression. Giraffe have not extended their range, though (government correspondence, 1971).

ANGOLA

In 1968 there were estimated to be about 200 giraffe near Mucusso, about 100 near Cafima, and about 30 in the Mupa National Park on the Cunene River (government correspondence, 1971). The northern areas are too mountainous and forested to support giraffe.

RHODESIA

The vegetation and climate of much of Rhodesia would seem to be suitable for giraffe, but these animals have never been widespread there. There are no records of giraffe at all from the north and eastern parts of the country, north of the Lundi River. In the southeastern corner of Rhodesia the 1,700 or so giraffe are almost entirely restricted to the extensive European ranching areas between West Nicholson and the Lundi River, although a small and entirely separate population exists in the Gona-re-Zhou complex. These animals are numerous enough that limited culling has been or will be required. No giraffe exist on the Tribal Trust Lands, where there is a high density of African people (government correspondence, 1971). In 1960 there were about 3,000 giraffe in the Wankie Game Reserve and in the area south of Victoria Falls railway where the giraffe range over 13,000 sq km including the Victoria Falls National Park (government correspondence, 1960; correspondence with Prof. E. B. Edney, 1960). Giraffe are also present south of Gwanda and have been introduced from Wankie into the Matopos and McIlwaine National Parks. At McIlwaine 11 giraffe were introduced between 1960 and 1963; six of these had died and eight young had been born by 1971. In Matopos National Park six of the first eight introduced there in 1960 and 1962 soon died (Wilson, 1969), but there were four giraffe by 1971. In the 4860-ha fenced Kyle National Park giraffe and progeny introduced in 1962 and 1964 numbered 10 in 1971 (government correspondence, 1971). At Matopos there are many cave paintings of giraffe, so that these animals may formerly have lived in this region.

ZAMBIA

Giraffe, which have never ranged through much of what was Northern Rhodesia, are isolated in two areas. The 300 in Barotse live between 16° 30' south and the Caprivi Strip west of the Zambezi River (Ansell, 1974). Their range probably once extended north to 15° 40' south.

The *thornicrofti* race, a relict population of about 300, lives on the Luangwa River, mostly on the east bank as far north as 11° 50' south. Its numbers have increased recently on the west bank in places which were previously sparsely inhabited (Berry, 1973). (Races of giraffe are discussed in Appendix A).

MOCAMBIQUE

There are few giraffe in this country, all in the southern part where the number has been decreasing annually. Giraffe were still found in 1960 south of the Save River in the region of Guija, Uanetze, Saute, and Funhalouro (government correspondence, 1960) from where some crossed into the Kruger National Park.

About 40 individuals lived north of the Save River (Dalquest, 1965). By 1971 the few remaining giraffe were restricted to the area between the Kruger National Park and the Limpopo River (Safrique, Mocambique, correspondence 1971).

TANZANIA

This country has the giraffe as its national emblem, a suitable choice since this animal ranges over most of the country except south of the Rufiji River where dense *Brachystegia* vegetation replaces the *Acacia* parklands. Schaller (personal communication, 1970) estimated that the population of giraffe in the Serengeti National Park was between 6,500 and 8,000. Douglas Hamilton (personal communication) believes the population in Lake Manyara National Park to be about 60. Giraffe, all belonging to the Masai race which has jagged spots, are also present in Mikumi National Park, Ngorongoro Crater Conservation Area, Ngurdoto Crater National Park, and Ruaha National Park (Williams, 1967). Recently giraffe were transported by ferry to an island in Lake Victoria where it is hoped that they will prove a tourist attraction as members of the 40-ha Saanane Island Game Reserve (Achard and McCulloch, 1967).

KENYA

As in Tanzania, much of this country provides suitable habitat for giraffe, but this animal has had a more checkered history here because of the more intensive colonization. With the arrival of white men and their guns toward the end of the last century, giraffe became an easy target that few hunters could resist. Thousands were slaughtered in Kenya, often in the name of sport. Along the Uaso Nyiro River where reticulated giraffe had once been abundant, so few survived by 1908 that a herd of 20 was a most uncommon sight (Dugmore, 1925). By 1925, after many years during which giraffe were protected by sentiment if not by law, their numbers had increased so greatly that herds of 50 or 100 giraffe were not rare. By 1965 about 400 reticulated giraffe ranged over 1,175 sq km in the arid northwest corner of the Samburu Game Reserve, even though there were also large numbers of domestic stock there (Bourlière, 1965). Reticulated giraffe also occur in the Marsabit National Reserve and in the Meru and Isiolo Game Reserves (Williams, 1967).

Giraffe have become scarce in the fertile areas of Kenya where more and more land has been taken over for agricultural purposes. For example, on the rich Uasin Gishu Plateau of Kenya Sir Harry Johnston saw large herds of giraffe standing about in 1902 as one might see cattle on a dairy farm. Fifty years later, with the plateau entirely developed for farming, the giraffe were gone except for a small herd of Rothschild's race that wandered from farm to farm (Simon, 1962).

There are probably fewer than 200 *rothschildi* remaining in Kenya, with most in the Soy area. When some of the farmers who own the land on which the giraffe lived decided that they no longer wanted them, the Kenya Game Department agreed to move some to another area. The new locality obviously had to be not only suitable for giraffe, but also giraffe-free, since *rothschildi* would interbreed with any other race and its unique characters would soon become drowned in a large population of another race. Consequently the department chose Maralal, about 300 km north of Nairobi, which is separated by at least 40 km from the nearest *reticulata*. Early in 1968 the Elsa Wild Animal Appeal fund helped to finance the translocation of 11 giraffe to the Maralal area, a substantial task because of the large number of overhanging wires along the 300-km route (Nesbit Evans, 1970). In 1974 there were plans to move more of these Soy giraffe to Nakuru National Park and possibly fence them in (Nesbit Evans, personal communication).

Many Masai giraffe still live in large areas of Kenya, both outside and within protected areas including the Mara Plains adjacent to Tanzania (750 giraffe; Darling, 1960), the Nairobi National Park (about 80 individuals; Foster and Kearney, 1967), the Amboseli Masai Game Reserve (a few hundred), Tsavo National Park, Lake Nakuru National Park, and near Naivasha and Lake Magadi (Williams, 1967).

UGANDA

This country is the most densely populated by man of the three East African countries, which largely accounts for the spotty distribution of giraffe. They were eliminated from Queen Elizabeth National Park area before it attained park status. Extreme southwestern Uganda is too forested to support giraffe, but Rothschild's giraffe are found in the parkland country along the eastern boundary of Uganda and on the plains north of Lake Kwania extending into the Murchison Falls National Park. Giraffe inhabiting the acacia woods in this park have been increasing recently. In 1958 there were 80 to 100; 1961: 150; 1966: 200. The Victoria Nile runs through the park, but no giraffe can cross this river and all are found on the northern bank (Bere, 1966). Elephants have removed most of the woody vegetation on the south bank, making the habitat unsuitable for giraffe. It is hoped that the cropping of elephant on the north bank will halt a similar trend there. Pitman (1942) cited an example of local extinction in Uganda. Of three well-known giraffe from Kasilo just east of Lake Kyoga, two were killed in an African hunt in 1920, and the survivor died when he fell into an old game pit in 1929. No giraffe have since been seen in this area.

Kidepo Valley National Park in northwest Uganda is the stronghold for giraffe in Uganda. Mr. Iain Ross, the warden, reported that there were between 300 and 400 there in 1967. Giraffe also occur in Debasien Animal Sanctuary (Williams, 1967).

BRITISH SOMALILAND

There are no giraffe at present in this protectorate (J. J. Lawrie, government correspondence, 1960) but the name for the giraffe in Somali is *geri,* a word which appears frequently as a place name and suggests that the giraffe may have become extinct fairly recently, perhaps because the whole country seems to be becoming progressively less fertile with overgrazing of livestock. (The last elephant died five years ago, and Clarke's gazelle has become extinct in regions where it was once common.) A cave drawing has been found at Caan Libah, about 9° 50' north and 44° 48' east which may be a giraffe but which may be a gerenuk (Burkitt and Glover, 1946).

SOMALIA

Most of Somalia is too arid to support giraffe, but some, perhaps many, live in the southwest corner along the Juba River (government correspondence, 1971). In 1905, about 200 giraffe roamed between the Webi and the Juba rivers, but now giraffe are rare there. Dracopoli reported reticulated giraffe in "astonishing numbers" in 1914 in Jubaland, and this race was also present in large numbers north of the Nzoia River (Simon, 1962). The total number of giraffe in Somalia has decreased greatly in the last 30 years, largely because of poachers who can sell the meat, skin, and tails of any giraffe they kill. Licenses may also be obtained to shoot giraffe legally.

ETHIOPIA

There are no giraffe in the central mountainous part of Ethiopia and few elsewhere. Bolton (1973) reported giraffe near the Dinder River, north of the Baro River and between the Gilo and Akobo rivers. Recently in the Omo Valley there were a few giraffe near the Mwi River, some in the Mago Valley and some north of Moyale. During tours through the Shakissa area of Bale and Ogaden, however, no giraffe were seen, despite rumors by local tribesmen that they were not uncommon there. Bolton feels the giraffe is probably seriously endangered over most of its range, although the government estimated in 1971 (government communication) that there were between 1,000 and 2,000 giraffe in Ethiopia. The recent drought has undoubtedly affected the giraffe population adversely.

SUDAN

The range of the giraffe in the Sudan is mostly in the south and east and more limited than in the past. As early as 1868 Baker claimed that the Arabs had slaughtered all the game on the west bank of the Atbara River, although there were many giraffe still on the east side of the river. Prof. H. Sandon, University of Khartoum (personal communication), wrote in 1960 that giraffe were fairly common in the acacia forests and savannahs of eastern Sudan bordering Ethiopia (Nubian race) and in the foothills and plains east of Kapoeta in Eastern Equatoria and the forests of southern Sudan (Rothschild race), but scarce in the acacia forests and savannahs in the western Sudan (Kordofan race). Giraffe were present then in some of the 14 game reserves and in two of the three national parks—the Dinder and the Southern but not the Nimule National Park (Schomber, 1962). Few giraffe are found north of latitude 12° north, except in the rainy season, when they may range to latitude 13° north (government correspondence, 1971).

ZAIRE

Most of this country is too forested for giraffe, but they are found in the extreme northeast corner in the Garamba National Park, the formation of which probably saved the giraffe from extinction in Zaire. There were about 60 giraffe in the hunting reserve in the south of Garamba National Park and altogether 300 or more in the entire park (Cornet d'Elzius and De Saeger, in Verschuren, 1958b). Backhaus (1961) estimated the number of giraffe in the Garamba National Park in 1957 as over 800 animals. In 1971 the government reported 589 giraffe in this park (government correspondence, 1971).

CAMEROONS, TCHAD, AND CENTRAL AFRICAN REPUBLIC

Giraffe are more common on the forested plains of these countries than elsewhere in west Africa, especially on the dry bush plains of Tchad and Oubangui. Recently they were common as far north as the eighth or ninth or even the twelfth parallel north (Blancou, 1958a). They were formerly recorded up to the eighteenth parallel in the Mourdi Depression; but there is no longer much water to the northwest of Lake Tchad, and no giraffe are now found there. Blancou (1958b, 1960) estimated the number of giraffe in French Equatorial Africa at between 5,000 and 6,000 head, mostly in the Oubangui-Chari provinces. Most of these giraffe were found in the latter province, which is less heavily wooded than Oubangui. With their protection (on paper) the giraffe seemed to be on the increase, but poaching has been considerable (Mahuzier, 1956), especially on the plains between Fort Archambault and Ati and by Arab horsemen (Bourgoin, 1958).

In Tchad, Happold (1969) reported that there were over 400 giraffe in the Zacouma National Park, over 100 in the Siniaka Minia Reserve, and that giraffe were common in the Bahr Salamat Reserve.

Giraffe are common in the northern section of the Cameroons. Jeannin and Barthe (1958) reported at least 1,000 head, 300 to 400 of them in the 1700-sq-km Waza Reserve in 1958. In 1960 about 2,000 giraffe inhabited the Waza Park (Waza National Park, 1962).

In the Central African Republic giraffe in 1968 were common in the Aouk-Aoukale Reserve, the Ouandjia-Yakaga Reserve, and the St. Floris National Park, but rare in the Yata N'Gaya Reserve and the Andre Felix National Park (Happold, 1969).

NIGER, MALI, AND SENEGAL

The number of giraffe in this huge area has decreased greatly in this century (P. L. Dekeyser, correspondence, 1960) and all giraffe may be facing extinction there now because of the recent droughts. About 1909, ninety giraffe were shot by Africans with carbines in one year (Lhote, 1946). Africans also used pitfalls, lassos, and nooses hung in the trees to catch giraffe. Their hides were sold in large numbers in Timbuctoo to make sandals, but none have reached the market there since before 1939. Haywood (1912) feared that so many giraffe were slaughtered annually along the Niger River that the species would soon be extinct there. Giraffe have been killed indiscriminately by military men stationed in outlying areas (Blancou, 1960), and by 1958 only a few dozen head were extant in the whole central territory (Bourgoin, 1958).

Giraffe still occurred in Niger in 1968 on the Niamey-Tillabery-Ansongo road which runs near the northern bank of the Niger River, and between Zinder and Agadez. They were most numerous near Tanout. In Mali there were some giraffe in the Ansongo-Menaka National Park, which was created to protect this species, and a few in the Boucle de Baoule National Park (Happold, 1969).

Giraffe once roamed in Senegal in the region of the Ferlo Desert, but they are no longer there. In 1932 a giraffe was killed on the Senegal River, and in 1935 a herd was sighted north of the railway line, where there are no longer any giraffe. In 1960 about 100 giraffe lived between 13° 30' and 14° 30' north latitude south of the Dakar-Bamako Railway (government correspondence). In 1968 giraffe were present in the Niokolo-Koba National Park, but their numbers were low (Happold, 1969).

NIGERIA

Giraffe are rare in Nigeria because the vegetation is generally too dense and the population too great—about 21 Africans per sq km. Giraffe have long been extinct at Lokoja, where the first Nigerian giraffe (race *peralta*) ever seen by Europeans was shot about 1898 (Rosevear, 1953). Giraffe may wander into northeast Nigeria from the bordering countries, and there are a few present in the Yankari Game Reserve in Bauchi Province in the north. The population there ranged between 40 and 50 individuals in 1960 (Sikes, 1964a); since then it has decreased so that few survive (Sikes, 1964b; Happold, 1969).

There is apparently suitable woodland savannah for giraffe south of the Niger and Benue rivers, but these waterways plus the Cameroons mountain range in the east and the Liberia–Ivory Coast forests to the west have prevented the giraffe from inhabiting it. These geographical barriers have also prevented giraffe from invading Sierra Leone, Guinea, Liberia, Ivory Coast, Ghana, Upper Volta, Togo, Dahomey, and southern Nigeria (Happold, 1969). Giraffe occurred in Gambia many years ago, but none exist there today (Sidney, 1965).

GENERAL DISCUSSION

The range of the giraffe in Africa has decreased recently because of increased aridity and because of modern man's encroachments on their habitat. Their future survival over large regions is probably assured, however, because giraffe are now important both as a tourist attraction and as a source of meat. Sometimes tourism is one of a nation's top sources of foreign income, earned because of the wild animals that live in the country.

Even while they serve as a tourist attraction, giraffe can be a potential source of protein to a country's human population. If giraffe are completely protected in national parks and game reserves, their numbers may increase beyond the ability of the land to support them because one of their natural predators, man, has been eliminated. If lions are also removed, a feature that some game management experts recommend for the harvest of game, the numbers of giraffe will increase even more sharply. These surplus giraffe can be shot and sold cheaply as meat to the Africans. The parks will not be degraded from too dense an animal population, while the giraffe will be admired during their lifetime, and be of use after their death.

The advantages of game management and cropping are numerous and especially apparent to those who have had experience in trying to raise cattle on marginal land (see Dasmann and Mossman, 1960, 1961; Bourlière, 1962; Matthews, 1962; Talbot *et al.,* 1965; Riney and Kettlitz, 1964; Roth, 1966; Foster and Coe, 1968; Funaioli, 1968; Brown, 1969). This land will support a far greater total weight of game than of cattle, since the game have evolved food preferences that largely eliminate competition: giraffe browse on vegetation that other ungulates cannot reach and consume thorny plants that most other mammals will not touch. Cattle compete with each other for their preferred foods, but even without such competition a cow living on unimproved marginal land is generally in worse shape than a game animal that is used to poor conditions. Open water is often at a premium in Africa, and cattle need more of it to survive than do many species of game animals. Even when they have consumed more water and more food, they are less efficient in changing them into meat; giraffe have a mean killing-out percentage of 58–63%, considerably greater than that of domestic cattle (Roth, 1966). Wild game are more resistant than cattle to prevailing insect-borne diseases such as trypanosomiasis.

Foster and Coe (1968) calculated that the total carrying capacity of the Nairobi National Park under present climatic conditions is about 6000 kg/sq km

(36,000 lbs/sq mi). Of this about 600 kg/sq km are of giraffe, which is only eighth in order of abundance of game, but third in order of biomass because of its large size. Some areas in East Africa have twice Nairobi Park's biomass in game animals (Lamprey, 1964), while in areas where domestic stock only is run, the biomass is generally less than one-half of the total biomass in Nairobi Park.

The amount of money that must be spent to realize a profit is an important factor to farmers. Given that vast amounts of money are available to improve the land of an area, cattle will do well in Africa. They can be managed along the most modern lines with the use of modern machinery. But such money is almost never available. One of the important aspects of game farming is that little investment is necessary. Initially fences need not be erected, since supposedly the game has always lived on the land and will continue to do so, and cattle-dips or showers need not be constructed, since game has built up an immunity to the diseases that ticks and mites carry which cattle have not. Nor need the land be fertilized or otherwise managed as it sometimes must be to make meat production of cattle efficient. Thus game cropping offers a future for the marginal areas of Africa for which there is at present no other use except occasionally tourism, and offers a valuable source of meat for the Africans who have too little protein. The giraffe, which eats leaves that few other mammals eat and provides nearly 450 kg of meat, will be an important part of such a scheme. (Brynard, 1967, underlines the importance of *not* building a meat-canning factory near national parks, as rumors have it that various governments plan to do. The cropping of game must always be carried out to the advantage of the species and the park, never to the demand of an idle factory.)

There are difficulties in any new schemes that must be worked out, but none of these are as insuperable as professional cattlemen who fear competition make out. These pessimists underline the gamy taste of the meat, its leanness (Africans prefer the fatter livestock), the fences that the game will break, the diseases that the meat will carry (which are the main obstacle to export), the possibility of spoilage of the meat, the difficulty of cropping and transporting the carcasses, and the various taboos some tribes have towards certain game meat. The culling will have to be done carefully, either at night or one complete herd at a time, to avoid making the animals more wary—of hunters or tourists.

All of these objections are valid at present. But with enough imagination and publicity giraffe steaks can become a specialty of a country rather than an inferior meat: inspectors can examine the meat to make sure that it is of top grade; research will determine where and how the animals may best be killed and their carcasses stored and transported to the markets; and biologists will need to study the life history of each species in detail, so that game ranchers will know how many animals they can remove from a population without jeopardizing its future or the future of the vegetation on which it feeds.

3 *The Giraffe and Its Environment*

The density of giraffe on various areas throughout Africa has been calculated (Table 3–1), but these values can only be approximate; the accuracy of ground surveys depends on such things as the season (Hirst, 1969a), and that of air surveys on the height of the surveying plane, the number of people involved, and the time they observed, the number of mammalian species counted, the area searched, the direction flown, and the time of day and season of the census (Pennycuick and Western, 1972; Sinclair, 1972). Some areas are undoubtedly overstocked, while others are understocked. Each density also depends on the vegetation of the area, the number of other animals that it supports, and outside forces that may prevent giraffe from leaving or alternately favor giraffe immigration.

On Fleur de Lys where giraffe were rigidly protected, 95 individuals lived on 40 sq km, a density of 2.4 giraffe/sq km (6/sq mi). This is a high density because species of trees that giraffe preferred to eat were completely defoliated by them. It is probably an abnormal one. Fleur de Lys locally was surrounded by ranches that more or less valued their giraffe. The Bantu Reserve area several km to the south prevented giraffe from migrating south, and the 1200-meter-high Drakensburg Range 13 km to the west prevented them from moving in that direction. On the ranch itself lion were shot on sight to protect the cattle, so that the giraffe population was free to increase as much as it could.

TABLE 3–1 DENSITY OF GIRAFFE IN DIFFERENT REGIONS OF AFRICA

Number of giraffe per sq km	Area	Area sampled (sq km)	Reference
14.1	Main camp area, Wankie Nat. Park, Rhodesia	—	Dasmann, pers. comm., 1960
5.3	Timbavati (part), South Africa	53	Hirst, 1969a
2.6	Timbavati Private Nature Reserve, South Africa	550	Hall-Martin, 1974b
2.4	Fleur de Lys, South Africa—bush veld	40	Innis, 1958
2.1	Arusha National Park, Tanzania—thick bush	—	Spinage, pers. comm., 1974
1.9	Longido Game Controlled Area, Tanzania	1,105	Spinage, pers. comm., 1974
1.45	Eldoret, Kenya	72	MacTaggart, pers. comm., 1959
1.23	Hans Merensky Nature Reserve, South Africa	52	Oates, 1970
1.13	Tarangire Game Reserve (transects)	ca. 100	Lamprey, 1964
1.1	Robin's Camp area, Wankie Nat. Park, Rhodesia	—	Dasmann, pers. comm., 1960
1.0	NW corner of Nairobi Nat. Park—plains	10	Wyatt, 1969
0.99	Sabie Sand Wildtuin, South Africa	550	Graupner, 1971
0.88	Akira Ranch, Rift Valley, Kenya	316	Blankenship and Field, 1972
0.87	Isiolo, Kenya	1,140	Stewart and Zaphiro, 1963
0.76	Serengeti woodlands, Tanzania	7,396	Sinclair, 1972
0.72	Nairobi National Park, Kenya 1961	100	Bourlière, 1963
0.72	Nairobi National Park, Kenya 1966	122	Foster, 1966
0.67	Manyara National Park, Tanzania	90	Schaller, pers. comm., 1969
0.65	West Nicholson, Rhodesia	125	Dasmann, pers. comm. 1960
0.6	Serengeti National Park, Tanzania	12,500	Kruuk, 1972
0.51	Mkomazi Game Reserve, Tanzania—Commiphora bush	100	Spinage, pers. comm., 1974
0.27	Mara Plains, Kenya	2,560	Darling, 1960
0.22	Wamba, Zaire	1,680	Stewart and Zaphiro, 1963
0.22	Loliondo controlled area, Tanzania	6,734	Watson et al., 1969
0.16	South of Garamba Park, Zaire	—	Backhaus, 1961
0.16	Kruger National Park, South Africa	19,000	National Parks Board, 1970
0.13	Garamba National Park, Zaire 1960	4,800	Bourlière, 1965
0.09	Garamba National Park, Zaire 1963	4,800	Bourlière, 1965
0.01	Serengeti plains, Tanzania	10,000	Grzimek, in Bourlière, 1963
0.01	Baragoi, Kenya—desert	2,040	Stewart and Zaphiro, 1963

The only densities higher than the density at Fleur de Lys were those at the Main Camp area in the Wankie National Park, Rhodesia, and at Timbavati, eastern Transvaal. The density of giraffe at Wankie, which is undoubtedly far above the continued carrying capacity of any area, is difficult to explain. Even though it was calculated for the dry season, there is little evidence that giraffe congregate then, as some game species do, wherever water is available. The densities cited for Timbavati are also abnormally high, since later, during the dry season of 1965, following a season of low rainfall, 182 giraffe (over 15% of the population) died from starvation and malnutrition (Hirst, 1969b). Hirst also noted deaths from the same causes, and increased lion predation on giraffe, during the late dry seasons of 1964 and 1966.

The most reliable density values are probably those for the Nairobi Park. Since the density of giraffe there has remained constant at 0.72/sq km (2/sq mi) for at least seven years, this value is likely close to the carrying capacity of the park under the present conditions of climate and predation. If giraffe average 800 kg each, their biomass here is 576 kg/sq km, far greater than the value of 180 kg/km quoted for giraffe introduced to the arid steppes bordering the Volga River in the USSR (Bannikov and Zhirnov, 1970).

From Bourlière's report (1961) that more male giraffe are born in captivity than are females, one might expect males to predominate in the wild, as apparently causes of death do not discriminate against one sex more than the other, except in the very rare cases when a male giraffe is killed in a fight with another male or a female dies during parturition. At Fleur de Lys only 28% of the giraffe were females. Perhaps the males were less disturbed by a car and therefore more likely to be seen and counted, but a similar disproportion between the sexes was reported for the Amboseli Game Reserve in Kenya, where, of 85 giraffe counted in 1959, only 41% were females (Bourlière, 1961). However a chi-square test indicates that this is not significantly different from an equal sex ratio, although the Fleur de Lys ratio was ($P < .01$).

The ratio of males to females was close to unity in Nairobi Park, taking into account the fact that the males tended to remain obscured in the wooded areas while the females and immature giraffe frequented the open spaces (Foster, 1966). Here 61% of giraffe in a survey taken between October 1960 and February 1961 were females (Bourlière, 1961), although later percentages for the park determined from Foster's "known" animals give a figure of 52.6% females.

The sex ratios observed in Rhodesia were 66% females on Henderson's Ranch, and 56% females in Wankie National Park (Dasmann, personal communication). The number of young in these populations reflected this predominance of females.

Since giraffe sometimes divide the habitat between the sexes, with most males living in the more heavily wooded country and the females and young on the plains, this factor could influence the determination of sex ratios if only part of the population were examined. In any case many samples are too small to be statistically significant. Most natural populations of giraffe are probably close to a 1:1 ratio.

It is probably true to say that game prefers to live in one area, but that if this is not possible it will migrate (Hediger, 1950). Game generally moves some distance during each day—while browsing or to visit a waterhole—but migrations are usually seasonal so that the animals can take advantage of food in a different area (Hall-Martin, 1974a). On Fleur de Lys a herd of about 13 giraffe stayed for at least a year in an 8-sq-km paddock. With plenty of food and water, there was no reason for them to leave. They were joined for a brief period by a group of emaciated giraffe that had presumably migrated from the drought-stricken area to the north. In the only other instance of migration noted on Fleur de Lys, a group of giraffe forced south by a veld fire passed through the ranch.

The daily movements of giraffe in the paddock on Fleur de Lys were small. During three months at the beginning of the growing season they covered an average of 1.1 km in 20-hour periods that included the night (range 0 to 2.6 km for 23 observations). There was no observed correlation between these distances traveled each day and the date, rainfall, sunshine, temperature, or humidity. During the daytime the animals usually moved slowly while browsing. Their speed averaged 0.21 km/hr (range 0 to 0.76 km/hr for 26 observations). The observations of Backhaus (1961) on the giraffe in the Garamba National Park were similar to those of Dagg.

Nairobi Park harbors about 80 giraffe at any one time. However, since 241 different giraffe have been identified there by Foster, it is obvious that there is considerable migration to and from the vast plains lying on the south side of the park. Even after two and a half years of study, Foster was still discovering "new" adult giraffe. While he was generally able to identify any giraffe in the park, he was often unable to locate a given individual. It could have been nearby, hidden by a valley or dense vegetation, or it could have moved many km away. One adult park male for example was sighted 50 km south of the park's borders near Kajiado.

Figure 3–1 gives an example of the home range of one giraffe in and near Nairobi Park. While the total area shown was probably quite accurate, the concentration of visual observations was a result of the route which Foster most commonly took across the north end of the park. The size of the home ranges calculated for the 10 most commonly seen males and females was 62 and 85 sq km respectively. Some home ranges may be larger than those calculated, since it proved difficult to identify giraffe in the rough, trackless area south of the park. The home ranges of adult males (22.8 sq km), adult females (24.6 sq km), and juveniles (12.8 sq km) in Timbavati Private Nature reserve were much smaller, perhaps because this area has a greater density of giraffe (Langman, 1973b).

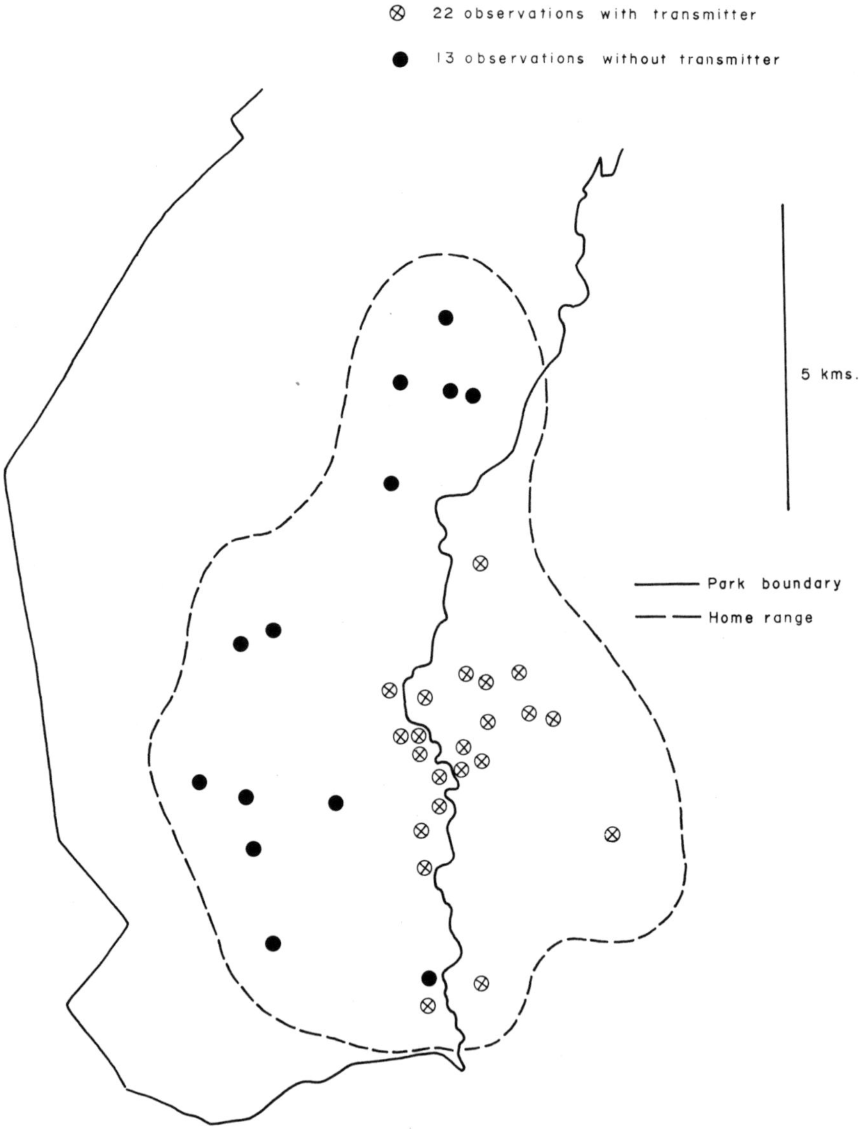

Fig. 3–1 Home range of T27 (young female) in Nairobi National Park.

In order to be able to trace the movements of a giraffe without continually following it, Foster placed a radio transmitter on a giraffe near Nairobi Park. Dr. John King of the Game Capture Unit of the Kenya Game Department carried out this operation using a powder-charged Palmer Cap-tur gun which projected a drug-filled dart. (References on drug use in giraffe include Binkley, 1959; Buechner *et al.*, 1960; Harthoorn, 1960; Talbot and Talbot, 1962; Van Niekerk *et al.*, 1963; Van Niekerk and Pienaar, 1963; Harthoorn, 1965, 1966; Hirst, 1966; Pienaar, 1968; Williamson and Wallach, 1968; Wallach, 1969; Langman, 1973a). Special sturdy darts had to be made in order to penetrate the giraffe's thick skin. The dart was filled with the "cocktail" invented by Pienaar *et al.* (1966). For a young giraffe in the 270–550 kg class (600–1200 lb) it consisted of the following: 2 mg of the main immobilizing agent M183, a morphine derivative; 20 mg of acetylpromazine maleate, a sedative; and 50 mg of hyoscine hydrobromide, an alkaloid with parasympatholytic action, having the effect of dilating the pupil, thereby making the animal temporarily blind by being dazzled with too much light and less liable to fright. For adult animals (900–1350 kg) the dose of M183 was increased to 4–5 mg. Pienaar *et al.* consider M183 to be a safer drug than the related more potent M99, but King has used the latter with success. However, the effect of M99 on cardiac function and respiration may be more drastic; the drug often causes a sudden fall in blood pressure which is sometimes associated with cardiac failure in giraffe in poor condition. Pienaar *et al.* believe that it is essential to give a dose of narcotic which will keep the animal on its feet, as a giraffe may experience great difficulty in rising from the ground in a drugged state and may succumb to the exertion. However, in the Nairobi area men were always able to help the six lightly tranquilized animals that had been darted to rise (Fig. 3–2).

To fasten a collar equipped with radiotelemetry equipment onto a giraffe, it was shot in the rump or shoulder with a drug-filled dart. When hit, the animal gave a short jump, but then often continued to feed. Within a few minutes it began to walk, generally without pausing; in 10 to 15 minutes it was taking short steps while holding its nose high, its tongue sometimes extended. Rangers from the Game Department then ran ahead of the giraffe with a long rope to catch the animal across the chest with it while the men pulled on either end. Hopefully, the giraffe was slowed to a halt. If it was underdrugged, it could easily pull a dozen men behind it. After a daring ranger had caught a hind leg in a second rope, the animal was eased down onto its brisket. The men then rushed up to keep the animal from toppling on its side (Fig. 3–3). This was done both to prevent the animal from hurting itself in the fall and to prevent the stomach contents from being regurgitated and perhaps sent down the trachea and into the lungs with fatal results. The collar was then rapidly placed around the neck so that the transmitter rode comfortably on the chest of the animal.

The transmitter consisted of a transistor, a resistor, a tuning capacitor, a crystal, and mercury batteries. It transmitted at 52.4 megacycles. The transmitter

Fig. 3–2 Helping a female tranquilized giraffe to regain her feet.

was embedded in dental acrylic and fastened to the polyester collar. The aerial ran around the collar to form a loop. The whole collar was then covered with black plastic tape to keep out moisture. The batteries contributed most of the weight of the approximately 1-kg collar; the more batteries there are, the longer the transmitter will function.

Once the collar had been placed on the giraffe, its body measurements had been taken, and its teeth had been examined, the antidote M285 was injected into the jugular vein while a continuing check was kept of the pulse and rate of breathing. Intramuscular injections of 100–200 mg of hydrocortisone and 12 million IU of long-acting penicillin were often injected. As the giraffe recovered, it was helped to rise—no mean feat with a large giraffe—and the animal slowly walked away. Within an hour it was often browsing, but a watch was kept for several hours as the animal was still especially vulnerable to predation. By the next day its reactions appeared to be normal, and the giraffe was apparently oblivious to its new ornament (Fig. 3–4).

For a half-grown female giraffe "instrumented" in this way in the Nairobi Park,

Fig. 3-3   Keeping the tranquilized giraffe from collapsing completely.

Foster went each day to where the giraffe had been seen on the previous day and raised a large high-gain antenna. This antenna was swung around until the distinctive "beep beep" signal was heard. Once the direction of the signal was known, it was generally easy to locate the giraffe. Usually it had moved from 1 to 4 km from where it had been the previous day. For the first week the giraffe remained with a herd consisting of two adult females and two young in their first year, but after that it was found with various mixed herds. Every few days it deserted the park for the plains outside its borders (Fig. 3-1). It circulated around an area of about 17 sq km over a period of 63 days while the radio functioned. The giraffe that Langman (1973b) tracked by radiotelemetry remained in even more confined areas.

SENSES

As in most open-country game species, the sight of giraffe is excellent, and they apparently have some color vision (see Appendix B). They are able to see

Fig. 3–4 Female giraffe fitted with collar containing transmitter.

a man 2 km away (Dugmore, 1924), and, if bushes obstruct their sight, they may stand on an ant hill to obtain a better view (Johnston, 1902). Like most animals the giraffe probably only becomes alerted when an object moves; if a man remained immobile while a giraffe was looking in his direction, it might not notice him.

The giraffe's hearing is at least as sharp as man's, though nobody has tested it accurately. On Fleur de Lys any sound that Dagg heard was also heard by giraffe near her; when she heard a car, laughter in the distance, the cough of a sable antelope, or a far-off train whistle, the giraffe, too, turned to face these noises, holding their ears forward.

Some naturalists claim that the sense of smell of the giraffe is excellent (Stevenson-Hamilton, 1947; Mahuzier, 1956). Others, like Grzimek (1956b), believe that it is not very good. Dugmore (1925) wrote that while he was hidden under a bush in the veld, a giraffe wandered over and browsed on the very plant under which he crouched without seeing or scenting him. However, in the London Zoo several giraffe have at first refused to eat food that had been prepared by a person who had previously been handling mice. One giraffe also refused an apple out of which his keeper had taken a bite, possibly because the keeper chewed tobacco (Aflalo, n.d.). All of the senses of the giraffe must be tested experimentally before we can draw any definite conclusions about their keenness.

Occasionally the response of giraffe to unusual circumstances is tested in the wild. With the encroachment of farming into wild-game country in Africa, the giraffe have recently been confronted with fences, which in both South Africa and Kenya they have learned to get over within three or four years of their construction (Innis, 1958; Churcher, personal communication). At first the giraffe ran through the fences, tearing them down and causing much damage. Gradually, to the farmers' relief, they learned to go over instead of through such barriers, many of them 1.4 meters high. Usually the animal lifted one foreleg over the fence and then the other. Then it shifted forward and hopped its hind legs over together, sometimes catching one foot on the top wire in the process (see below, Fig. 8–11). Churcher watched a medium-sized giraffe chased by a large male jump a one-meter fence in full flight as would a horse. When the male was about 50 meters from the fence he wheeled slightly so that he approached the fence at right angles. He changed his gait somewhat as he neared the barrier and then took off, his forelegs stretched out and his hind legs giving a strong kick behind. He landed with his forelegs first and then ran about 10 meters before he slowed down and stopped. The performance was smooth and practiced.

In Kruger National Park where a 2.5-meter fence was recently erected along part of the boundary to keep wild animals in and poachers out, the fence was soon broken three times by giraffe, but in general it forms an effective barrier (Brynard and Pienaar, 1960).

Giraffe make no apparent effort to conceal themselves among vegetation when danger threatens. Although the coat pattern of a giraffe camouflages the animal very effectively among trees and bushes, two of its characteristic actions attract attention to itself rather than do otherwise. When a giraffe was approached on Fleur de Lys, it often retreated behind a low bush so that although its body was virtually invisible, its neck and head, with ears erect, stood out strikingly, often silhouetted against the sky. In no instance did a giraffe move behind a tree or tall shrub where it would have been better hidden, although its view of danger would have been restricted. The giraffe also often swished its tail back and forth vigorously. Had not one been attracted by its periscope-like neck, one would certainly have noticed these jerking movements.

When danger threatens, as when a lion is sighted, giraffe (and other plains game) seem to be far more concerned in having a clear view of the predator than in being camouflaged. Should a lion be sighted by a herd of giraffe, the giraffe tend to crane their necks to see better. Often some will walk in the direction of the predator to obtain a better view. But lion probably rarely attack prey if they know they are being closely watched.

Because of their good vision and lofty view, giraffe are often first among a group of ungulates to notice a potential danger. For this reason, if one is looking for predators, even ones like the cheetah which would rarely harm giraffe, it is always worth while watching the behavior of giraffe. A herd with its members standing motionless, erect, and facing one direction is generally a clue to the presence of a predator.

Giraffe are very curious. One morning at dawn Dagg was checking the activities of a herd of giraffe browsing on a hill 1 km away. As this only involved looking at each giraffe through field glasses every five minutes to see what it was doing, she spent the remaining time doing ballet exercises on the far side of the car from the giraffe. When she had limbered up for several minutes, she suddenly noticed a female giraffe she had not seen before approaching on the right. This giraffe stared at Dagg fixedly, edging forward every few minutes until it was within 20 meters of the car. It did not retire until Dagg had retreated into the car.

A giraffe may react to an unknown object not by inquisitiveness but by flight, if the object is within the species' flight distance. This distance varies with almost everything including the number of giraffe present, their mood, the time of day, the nature of the terrain, the kind of object, what it is doing, and how well the giraffe recognize it. As an example of the latter, when hunting with guns was at its peak early in this century, many giraffe would not allow a man to approach closer than 450 meters before they fled (Madeira, 1909). Now, where giraffe are protected, they are far more tolerant of men. Similarly giraffe were stampeded by airplanes flying overhead when they were unused to them (Johnson, 1935). By the 1950s the Grzimeks' (1960a,b) overhead plane caused giraffe to run only 50 meters off, or even was ignored if the animals were among trees. Today giraffe do not even look up as the jets approaching the Nairobi International Airport sweep overhead.

Giraffe have become equally blasé about vehicles. They do not bother about cars parked 30 meters away. If one drives within 15 meters, a giraffe may move slowly away, and it may gallop off if the car approaches more closely, but Foster found that he could drive within one meter of old George. In general Foster could tell whether a giraffe was new to the park by its tameness; those not used to tourists had a much greater flight distance.

Some giraffe in Africa have lost all fear of vehicles. Mr. Whittingstall of Acornhoek (personal communication) told of a bull giraffe that kicked in the radiator of his car more or less in self-defense after the animal had decided to charge across the road directly in front of the vehicle but had misjudged the distance. (Why so many game animals, including the giraffe, have the urge to race alongside a moving vehicle and then cut across in front of it, sometimes to their peril if they are not quick enough, is a puzzle.) Another giraffe in the Hluhluwe Reserve smashed in the rear window of a safari bus (Huxley, 1963). It had become so used to cars that it had walked almost over this vehicle. One giraffe on the road, annoyed when a car blew its horn, turned on the Anglia, knocked it over, and kicked it vigorously (W. Stephenson, personal correspondence). Another car, traveling at night in South Africa, stopped and dimmed its lights at the approach of two giraffe. One giraffe left the road, but the other walked up to the car, turned its back, and kicked the radiator three times with both feet before the driver could back away (Dr. D. Serfontein, personal correspondence). Stokes (1942) recounted a similar story.

Giraffe are more wary of men on foot than they are of men in cars. On Fleur de Lys they usually fled if Dagg approached nearer than 50 meters in the parkland area. In dense bush veld areas she could walk much closer to them than this. Their confidence in the bush is probably misplaced, as they seem to be more vulnerable to lions there than in open areas.

PREDATORS

Excluding the attentions of man, other animals either prey on giraffe or live harmoniously with them. Giraffe are rarely killed by crocodiles, cheetahs, and leopards; but the larger an individual grows, the less it has to fear from these predators. It remains vulnerable to lions for its entire lifetime.

The most extensive study of large African predators has been done by Pienaar (1969), who studied 46,181 kills in the Kruger National Park from 1933–46 and 1954–66. During these periods 675 giraffe were killed by lion, two by crocodiles, and two young calves by cheetah. In the two following years lions killed 108 giraffe, 56% of which were identified as males and 31% as females. Of the total number, 64 (60%) were adults, 18 were subadults and juveniles, 12 were suckling young, and 14 were unidentified. These figures resemble the age composition of the stable population of giraffe in the Nairobi Park. Therefore, it seems that lion choose their giraffe prey at random according to age, not predating any one class significantly. They may kill males more than females because the bulls are more often alone and less likely therefore to be warned of approaching danger. Pienaar calculated the Preference Rating of lion for giraffe as opposed to other game

$$(= \frac{\text{Kill Percentage}}{\text{Percentage Abundance}})$$

as 3.01. The only ungulates which were more favored by lion as food were waterbuck (Preference Rating 6.05), kudu (3.82), and wildebeest (3.06). The Preference Rating by cheetah for giraffe was 0.14, the lowest for any of their prey species.

Other studies have also shown the lion to be the only important predator of giraffe. Wright (1960) reported that of 211 kills in Tanzania six were of giraffe that had all been killed by lions. Kruuk and Turner (1967), who compared the predation of lion, leopard, cheetah, and hunting dog in Serengeti National Park, found that lion only had been known to kill giraffe. Of over 125 lion victims discovered between 1957 and 1965 only six were giraffe, and all of these were killed in bush areas. (These kill records are biased in favor of large prey, since small animal remains are less likely to be located and counted.) In Seronera, Schaller (personal communication) knew of only two giraffe which had been killed by two local prides of lion in over a three-year period. In the Nairobi National Park where about 80 giraffe and 25 lion live, five giraffe were known to have been killed by lion in 1965, three in 1966, and two in 1967. Lion also probably accounted for the disappearance of most of the young giraffe born in the park, but there would be little trace of such kills after a few hours. Berry (1973) felt that lions were the main predator of giraffe in the Luangwa Valley, but that few giraffe were killed. Carcasses were usually found in thickly vegetated terrain.

Giraffe are big and strong enough that a lion may itself be in jeopardy if it attacks one. Russell Douglas of Tanganyika Safaris (personal communication, 1957) once spotted a large bull giraffe with blood spattered over it but not seriously injured. He retraced the trail of the animal until it led to what looked like a blood-stained rag. On closer examination this rag was found to be the remains of a lion that the giraffe had trampled into oblivion.

In another skirmish between a female giraffe with her young and a lion, the giraffe killed the lion with a kick from her forefoot. The men who watched from a distance only needed a knife to finish severing the head completely. One of the Africans in the party reportedly recalled another mother giraffe that had also kicked off the head of an attacking lioness (Campbell, 1951). Puxley (1929) reported that in Tanzania a lion was found lying dead under a dead giraffe. The lion seemed to have severed the neck vessels of its prey, but the wounded giraffe fell on the predator, crushing it.

Such stories of course are exceptional, since almost all lion that kill giraffe survive to consume them. In Nairobi Park the giraffe, like other large prey such as wildebeest and zebra, are usually suffocated by the lion. The lion either grasps the throat or completely encloses the mouth and nostrils, holding on until well after the animal collapses. Schaller (personal communication) found two adult giraffe in the Serengeti that had been strangled by lion.

A powerful kick is the giraffe's defense against attackers. The giraffe can kick its hind foot with a cow-like swing, chop-kick with its forefoot like a horse, or strike with a stiff foreleg. One giraffe missed her aim while kicking out at an attacking lion and hit her young instead, breaking its neck and killing it (Tjader, 1910). Other calves have had their backs or their legs broken accidentally by their mothers which have kicked out at a predator (Percival, 1924).

Putnam (1947) told of a lion that stalked a herd of six giraffe which included one calf and its mother. When the other giraffe saw the lion they raced away in a body. Although the mother tried to push her young one in front of her and so follow them, the baby was too slow; instead she was forced to tuck her calf between her fore and hind legs and face the predator. The lion circled the pair at 30 meters while the mother slowly wheeled to continue facing him. When the lion ventured closer than 30 meters, the mother struck out at him so forcefully with her forelegs that the lion retreated. The lion circled his prey for an hour before finally giving up. When he had gone, the two giraffe slowly followed after the rest of the herd. Similarly another giraffe was able to escape from two lionesses and their eight cubs by kicking out continually at them (Roberts, 1969).

Leopards are rarely considered predators of giraffe, but encounters between these species have been reported. Grzimek (1972) related how a male giraffe browsing in a tree had disturbed a leopard there which jumped and damaged the giraffe's neck so badly that it soon died. Hart (1972) recorded that a leopard had dragged the carcass of a young giraffe three meters up on to the branch of a tree. Berry (1973) reported that a very young giraffe carcass was eaten by a leopard in Zambia, and cited an earlier incident in Matabeleland where two leopards had managed to claw a young calf before its mother had driven them off.

A new view of the hyena by Kruuk (1972) shows this carnivore to be far more of a predator than a scavenger in some areas. It is possible that hyenas too could kill a young giraffe, but as yet there is no evidence for this.

OTHER INTERSPECIFIC CONTACTS

Different species of plains game are frequently found consorting together. In general giraffe ignore other animals; the smaller species would gain more benefit from the giraffe's eyes and vantage point than vice versa. However one male giraffe stayed with two elephants in a forest near Kilimanjaro for several weeks (Schillings, 1905), and other giraffe, again often solitary males, have joined forces with groups of eland, zebra, wildebeest, and ostrich (see Ziccardi, 1960), perhaps because there is greater safety in numbers.

Occasionally giraffe become more closely involved with other species. One female apparently suckled a zebra foal that had lost its mother. This foal retreated between the giraffe's forelegs whenever there was danger (Stevenson-Hamilton, 1947). However one wonders how the foal could reach as high as the giraffe's udder.

Interspecific behavior with more sexual overtones was noted at Fleur de Lys in 1952 when a bull giraffe took over a harem of 60 domestic cows, refusing to let the domestic bulls near them for a month. It has also been seen in zoos. When a male eland in captivity sniffed at a female giraffe's genital area, a male giraffe approached and hit the eland with its horns several times so vigorously that it broke the eland's shoulder blade (Backhaus, 1961). In this instance, since the giraffe used its head rather than its feet to attack the eland, he regarded it as a rival rather than an enemy in the more restricted sense. This prognosis was correct, as the eland later tried to mount the giraffe.

Several types of birds live commensally with the giraffe, often perched upon their necks or trunks (Fig. 3–5). These include the buffalo weaver *(Texor niger)* (FitzSimons, 1920) and two tick birds: the red-billed oxpecker *(Buphagus erythrorhynchus)* and the yellow-billed oxpecker *(B. africanus)*. The former oxpecker has been reported on giraffe at Fleur de Lys, in Wankie National Park, in Barotseland, and in the Luangwa Valley (Attwell, 1966). Berry (1973) reported that the yellow-billed oxpecker also frequented giraffe in the Luangwa Valley, but that it did so less commonly than the other oxpecker. Attwell reported that oxpeckers call out at the approach of a man, so raising an alarm, but he did not know if they did this also at the approach of a carnivore. These birds are useful to giraffe in that they search through their hair for ticks, which they eat. In the process they clean the giraffe's hide by removing dirt and bits of dry skin. If the giraffe has open sores, tick birds have been seen to peck at and aggravate these wounds; possibly here too, however, the bird is beneficial in that it may remove maggots from the area.

Fig. 3–5   Red-billed oxpeckers on giraffe's shoulder.

Normally four or five oxpeckers may perch on one giraffe. Dowsett (in Berry, 1973) reported that one group of giraffe were accompanied first by seven yellow-billed oxpeckers and later by four red-billed oxpeckers. (Whether individual birds stay with one herd remains unknown.) The former birds were observed to perch on adult cows only.

DISEASE AND ACCIDENTS

Epidemics that sweep through Africa may kill large numbers of animals and affect the distribution of species for many years afterwards. This was true for giraffe and the rinderpest epidemic at the end of the last century. Before this time rinderpest had never occurred in Africa, which explains the virulence of the disease when it was finally introduced, either by the cattle brought in from India and Aden to feed the Italian army in Italian Somaliland in 1889, or by cattle imported from Russian ports and shipped up the Nile to Khartoum for the 1884–1885 British campaigns (Spinage, 1962).

Whatever the source, by 1890 rinderpest had progressed south to Lake Tanganyika, killing both domestic and wild ruminants in its path (Hobley, 1929). Giraffe were less susceptible than buffalo, eland, and warthog, but even so hundreds died. Those that did not were sometimes temporarily blinded and thus became easy prey for lions (Simon, 1962). By 1892 the epidemic had spread to Lake Nyasa and by 1896 to South Africa, but by 1903 Africa seemed temporarily free of the disease (Grzimek, 1956b). Since then there have been various scattered outbreaks of rinderpest throughout Africa, a particularly severe one in northern Kenya in 1960 killing about 40% of the giraffe there (Simon, 1962), then dying down after 1964 (Stewart, 1968).

Other diseases have not proved as serious as rinderpest. In northern Kenya many giraffe died in an epidemic of gastroenteritis over 45 years ago, but it did not spread over a larger area (Percival, 1924). Recently an outbreak of anthrax threatened game in southern Africa. Giraffe died both in Botswana and in the Transvaal (Pienaar, 1961), but the epidemic was suppressed by disinfecting the water sources responsible for the spread of the infection (Payne, 1961). Giraffe may have antibodies to the Allerton-type herpes virus (Plowright and Jessett, 1971).

If the giraffe are already in poor health, changeable weather may contribute to the death of large numbers. On Fleur de Lys in 1957 such weather killed eight giraffe, about one-twelfth the total population, during the dry season. Two years later, following a long drought when grazing and browsing had been scanty and the animals were in very poor condition, 51 head of game including 21 giraffe died one winter weekend. During these two days the temperature dropped from 30° to 7°C, accompanied by a strong south wind and cold rain (A. Matthew, personal communication).

Other giraffe in the wild are killed in an assortment of miscellaneous accidents. On Fleur de Lys a giraffe broke its neck when it fell into a ditch, and another giraffe found dead had several .22 bullets embedded in its skull, apparently from motorists on the highway who had used the animal for target practice. A giraffe was killed when it slipped on the steep stony slopes of the Loskop Reserve in South Africa to which it had been introduced (Riney and Kettlitz, 1964); another South African male died in a veld fire (Brynard and Pienaar, 1960); and Grzimek (1964) gives a photograph of a dead giraffe, its head caught in the fork of a tree. Apparently while that animal was browsing in the tree its foot slipped from the bank of the river on which it had been standing, and it was unable to climb back onto firm ground.

Giraffe also suffer a variety of ailments in the wild which may impede or debilitate them, but which are not fatal. On Fleur de Lys a number of giraffe had growths about the size of golf balls scattered over their bodies. Stevenson-Hamilton reported such growths on giraffe in the Kruger National Park in 1947, and similar papillomata on giraffe in 1958 disappeared at the end of that winter (Brynard and Pienaar, 1960). Giraffe are susceptible to lumpy skin disease both in the wild and experimentally (Young et al., 1970; Anon., 1973). Other giraffe have had gray scabs on their bodies or other skin diseases such as actinomycete lesions (Woodhouse, 1913; Austwick, 1969). One South African giraffe had suffered a broken neck but appeared in excellent health except for a large bulge on the side of the neck 75 cm below the head where the break had healed (Brynard and Pienaar, 1960). Another adult in Arusha National Park had the distal half of one of its front legs missing, but still managed to survive (Vesey-Fitzgerald, personal communication).

Poachers not only kill some giraffe, but they disable many others. Two giraffe on Fleur de Lys limped badly because of wire snares in which their feet had become caught. In each case the giraffe had pulled free, but the wire remained on its leg. Many such giraffe die eventually of blood poisoning, but in one instance in which the giraffe was killed later by lions, an examination of its leg showed that the bone had begun to grow over the wire (Madel, 1964). Another giraffe in Kenya had a wire snare caught around its neck. This animal was darted, immobilized, and cut free from the snare before it became asphyxiated (Hart, 1972).

Giraffe, like other game, are plagued by parasites. Ticks are found on all parts of the giraffe, but especially around the anus and the genitalia where the skin is relatively thin. They suck the blood of the giraffe, debilitating the animal to some extent and perhaps spreading diseases to them. (Heartwater fever, redwater fever, and East coast fever are spread to cattle by ticks, but no one knows the susceptibility of giraffe to such diseases.) Ticks that have been found on giraffe are listed in Table 3–2. Internal parasites and diseases identified from wild giraffe are given in Table 3–3. Giraffe may also be annoyed by tse-tse flies (Child et al., 1970).

TABLE 3-2 TICKS OF GIRAFFE[a]

	Ethiopian region, Theiler, 1962	Tanzania, Yeoman and Walker, 1967	Kenya, Walker, 1974	Sudan, Hoogstraal, 1956	Other areas, with references
Amblyomma cohaerens	*		*		
Amblyomma eburneum	*				
Amblyomma gemma		*	*		Imported on captive giraffe into New York, Becklund, 1968
Amblyomma hebraeum	*				
Amblyomma lepidum	*		*		
Amblyomma sparsum	*		*	*	
Amblyomma variegatum	*		*	*	Transvaal, Innis, 1958
Boophilus decoloratus	*				Imported on captive giraffe into New York, Becklund, 1968
Hyalomma albiparmatum		*	*		Transvaal, Innis, 1958 Imported on captive giraffe into New York, Becklund, 1968
Hyalomma marginatum rufipes	*	*	*	*	Zambia, Colbo, 1973
Hyalomma truncatum	*		*	*	
Margaropus reidi	*			*	
Margaropus wileyi					Kenya, Walker and Laurence, 1973

TABLE 3-2 (continued)

	Ethiopian region, Theiler, 1962	Tanzania, Yeoman and Walker, 1967	Kenya, Walker, 1974	Sudan, Hoogstraal, 1956	Other areas, with references
Rhipicephalus appendiculatus	*		*		
Rhipicephalus camelopardalis	*	*	*		
Rhipicephalus compositus		*	*		
Rhipicephalus evertsi	*				
Rhipicephalus evertsi mimeticus	*				
Rhipicephalus evertsi evertsi			*		
Rhipicephalus hurti			*		
Rhipicephalus longicoxatus			*		
Rhipicephalus mühlensis	*	*	*		
Rhipicephalus neavei (= R. kochi)		*			
Rhipicephalus pravus	*	*	*		
Rhipicephalus pulchellus	*	*	*		Imported on captive giraffe into New York, Becklund, 1968
Rhipicephalus senegalensis	*				
Rhipicephalus simus		*	*	*	
Rhipicephalus supertritus		*			
Rhipicephalus tricuspis	*			*	

aWe are extremely grateful to Dr. J. Walker and to Dr. H. Hoogstraal who sent us the information for this table.

TABLE 3–3   INTERNAL PARASITES AND DISEASES OF WILD GIRAFFE

	Location	Reference	Comments
Cooperia pectinata	South Africa	Ortlepp, pers. comm.	
Cooperia punctata	South Africa	Ortlepp, pers. comm.	
Haemoncus contortus	South Africa	Ortlepp, pers. comm.	
Haemoncus mitchelli	South Africa	Ortlepp, pers. comm.	
Parabronema skrjabini	South Africa	Ortlepp, pers. comm.	
Trichuris globulosa	South Africa	Ortlepp, pers. comm.	
Monodontella giraffae	East Africa	Leiper, 1935	
Trichuris giraffae	East Africa	Leiper, 1935	
Rhinoestrus sp. larvae	East Africa	Laurence, 1961	In throat and nose
Rhinoestrus giraffae	Tanzania	Sachs, 1970	
Trichina	East Africa	Fortie, 1938	In flesh
Fasciola gigantica	Kenya	Hammond, 1972	
Trypanosoma (Duttonella) uniforme	East Africa	Baker, 1969	
Hydatid cyst (in liver)	East Africa	Sikes, 1969	
Babesia sp. (in blood)	East Africa	Sikes, 1969	
Cytauxzoonosis	South Africa	McCully *et al.*, 1970	
Sarcocystosis	East Africa	Kaliner *et al.*, 1971	
Protostrongylid larvae	East Africa	Dinnik and Sachs, 1968	In feces

4 *Taxonomy of the Giraffe*

In 1758 the giraffe, along with other known animals and plants, was finally given by Linnaeus an official scientific name and in turn a scientific relationship with other animals. However, with no giraffe to look at and no material to work with, Linnaeus named the giraffe *Cervus camelopardalis,* placing it in the same genus as the American elk and the red deer. His description of the animal was taken from that of Belon, who had seen a captive giraffe in Cairo over 200 years earlier. This particular northern giraffe became the type specimen for which the species was named. (See Table 4–1 for a complete taxonomic review of the giraffe.)

It was soon apparent that although the giraffe might be as nearly related to the deer as to any other ungulate, this relationship was not close. In 1762, Brisson renamed the giraffe *Giraffa giraffa,* and in 1848 this was amended to *Giraffa camelopardalis* (Linnaeus), the name in use today.

Just at the time that the northern giraffe was given a scientific name by Linnaeus, a second kind of giraffe was reported in Europe. All the giraffe seen in Europe up until this time had been from the headwaters of the Nile, but with Dutch explorers pushing northward in southern Africa, a southern giraffe was killed near the Orange River in 1761 and its skin sent back from Cape Town to Leyden University in the Netherlands by the Governor of South Africa. The Dutch proved as unfamiliar with giraffe as Linnaeus had been. One scholar wrote, ''I saw the skin of a young one [giraffe] at Leyden, well stuffed and

TABLE 4-1 TAXONOMY OF THE GIRAFFE[a]

Giraffa Brünnich, 1772

Giraffa Brünnich, 1772:36. Type species *Cervus camelopardalis* Linnaeus, 1758, by monotypy. *Giraffa* Brisson, 1762, although frequently cited, is in a work that is not consistently binomial and is therefore unavailable for purposes of nomenclature unless specifically validated by the International Commission on Zoological Nomenclature, a step that has not been taken, although some have advocated it.

Camelopardalis Schreber, 1784:pl. 255. Type species *Camelopardalis giraffa* Schreber, 1784, by monotypy.

Orasius Oken, 1816:744. Type species *Cervus camelopardalis* Linnaeus, 1758, by monotypy. Ruled unavailable, because in a work not consistently binomial, by the International Commission (Opinion 417, 1956, Bull. Zool. Nomenclature 14:1).

Trachelotherium Gistl, 1848:81: Proposed as a replacement name for *Camelopardalis* Schreber, 1784.

CONTEXT AND CONTENT. Order Artiodactyla, Suborder Ruminantia, Infraorder Pecora, Family Giraffidae, Subfamily Giraffinae. There are only two living giraffids, the okapi, *Okapia johnstoni*, and the giraffe, *Giraffa camelopardalis*.

Giraffa camelopardalis Linnaeus, 1758

Cervus camelopardalis Linnaeus, 1758:66. Type locality "Sennar and Aethiopia."

Camelopardalis Giraffa Schreber, 1784:pl. 255 only, rather than Boddaert, 1785: 133 as usually cited. Type locality of Schreber not given, Boddaert gave "Cape of Good Hope," but no giraffe have been found that far south; here restricted to Warmbad, where Brink (1761) encountered and described giraffe just north of the Orange River.

Cameleopardalis antiquorum Jardine, 1835. Type locality "Sennar and Darfour," restricted to Baggar el Homer, Kordofan, about 10°N and 28°E by Harper (1940).

Camelopardalis aethiopica Ogilby, 1837:134. Type locality undesignated, by inference Ethiopia.

Camelopardalis capensis Lesson, 1842:168. Type locality Cape of Good Hope.

Giraffa senaariensis Trouessart, 1898:902. Type locality interpreted to be south of Sennaar, Anglo-Egyptian Sudan by Allen (1939:468).

Giraffa tippelskirchi Matschie, 1898:78. Type locality Lake Eyassi, southeast of Victoria Nyanza, Tanganyika Territory (now Tanzania).

Giraffa schillingsi Matschie, 1898:79. Type locality Taveta, Kenya.

Giraffa infumata Noack, 1908:356. Type locality Barotse, middle Zambesi region, Northern Rhodesia (now Zambia).

Giraffa hagenbecki Knottnerus-Meyer, 1910:800. Type locality Gallaland, southern Abyssinia (now Ethiopia).

CONTEXT AND CONTENT. Context noted in generic summary above. Nine subspecies are recognized (Ansell, 1968) as follows:

TABLE 4–1 (continued)

G. c. camelopardalis (Linnaeus, 1758:66), see above (*biturigum* Duvernoy, *aethiopica* Ogilby, and *typica* Bryden are synonyms).

G. c. antiquorum (Jardine), 1835:187, see above (*senaariensis* Trouessart and *congoensis* Lydekker are synonyms).

G. c. peralta Thomas, 1898:40. Type locality near Lokoja, at the junction of the Niger and Benue rivers in Nigeria, probably north of the confluence (Happold, 1969).

G. c. reticulata de Winton, 1899:212. Type locality the Loroghi Mts. in Kenya (*hagenbecki* Knottnerus-Meyer and *nigrescens* Lydekker are synonyms). Mertens (1968 a, b) pointed out that *reticulata* de Winton, 1899, was a junior homonym of *reticulata* Weinland, 1863, but requested validation of de Winton's name and suppression of Weinland's by the International Commission on Zoological Nomenclature under their plenary powers, because Weinland's type locality was within the range of *antiquorum* rather than that of *reticulata* as these names have been used recently. This has been given by Opinion 944. The name *australis* Rhoads is also a synonym (Ansell and Dagg, 1971).

G. c. rothschildi Lydekker, 1903:122. Type locality, as given originally, Uasin Gishu Plateau east of Lake Baringo, Kenya, corrected to west of Lake Baringo (Lydekker, 1908) (*cottoni* Lydekker a synonym).

G. c. tippelskirchi Matschie, 1898:78, see above (*schillingsi* Matschie a synonym).

G. c. thornicrofti Lydekker, 1911:484. Type locality Luangua Valley, Petauke, Eastern Province, Northern Rhodesia (now Zambia).

G. c. angolensis Lydekker, 1903:121. Type locality by the Cunene River 240 km southwest of Humbe, Angola (*infumata* Noack a synonym according to Ansell).

G. c. giraffa Schreber, 1784:pl. 255, see above (*capensis* Lesson, *australis* Swainson, *maculata* Weinland, and *wardi* Lydekker, are synonyms).

[a] Based on Dagg (1971).

preserved; otherwise might possibly have entertained doubts in respect to the existence of so extraordinary a quadruped."

By 1800, both northern and southern giraffe were known in Europe, but no one wondered if they were the same or not. Drawings and descriptions of the southern giraffe appeared in Levaillant's account of his travels in southern Africa which was published in Paris in 1790, so that this type of giraffe was relatively well documented. The northern giraffe ought to have been better known by virtue of its repeated introduction earlier into Europe and by its proximity to Europe, but the only scientific description of it was the second-hand one of Linnaeus.

The northern giraffe became much better known in 1827, the year that the gifts of giraffe from Egypt reached the kings of England and of France. The French giraffe was the animal that made French zoologists decide there were two kinds of giraffe. Before her arrival in France, St. Hilaire had concluded that there was only one species—that described by Levaillant from southern Africa. He had studied the remains of a southern giraffe sent home by Levaillant and exhibited in the Paris Museum. In 1827, after he had had a chance to study the new arrival from northern Africa, St. Hilaire decided that there were two species. Sir Richard Owen agreed with him formally in 1841 after he had inspected skulls of the Nubian and of the Cape giraffe.

Following Swainson (1835) and Ogilby (1836), Sundevall claimed in 1842 that the two kinds were two variations of one species. The major difference between them he found was in the coat; the Cape giraffe had longer hairs, probably because of the colder climate in the south. His hypothesis was later confirmed by Carl Hagenbeck, who kept giraffe in unheated stables in Germany where the temperature was only a few degrees above freezing, a novel experiment at a time when it was believed that all tropical animals should be kept in hot-house conditions. Hagenbeck's giraffe thrived and by the end of the winter had grown a thick crop of hair two and a half times the normal length (Street, 1956).

Lesson (1842) disagreed with Sundevall's conclusions and reasserted St. Hilaire's conviction that there were two species of giraffe. He named them *Camelopardalis giraffa* from Nubia and Sennar in the north and *Camelopardalis capensis* from the Cape of Good Hope. The latter species was based on Levaillant's description of the giraffe from the Orange River area. Wild giraffe apparently never came closer than 700 km to the Cape, so Lesson's location for it was a misleading one rather than otherwise.

The giraffe vacillated between being one and two species for over 50 years, until the last part of the nineteenth century. At that time more information about giraffe became available as Africa was being opened up on a large scale by hunters and explorers. Many of these adventurers sent the skins and skulls of giraffe they had shot to European museums. With giraffe material arriving from newly explored parts of Africa where giraffe had not been collected before, the taxonomists renewed their interest in the classification of the giraffe. Nevertheless, Schillings reported that even in 1903 with professional help the skin of a male giraffe "withstands every art of the taxidermist who finds it one of his most difficult tasks in the tropics, without the employment of salt and alum baths, to preserve it for safe transport to museums at home" (Podmore, 1958).

Thomas (1894) was the first to separate giraffe on the basis of their spotting. He contrasted the *blotched* giraffe which inhabited most of Africa and had blotches or spots separated by broad bands of the lighter ground color with the *reticulated* giraffe which lived only in the northeastern part of the continent. The first of the latter striking animals had been shot the previous year at Lake Rudolph. They had polygonal spots placed so closely together that the ground color was present only as a narrow light network rather than as broad bands.

Thomas decided this pattern difference merited subspecific ranking for the two kinds of giraffe.

Thomas was less justified in instituting a new subspecies for a giraffe shot in Nigeria. This race was established on the basis of the skull, skin, and leg bone of a single female giraffe sent from Nigeria to the British Museum. The female skull measured over 66 cm, which is long, but not so long as to merit Thomas's name for his subspecies—*Giraffa camelopardalis peralta*—indicating an exceptionally tall variety of giraffe.

In 1899 De Winton agreed with Thomas that the reticulate giraffe deserved a subspecific ranking, but he divided the giraffe into two other species, *G. camelopardalis* and *G. capensis* on the basis of the number of horns they possessed. He decided that the former northern giraffe had three distinct horns in the adult male at least, the third being the median horn on the nose, while the latter southern giraffe had only two horns. Unfortunately we know now that these distinctions are not constant, and therefore not all his conclusions are tenable.

Lydekker reviewed the entire classification of the giraffe in 1904. From a thorough examination of the horns, coat pattern, and coat coloration of all the European specimens that had been collected over the years he concluded that there were two species, this time the reticulate giraffe *G. reticulata* and the blotched giraffe, *G. camelopardalis*. He divided the latter species into 10 subspecies, each with a distinct range (Fig. 4–1). Lydekker's work was competent, since his names and subspecies are more or less the ones still in use today (Appendix A). But the giraffe material to which he had access was limited, with barely enough specimens to describe even one race thoroughly. At best it was hoped that no important racial characters were attributed to individual idiosyncracies. He felt that for giraffe in a cline from north to south the frontal horn decreased in size and the lower legs became more fully spotted. These clinal changes are not accepted as valid today.

Although Lydekker was primarily a taxonomic "splitter," he lumped some races together. When he realized that two species had been described from locations within 300 km of each other, *Giraffa tippelskirchi* from southeast of Lake Victoria and *Giraffa schillingsi* from Taveta in Kenya; that giraffe wandered freely between these two areas; and that these two species looked very like all the other giraffe in the area, he combined them into one subspecies, *Giraffa camelopardalis tippelskirchi*. (It was not difficult for Lydekker to make the comparison as these two "species" had been described on successive pages in the same Berlin journal of 1898.)

Many of Lydekker's other races were established from groups of animals that could also interbreed if they wished. In southern Sudan alone in an area about 800 km square there are four subspecies of giraffe which are not separated from each other by an impassable river or any other physical barrier (Fig. 4–1).

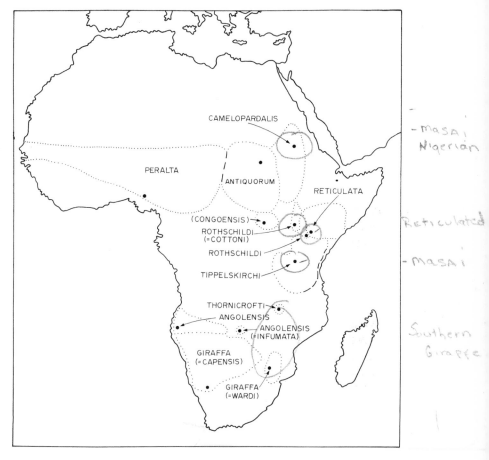

Fig. 4–1 Maximum ranges of subspecies of giraffe, often now much reduced.

Probably there is interbreeding, as Stott (1959) and Dagg (1962c) have suggested, since the subspecies of the Sudan look similar. Droughts are not so rare in the Sudan and in other parts of Africa that they do not cause occasional large-scale movements of giraffe.

Lydekker confused matters further by giving two subspecies an overlapping range, Linnaeus's giraffe *G. c. camelopardalis* from "Aethiopia and Sennar" and *G. c. antiquorum* from "Senaar and Darfour." In the past much time has been spent trying to prove that one or the other of these two races is misrepresented in its range. With some hesitancy the former is now said to come from east Sudan while the latter comes from southwest Sudan, apparently where the first French giraffe was captured (Setzer, 1956). More probably both races belong in a single group.

Lydekker's species *G. reticulata* has provided the most controversy. This animal is now generally considered as a subspecies rather than as a distinct species because these giraffe breed freely with other varieties in zoos, producing fertile young. They also interbreed with other races in northern Kenya, such as with Masai giraffe between the Tana and Athi Rivers, so that some "hybrid" individuals may have reticulated legs and blotched necks while others have spotted legs and reticulated necks. Several specimens have been briefly glorified with their own name before being incorporated again into the reticulated race —forms such as *Giraffa hagenbecki* and *Giraffa reticulata nigrescens.* The most extreme example of a reticulate giraffe being given another name is that of the original *G. c. australis.* The type specimen was shot near Lake Rudolph by Dr. Donaldson Smith, an American on a hunting trip to Africa, from where the head and neck of the animal were sent to Philadelphia. In 1896 a Mr. Rhoads there, who had had no previous opportunity of studying giraffe since so few of these animals reached the New World, originated a new subspecies for it, despite the fact that other giraffe had been collected from Lake Rudolph and he had no reason to believe that his giraffe differed markedly from them. To compound the confusion, the *australis* giraffe has become listed more recently as a kind synonymous with the Cape giraffe of South Africa, undoubtedly because "austral" means "southern." In reality the *australis* specimen was from the extreme north of the giraffe's range and therefore theoretically as unlike the Cape giraffe as possible (Ansell and Dagg, 1971).

Since Lydekker's revision two new giraffe races have been reported: *G. c. infumata* in 1908 from a small group of giraffe in Barotseland and *G. c. thornicrofti* in 1911 from a single herd on the east bank of the Great Luangwa River in Zambia. *Infumata* referred to the smoky spots of the former giraffe, and Thornicroft was the name of the man who supplied a specimen from the latter range. Some zoologists claim that these two subspecies are true ones, others that they should be together in one race, and the most sceptical that they belong to the other groups in southern Africa and do not need a new designation.

Krumbiegel (1939) has studied the taxonomy of the giraffe in detail, but his conclusions often follow those of Lydekker, and those that differ have not been widely accepted. Because of lack of skeletal material, Krumbiegel based his races on the patterns of the giraffe coats, using many skins and a great number of photographs to reach his conclusions. He ignored coat color, which changes with the age of the individual and with its death, and also the face and head spots, which he found were often variable among individuals, although Lydekker had depended strongly on these features in his classification.

Most of the taxonomic work on the giraffe has been based on coat pattern, although the inheritance of spotting is not clearly understood, and many giraffe have nondescript spots which could belong to any of a number of subspecies. Also the coat patterns of the individuals in a group may vary greatly. As early as 1911 Rothschild and Neuville commented on the reserve with which the spots must be regarded as a basis for subspeciation; Kollman (1920) and Shortridge (in Fox, 1938) felt that Lydekker's races were not all justified; and Grzimek (1960a) wrote that "working on single skins in museums led Europeans to believe at one time that there were several subspecies [of giraffe]."

Even though markings are not good criteria for subdividing the giraffe into all the present races, some races of giraffe have such distinctive spots that they can be identified even by laymen (Fig. 4–2). The most obvious examples are the Masai (*G. c. tippelskirchi*) and the reticulated (*G. c. reticulata*) subspecies. Dagg (1968) studied the spot inheritance of the nine giraffe at Taronga Zoo whose parents were known. Her analysis indicated that the number of spots, the total area of spotting, and the shape of the spots—the three ways in which the spots of an individual could be defined numerically—were all apparently inherited, although not by a small number of genes, as Spinage (1968a) suggested. Some of these characteristics could probably be used to define a race. For example, the total area of spots on the trunk and neck was 80% on a typical reticulated giraffe but only 60% in the average of the mixed herd of Taronga giraffe. Using such a characteristic, one could also assess the geographic area over which races of reticulated and neighboring giraffe had interbred. Dagg also concluded

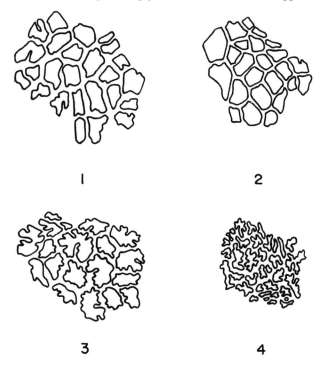

1   2

3   4

Fig. 4–2   Tracings of trunk spots of giraffe belonging to three races. 1. *G. c. rothschildi;* 2. *G. c. reticulata;* 3. and 4. *G. c. tippelskirchi.* After Dagg, 1968

from this study that the racial characteristics presently in use do not run in clines geographically as Lydekker had suggested, nor do they shed any light on the early dispersion of the species throughout Africa.

The horns are the other criterion on which races have been based. Except for the universal main pair, the number of horns in giraffe is not constant. Although the median horn has been described as the most important skull character in giraffe (northern ones with and southern ones without), this is a fallacy. Some northern individuals have a small median horn, while southern giraffe may have a strongly developed one. Fourteen skulls from Namibia showed a great variety in their horn development, several of them possessing well-developed median horns (Stevenson-Hamilton, 1912). Some median horns were originally separate bones which became fused onto the skull as the giraffe developed into an adult, exactly as do the main horns. Other median growths are only bumps on the nose. Similarly, bone outgrowths ("mizzen horns") at the back of the skull may be prominent on some individuals in a population but not on others. Bony growths may jut out over one or both eyes, and smaller bumps may develop about the head. It is difficult therefore even to decide what constitutes a true horn.

Extra facial bony growths occur commonly in males, apparently caused by the trauma of the head-hitting fights (Dagg, 1965). Lydekker did not worry about such sexual variations in the horns, although there are marked differences between male and female horns, as Singer and Boné (1960) have emphasized. Among other things, the main horns are smaller and more slender in the female than in the male, the median horn is less prominent in the female, and there are no additional bony growths on her head. As with the coat pattern, it seems safe to say that the horns of individuals are so variable that they should not be used for taxonomic work.

In summary, it seems that both horn growth and spotting are of doubtful use in the taxonomy of the giraffe. Skull characters other than the horns may offer the surest basis for systematics. However, there are too few skulls available for study as yet to enable a complete survey of the races to be made, although some skull measurements have been published (Thomas, 1901; Rothschild and Neuville, 1911; Lönnberg, 1912; Kollmann, 1920; Granvik, 1925; Broman, 1938b; Roberts, 1951; Singer and Boné, 1960). Without a thorough study any attempt to divide the species into further races or to telescope several races into one would only add further confusion to the already confused nomenclature.

5 The Okapi and Fossil Giraffids

The family Giraffidae to which the giraffe belongs includes one other living species, the okapi *Okapia johnstoni,* and various fossil members. Although the giraffe and the okapi are anatomically similar enough to be grouped in the same family, superficially they are very different, with the former being a creature of open woodlands and the latter of dense rain forests. Because of its dense forest habitat, the okapi was only discovered in 1901 by Sir Harry Johnston, the British explorer and empire builder. Johnston had been curious about this creature since 1883, when Henry Stanley had mentioned the possibility that a large unknown ungulate living in the Belgian Congo was hunted by pygmies.[1] The pygmies had described the okapi as being striped like a zebra and shaped like a mule, which made Johnston believe that it was an equid, despite the fact that other equids all live in open-country habitats.

By 1900, although Johnston had still not seen an okapi, he had acquired two pieces of okapi hide which he sent to Dr. Sclater at the British Museum in London, along with a letter detailing what he knew of this animal. This information, plus the zebralike white stripes on the black hide persuaded Dr. Sclater to include the okapi provisionally in the horse family; he named it *Equus? johnstoni.*

[1] *Okapi* was a pygmy word for this animal.

55

Shortly after this a Swedish officer in the Belgian service sent Johnston two okapi skulls and one complete skin, since Johnston had shown interest in the animal. As soon as he saw these, especially the male skull with its horns, Johnston realized that the okapi was quite unlike the horse but very like the giraffe. Among other things, horses have upper incisors while giraffids do not. In fact, the skulls were very similar to that of the extinct giraffid *Helladotherium* whose fossil remains had been discovered in Greece. When he sent these new remains to the British Museum, he suggested that the okapi be called *Helladotherium tigrinum,* the specific name referring to the white thigh stripes. But Professor Ray Lankester of the British Museum decided that this new animal was about as closely related to the giraffe as to *Helladotherium.* After careful study he established a new genus for the animal, renaming it *Okapi johnstoni* Sclater. Today the close relationship of the giraffe and the okapi has been confirmed by a technique not available at that time, namely a comparison of the protein serums of the blood of these two species. Van den Berghe and Boné (1944) tested the antigen relationship of both the serum and the globulins of fresh blood of these two animals and showed their affinity. Members of the deer, bovine, and horse families showed no close relationship with either the giraffe or the okapi.

As soon as the existence of the okapi was established, scholars tried to prove that it had been known for thousands of years. It was recognized in Neolithic rock-carvings in the Sahara, on early Egyptian painted vases, and on a Sumerian chariot ring (Colbert, 1936). Whether or not these representations are of the okapi, indicating that they were more widespread in Africa in earlier times than they are today, or whether they were of a similar animal such as *Sivatherium,* an extinct giraffid, remains unknown.

The most important similarities between the giraffe and the okapi—features that immediately enabled Lankester to classify the okapi as a member of the giraffe family—are the more or less skin-covered horns and the lobed canine teeth. Because the horns are covered with skin, they superficially resemble deer antlers in velvet, but instead of being shed each year as antlers are, the horns of the giraffids are permanent. In this they resemble the horns of bovids. These features of the horns set the giraffids apart from all other ungulates.

The unbranched horns of the two living giraffids look fairly similar. At 30 cm those of the male giraffe are over twice as long as those of the okapi, but the giraffe is over twice as tall as its 2-meter relative. Both types of horn rise from the top of the head behind the eyes. The horns of the giraffe retain their girth right up to the tip, although those of the female often narrow in the middle; those of the okapi taper into sharp points. These tips in the male okapi are of smooth polished skinless bone. The round top of the male giraffe's horns are also hairless, the circlet of black hair that surrounds the horns in very young giraffe having been worn off in the frequent head-hitting matches of the males. The okapi's horns point backwards while those of the giraffe stand more nearly erect.

The female okapi has no horns, although bumps on her head mark the place where her horns would have grown. The female giraffe has smaller horns than the male, which retain the jaunty black hairs that stick up beyond the bone itself. The okapi uses its horns to some extent intraspecifically (Walther, 1962). The bull giraffe also uses its horns to fight other bull giraffe, but never to fend off enemies. For that they kick with their legs. The female giraffe has no apparent use for her horns.

The second distinction of these two species is the lobed canine teeth, sometimes erroneously called fourth incisors or first premolars. Their presence in the lower jaw beside the row of incisors increases the width of the front teeth considerably. Instead of grasping a twig or leaf in its mouth and snipping it off briskly as most antelope do, a giraffe or an okapi usually grasps a twig between its jaws and combs off small twigs or leaves from the main stems. (The jaws of the giraffids are so long and slender that they are probably not powerful enough to break large twigs with their teeth.) The great width of the "comb" created by the incisiform nature of the canines and their additional lobe increases the efficiency with which the giraffe and okapi can browse.

The lobed appearance of the canine is so distinctive that any large fossil remains can be positively identified as belonging to the giraffe family if they possess it. The okapi's canine possesses two lobes, but in some giraffe three or even four lobes may be apparent on the inner face. Ansell (personal communication) is the first to suggest that the lobed canine may vary with the races of giraffe. His preliminary evidence is that three adult *thornicrofti* males had tri-lobed canines, while five males and one female from Rhodesia had bi-lobed canines. A second Rhodesian female had one bi-lobed canine and one nearly tri-lobed. Further research will reveal if these differences are truly racial or not.

The lobulations are most obvious in young giraffe whose teeth are not very worn down. These juveniles also have fine serrations on the free edges of both their milk and their permanent teeth (Neuville, 1930). The serrations plus the grooves present between the lobes of the canines help the giraffe to browse as effectively as possible at an age when they are changing from a milk diet to one of solid foods.

It is interesting to compare the early dentition of the giraffe and the dromedary, both animals adapted to dry conditions (Neuville, 1931–32). These animals eat the leaves found at the end of branches, grasping an entire twig in their mouths in the same way. But in the dromedary all of the lower incisors are denticulated, both in the milk and in the permanent dentition. The young dromedary also has incisiform milk canines lateral to the incisors which underline the importance of a wide front row of teeth, especially in young animals. These factors would seem to make the dromedary even better adapted to browsing than the giraffe.

The most unusual characteristics of a giraffid skull which have already been discussed—skin-covered horns and lobed canines—are shared by both the giraffe and the okapi. So are the low-crowned rugose cheek teeth with rough vertically plicated enamel coverings. Since the enamel ridges run lengthwise with the jaw, the movement of the jaw when cudding is sideways and therefore at right angles to these ridges.

Both giraffids also have air spaces beneath the horn region. These are relatively larger than the pneumatic sinuses in most ungulates and are especially extensive in the giraffe. Their main use is probably to lighten the weight of the skull which must be carried on such a long neck. As it is, the weight of a male's head and neck presents the animal with a permanent pull of about 253 kg (557 lb) along the back of the neck that must be counteracted by the resilient nuchal ligament which extends over 2 meters from the back of the head to the thoracic vertebrae. (Elephants and rhinoceros have large skull sinuses too, presumably also to decrease the weight of their heavy heads.) A second function of the sinuses may be to mitigate the effects of blows exchanged in the head-hitting matches of the males. For example, mountain sheep (*Ovis canadensis*) which fight by clashing their horns and skulls together have a 5-cm width of air-pocketed bone present over the brain (Geist, personal communication).

Long legs are another feature that giraffe and okapi share, with the forelegs longer than the hind legs unlike those in most other ruminants (Colbert, 1938). When Georges Buffon first saw a giraffe, he noted that the forelegs were twice as long as the hind legs. Baudier (1623), after seeing a giraffe in Constantinople, reported that the forelegs were four or five times as long. In reality the legs of the giraffe are of nearly the same length, the apparent inequality being caused by the marked slope of the back. The withers are considerably higher than the rump because of the long neural spines and massive musculature which is present around the shoulders to help support the head and neck. Especially long forelegs enable the giraffe to balance the weight of its head and neck readily. The okapi occupies a position between the giraffe and other ruminants, which have slightly longer hind legs than forelegs. Because of their long legs, the giraffe and the okapi execute the same type of walk in which the legs on one side of the body are swung forward more or less together, preventing them from hitting each other (Dagg, 1960). When galloping the hind legs pass to the outside of the front ones.

The similarities in the anatomy of the giraffe and the okapi are masked by the differences in superficial aspects of these animals. Few laymen would relate the two animals, even if they saw them side by side at a zoo. Each species has a coloration that helps camouflage it; but since their habitats are completely different, their coloration is too. The brown spotting of the giraffe blends well with sun and shadows present in open forested areas, but no better than the dark coat, striped on the hindquarters to break up the shape of the animal visually, suits the okapi for its life in the dark forests.

Because of its forest habitat, the okapi has acquired various adaptive features that differ from those of the open-country giraffe. In forest life, eyesight is of limited value when it is possible to see only short distances anyway, and the sense of hearing and smell are proportionately more important. Conforming with this, the okapi has less specialized eyes but relatively larger ears and tympanic bullae than those of the giraffe (Pocock, 1936). The giraffe is active during the daylight, when good vision is essential, while the okapi is largely nocturnal (Wilmet, 1913).

The social habits of the two species are also different. Giraffe are usually found in groups, as are many other open-country ungulates that rely on numbers and many pairs of eyes as protection against predators. The okapi is largely solitary, since in forests there is no advantage in numbers which merely attract attention to an animal that would rather evade notice. Both species can make vocal noises, but both are normally silent. Perhaps because of its more solitary nature, the okapi is more wary of human beings.

Although not many matings of giraffe and okapi have been observed, the social nature of the giraffe apparently simplifies this behavior in this species (Table 5-1). The "Approach" and "Demonstration" phases as defined by Walther (1960) are important in the okapi in quietening the defense reactions of the female, but they are either not present or not emphasized in giraffe, in which the animals are used to each other's presence. The "Chasing" and "Copulation" phases are similar in these two species and indeed also in many antelope (Walther, 1960).

A number of comprehensive studies have been made of fossil giraffids (Pilgrim, 1911; Bohlin, 1927; Matthew, 1929; Colbert, 1935a,b; Joleaud, 1937; Pairó, 1952; Singer and Boné, 1960; and Churcher, in press). In general the giraffe is considered the most specialized giraffid because it shows the most extensive development of many features present but less evolved in earlier giraffids (Major, 1902a,b; Bohlin, 1927; Colbert, 1935a, 1938). These include:

a. horns more posteriorly placed on the skull, partly at least on the parietals rather than entirely on the frontals
b. a broad rather than a narrow frontal region
c. more telescopic eye orbits
d. eye orbits shifted more posteriorly
e. increasing development of air spaces within the skull

An exception is the size and number of horns, which are often larger and more numerous in extinct species than in the giraffe (Fig. 5-1). For example *Bramatherium, Sivatherium,* and *Giraffokeryx* all had four horns, most of them larger than those in the giraffe. Curiously however, female giraffe have acquired horns that many female ancestors did not have, despite their apparent lack of usefulness. Although bull giraffe do not have more than two large horns, they usually have a number of other bony skull growths that are often called horns even though it is doubtful if most possess centers of ossification.

TABLE 5-1 COMPARISON OF MATING IN GIRAFFE AND OKAPI

Phases	Mating behavior of two captive okapi (after Walther, 1960)	Comparison in giraffe (from Dagg, pers. obs.) of one mating in wild and two in captivity
Approach	—m and f explore each other's anal regions —male flehmens —f aggressive if m touches her body but allows m to lick her face —if frontal approach, both raise noses to display white throats	—m explores anal region of f with his nose —male flehmens several times —f never aggressive —no such display and no such markings to be displayed
Demonstration	—m raises neck with head horizontal to demonstrate dominance —m kicks front leg forward —f may lower head and is no longer defensive —m approaches f at right angles usually	—male raises neck, presumably to increase height and impress f —m does not kick front leg —f ignores m —m makes no efforts to appease f
Chasing	—m follows f and stands behind her; f runs a few steps forward often —m follows, raising and lowering head and kicking with a foreleg behind her —m may touch f's flank with his forehead	—m follows f and stands behind her; f walks a few steps forward often —m follows persistently, without kicking —m may touch f's body with his head; once f licked m's trunk
Copulation	—m behind f, leans forward to lick f's neck —before mounting, m raises head and neck and one foreleg and bends hind legs —m mounts with head high —f's neck stretched forward and ears spread sideways —after mating, f quickly becomes defensive again and m responds aggressively	—m behind f, often with penis unsheathed —before mounting, m bows head down over f one or more times, and gently touches f's hind legs with his front leg; moves hind legs closer to front legs —m mounts with head high —f's neck at usual angle —after mating, f moves quietly away; m stayed close to her and mating occurred 3 times in captivity during a 3-hour period

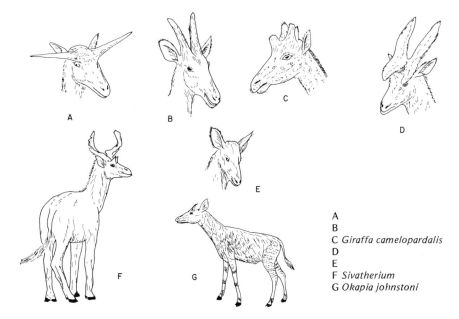

A
B
C *Giraffa camelopardalis*
D
E
F *Sivatherium*
G *Okapia johnstoni*

Fig. 5–1   Fossil and living giraffids. (After Churcher, in press)

The skulls of extinct giraffids confirm the diagnostic characteristic of the lobed canine teeth. These teeth are present in all the fossil species, indicating that all of them were browsers like the giraffe and the okapi rather than grass eaters. The teeth in general are similar in fossil giraffe, with the molars and premolars heavy and low, with deep folds. The more specialized giraffids tend to have slightly larger and broader teeth with higher crowns that provide wider and longer-lasting grinding surfaces. The general similar conformation of the teeth in giraffids is not surprising when it is remembered that the family has evolved only since the Miocene, a short period of time (about 15 million years) compared to that during which many mammalian families developed.

Other skeletal features shared by giraffids are the feet, in which the lateral metapodials and digits are atrophied more than in most other cloven-hoofed mammals. The latter modification is expected in animals that live in open country and need speed to survive. The legs are elongated in some giraffids but not in animals such as *Sivatherium,* which was as big as an elephant and so needed sturdy supports. Its cannon bones were only half as long as those of the giraffe (Singer and Boné, 1960).

Black (1915a,b) felt that the surface of the brain leaves an imprint on the inside of the skull which is retained as long as the skull itself remains. This is not necessarily so (C. S. Churcher, personal communication), and the fossil material that Black used was limited, but he found that the arrangement of grooves in the brain was more specialized in *Giraffa* than in *Okapia* and in *Okapia* than in *Samotherium*.

A study of fossil giraffids indicates that a close relative of the giraffe, *Giraffa jumae,* had evolved to a great height as early as the lower Pleistocene two million years ago (Leakey, 1965). Bones of the genus *Okapia* were also present at this time in the same Olduvai Beds of Tanzania, suggesting that the *jumae* giraffe and an extinct okapi occupied the same habitat, which the present-day okapi and giraffe do not do. Possibly the okapi, which remains strikingly similar to extinct giraffids like *Palaeotragus* and has not evolved greatly, has only been able to survive in the smaller and less favorable rain forest areas of Zaire (Joleaud, 1937).

There is controversy about where the very early giraffids evolved, just as there is argument about what Africa looked like in the past. Most palaeontologists think that the giraffe family evolved in the holarctic region of Europe and Asia, from where various forms since the early Miocene have migrated into Africa (Fig. 5–2). Arambourg (1963), however, considers it likely that the giraffids evolved in Africa and moved outward from there.

Other controversy exists over the type of mammal the giraffe evolved from in the Miocene. Three possibilities have been suggested: a cow- or antelopelike ancestor (*Bovidae*), a deerlike ancestor (*Cervidae*), or a pronghornlike ancestor (*Antilocapridae*). To mention the most unlikely first, the peculiarity of the horns of the giraffe caused Boas (1934) to relate the giraffe to the pronghorn antelope, even though the pronghorns are believed to have evolved entirely in the New

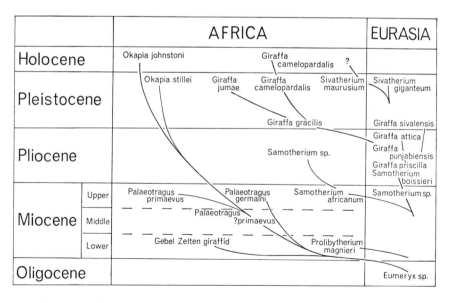

Fig. 5–2   Relationships and origins of African Giraffidae. (After Churcher, in press)

World while giraffid remains are confined to the Old World. Over their horn cores the pronghorn antelope have horny sheaths which are shed annually, unlike the bone core itself. Boas decided that the horny sheaths found partly over the horns in the okapi are a remnant of this same type of sheath. In the giraffe where there has been a further reduction of this sheath the wisps of hair round the horn may be regarded as the last vestige of it. Boas correlated the reduction of the sheath with the lengthening of the neck in the giraffe. Colbert (1935b), however, believed that the giraffids never had horny sheaths and that the hair-covered horns of the modern giraffe are a primitive character of ungulates.

Giraffe resemble *Bovidae* in several ways. Both have permanent horns which are not shed annually unlike the antlers of the deer, and many bovids have horns in both sexes as does the giraffe. The most valid suggestion for a possible relationship concerns the growth of the horns. Those of the giraffe are present as small lumps of cartilage under the skin over the skull at the animal's birth, unattached to the skull and soft, to make parturition easier. These lumps or ôssicones have their own centers of bone formation which ossify and fuse to the skull in the young calf. Frechkop (1946) and Geist (1966) suggested that the time of fusing is different in the bovids but the process is the same. In both families the horns develop from the ôssicones and the overlying skin in the region of the frontal (in bovids and the okapi) or slightly farther back (in giraffe). In giraffe the skin covering the ôssicone grows a hair coat; in bovids the skin becomes modified as a cornified layer of horn. Some extinct giraffids and some bovids also share a longitudinal groove of uncertain origin along the surface of the horn (Singer and Boné, 1960).

Lavocat (1958) felt that the members of the giraffe family were derived from the common stock of both cervids and bovids and so are equally independent of either, but most zoologists believe that the *Giraffidae* are more closely related to the *Cervidae* than to any other family of mammals (Linnaeus, 1758; Ogilby, 1836; Owen, 1841; Gregory, 1928; Loomis, 1928; Matthew, 1934; Colbert, 1955). As recently as 1836 Ogilby placed the giraffe in a group within the deer family, basing the relationship on such superficial considerations as the presence of four teats in the females and "horns" in both sexes in the giraffe as in the caribou. Giraffids and cervids also have in common more important characteristics such as those concerned with the teeth. Additionally, the horns of the giraffe are theoretically similar to the antlers of the deer when the latter are "in velvet," although the giraffe's covering resembles the rest of its coat unlike that of the deer (Spinage, 1970). However, deer lose first the skin covering and then the antlers themselves each year, while the giraffe's horns are never shed. Owen (1841) compared the horn covering of the giraffe with the skin over the frontal pedicles of the muntjak deer. (Owen had also first related the giraffe very closely to the deer family and to the elk in particular, but this was on the evidence of a fossil described by Duvernoy, 1844, which was later found not to be a fossil at all.)

6 *External Features of the Giraffe*

Its great size gives the giraffe a number of advantages. It can eat leaves between ground level and almost 6 meters while no other living mammals except elephants and arboreal species can reach above 3 meters. Giraffe can see danger from a greater distance than can other game animals; their height allows them to be greatly dispersed and to browse a large area as a herd, yet still be in contact by sight. They can run fairly fast and walk long distances. A giraffe's large size allows for efficient use of food, both in its storage and in its fermentation; its size eliminates most of the smaller potential predators and is of some advantage in temperature regulation. Larger species generally live longer than smaller ones, thereby permitting a greater accumulation of antibodies and experience, if these two disparate things may be grouped together.

Some zoologists have wondered why the giraffe did not stop evolving upward when it was, say, 3 meters tall (Darwin, 1859; Pincher, 1949; Wood-Jones, 1949). If dozens of species of antelope in Africa can survive on leaves growing below 2 meters, as each does in large numbers, there is surely enough food between 2 and 3 meters for the giraffe. The answer may be that when giraffe were evolving there were a number of high browsers to compete for what leaves there were—deinotheres, mastodonts, sivatheres, baluchitheres. These animals subsequently died out, leaving the food supply to the giraffe.

Brownlee (1963) presented a theory to help explain a giraffe's odd shape. Given that the giraffe is a massive animal weighing up to 1000 kg and living in a hot climate, its shape provides the most effective distribution of this weight against the heat. Animals in hot climates need as much surface area as possible where their body heat can be dissipated. The giraffe achieves this with its long legs and neck. (Schreider, 1950, suggests that the tall height of members of the Masai and Watutsi tribes may similarly help them to endure the hot climates of Africa where they live.) Unlike the more compact hippopotamus the giraffe does not need to keep cool by lolling in deep water, and unlike the rhinoceros, buffalo, and elephant it does not wallow in wet mud. Nor does it need to stand or lie in the shade, waving its ears, as elephant often do. Observations at the Taronga Zoo where shade was always available confirmed that giraffe are as relatively impervious to heat in captivity as they apparently are in the wild. In only 12% of 827 observations were giraffe standing or lying in the shade rather than in the direct sunlight (Dagg, 1970a). Only on the hottest day recorded, when the temperature was 54°C in the sun and 38°C in the shade, did most giraffe seek shade; even so six animals remained in the sun.

GENERAL COLORING

The spotting of giraffes' coats is so variable that different patterns have been used to separate this species into subspecies (Chapter 4). The description of each race (Appendix A) sometimes mentions the coloring as well as the spotting, although this varies with individuals and with age.

At Taronga Zoo the calves usually had light brown spots, although one male of six months had spots which were nearly black (Dagg, 1968). The three adult bulls all had spots which had darkened with age; those of the 24-year-old male called Jan Smuts were black. Most of the 11 females had light or medium brown spots, but one had dark spots similar to those of the youngest bull. The coloring of all the giraffe stayed the same or darkened with age. Many of the calves were born with spots that contained pale or white central areas. This area sometimes remained pale in the adult, or extra pigment was laid down during the growth of the animal so that it became darker than the rest of the spot. In at least one of the adult bulls the dark pigmentation had spread out from this central area, gradually covering the entire spot. This differential coloring was considered characteristic of the South African race to which Jan belonged (Krumbiegel, 1939). It was not noted for giraffe from Nubia where one of the female's parents came from, nor for the female herself.

Inheritance also affected the coloration of giraffe apparently. In the nine Taronga giraffe whose parents were known, the father being Jan, the spot color was always the same as the mother's or intermediate between those of both parents. This was also true of the background color, which was tan in Jan and tan or cream in the mothers. The tendency for the center of the spots to darken with age was also probably inherited through the father.

There are many records of white giraffe, some of which may have been albinos (Butler, 1912b; Johnson, 1928; McDougall, 1939; Goodwin, 1956; Hunter, 1957; Bere, 1958; Grzimek, 1966; Turner, 1969, Anon., 1971). One lived with a herd of 70 giraffe in Nairobi National Park (Stott, 1953). This giraffe had poorly defined reddish spots with interspaces of dusty white. Perhaps because of its poor sight, it tended to stay in the middle of the herd, presumably for protection against lions. Goodwin reported a white male from Masailand in Kenya in 1938. Its eyes appeared dark so that it may not have been an albino, although its coat was almost pure white with visible markings most strongly developed on the neck (Petzsch, 1950). In Murchison National Park, there was one white giraffe plus two individuals which were almost black (Bere, 1966). Caldwell (1923) reported another case of melanism in a male Kilimanjaro giraffe whose markings showed only faintly through its black coat. Blum (1957) photographed a young animal with an almost black band around its upper trunk. A pale brown unspotted calf was born to parents of normal coloration at the Ueno Zoo in Tokyo in 1967, the first such animal on record (Anon., 1968).

Because of the widely differing coat patterns and coloration in giraffe, apparently uniformity of coat color is not under as strong a selective pressure by predators as it may be in other species.

CAMOUFLAGE

Different writers disagree violently on the effect of the giraffe's coloring as a protection to it from its enemies, mainly lion and man. Supporting the stand that a giraffe is not protectively colored, Roosevelt wrote:

> Save under wholly exceptional circumstances no brute or human foe of the giraffe could possibly fail to see the huge creature if fairly close by; and at a distance the pattern of the colouration would be lost. The giraffe owes nothing to concealment; its colouration has not the slightest concealing effect so far as its foes are concerned. [in Lönnberg, 1912]

Roosevelt and Heller (1914) not only felt that its coloring was useless, especially when the giraffe's size and shape were so obvious, but that where its pattern was seen it advertised the giraffe and so in a small number of cases might be of disadvantage to it. In addition, they pointed out that the lion hunts its prey by night when appearance has no importance in any case. (This, of course, is the opinion of a member of a night-blind species.) Also individuals in one herd often vary so much in coloration that it is hard to believe that all the giraffe could be camouflaged in the same area at the same time.

Indeed, the giraffe does not try to conceal itself, usually whisking its tail about when it is suspicious and often peering curiously above or to one side of a tree so that it attracts attention to itself, rather than remaining behind the tree where it would escape notice. If the danger is great, the giraffe runs instead of standing motionless hoping to avoid attention.

Roosevelt and his followers must have seen giraffe mostly on open plains and in low bush areas rather than in more dense bush country. No one could miss a giraffe in an open field, but alternately giraffe are hard to recognize in a woods. We have driven within 10 meters of a herd of giraffe in light bush country before spotting any of them, and many others agree that giraffe are most difficult to see in such conditions when their legs resemble tree trunks and their bodies blend with the dappled light and shade of their surroundings (Debenham, 1953; Fortie, 1938; Haywood, 1912; Loveridge, 1945; Schillings, 1905; Tjader, 1910; and so on). Cumming (1850) wrote:

> I have repeatedly been in doubt as to the presence of a troop, until I had recourse to my telescope, and on referring to my savage attendants I have known even their practiced eyes deceived, at one time mistaking these dilapidated tree trunks for camelopards, and again confounding real camelopards with these aged veterans of the forest.

More explicitly, Trouessart (1908) argued that the giraffe's polygonal spots corresponded with the arrangement of *Acacia giraffae* branches. The branches are whitish and fork at more or less open angles, often forming polygonal figures which the minute leaves do not obscure and which resemble the spots of the giraffe. Such patterns could conceivably have evolved in Africa itself from an earlier monochrome giraffid, which is perhaps depicted in early Saharan cave drawings (Arnold, 1940). Lönnberg (1912) also believed that the ancestral giraffe type had a uniform coat color. He felt that spots arose from the concentration of pigment cells about scattered centers on the coat. They were at first fairly light and ill-defined but gradually became more compact, more distinct, and larger as more pigment collected at their periphery. Some spots merged, a fact which would account for the slight radiating lighter streaks in the spots of some present-day races such as *G. c. rothschildi*. Such spots may have several dark centers, a fact which also supports this theory of the confluence of primary spots. Thus the reticulated giraffe, where the spots are dark and so enlarged that only a thin network separates them from each other, is the most specialized form of the giraffe.

Since the reticulate coloring of the northern giraffe is quite different from the blotching of the giraffe farther south, reasons can be suggested to explain this difference. Goodwin (1956) postulated that in the reticulated giraffe the spots and interspaces are sharply separated and contrasted in color to match the sharp, bright equatorial shadows. The southern giraffe have less sharply defined spots to match the more diffuse shadows of the south. Alternately, Lydekker (1903) suggested that the coloring of the giraffe hide corresponded with the animal's habitat. The rich coloring of the reticulated giraffe and of Rothschild's giraffe harmonize with the bush and scrub among which they live, while the shading of the relatively pale, white-legged Nigerian giraffe blends with the sandy shades of the semidesert regions of the Saharan fringe.

Lydekker (1904) and Krumbiegel (1939) believed that the reticulated giraffe was the most original type of giraffe. They held that whole entire spots were the primitive condition with splintering of the spots a secondary adaptation and a forerunner to their further disintegration. The jagged spots of *G. c. tippelskirchi,* the leafy spots of *G. c. infumata* and the stellate spots of *G. c. wardi* thus denoted more specialized varieties of the giraffe. Which if any of the theories is correct can only be speculated.

HAIR

The coloring of the giraffe is of course a function of the hairs that cover the skin; a study of the microscopic structure of the five different types—flank, wrist, mane, tail, and eyelash—is given by Lochte (1952). Broman (1938a) studied the development of the mane, of which the origins can be identified microscopically in a giraffe fetus only 28 cm long.

The varying directions of hairs in a coat produces three types of hair arrangements—whorls, feathering, and crests. (A whorl is a spiral arrangement of the hair, feathering is a simple prolongment of the descending current of a whorl, and a crest is formed when two opposing hair currents meet so that the hairs run in sharply contrary directions.) The great amount of attention given to these features in the giraffe by Kidd (1900, 1903) and Rothschild and Neuville (1911) might seem to be excessive, were it not that Kidd felt they supported Lamarck's belief in the inheritance of acquired characteristics. He argued that the direction of the hair was correlated either with attitudes of rest, activity, or locomotion in any particular region of the body. Activity was restricted to the facial and spinal regions, while locomotion was correlated with the larger movements of the neck, chest, and legs. For example, the joint hairs are affected every time a giraffe gets up or lies down, so tufts and whorls soon appeared near the joints because of these actions. (Rothschild and Neuville, 1911, also noted the relationship between the muscles and the skin arrangements over them, although they agreed that such a correlation was odd when the skin is but loosely attached to the muscles underneath.) Thus the direction of the hair is determined in the living animal by physical conditions. Kidd argued that natural selection would not occur for a minor feature such as the direction in which the hair lies, yet the slopes were already present in the embryo giraffe, which had not been subjected to the same physical conditions as postnatal giraffe. He concluded that unless giraffe were divinely created, the hair slopes must have been produced in the ancestral giraffe during its lifetime activities and passed on from the adults to their young in classic Lamarckian manner.

Even if one cannot accept Kidd's conclusions, as most zoologists cannot, several of his observations are interesting. He found that the slope patterns in both the giraffe and the okapi, which has much less complex hair arrangements than the giraffe (Lankester, 1902, 1910), were more similar to those in the *Cervidae* than to those of any other ungulate, perhaps indicating a close relationship between these families. As in the cervids, the hair arrangements of the giraffids may be different on either side of an individual. He noted that the hairs of the mane were directed backward, while those on the middle of the back were directed forward. The crest where these currents met varied among individual giraffe but was much further back than it was in the cow, undoubtedly because of the greater encroachment of the neck on the trunk in the giraffe.

Lankester (1907) commented on other hair arrangements in giraffe, namely those around the face and horn region where the hair is differentiated into parallel tracts of dense hair which stands upright and intermediate tracts of smooth flat-lying hair. These ridges, which sometimes involve differential coloring of the hairs that makes them even more prominent, may vary among the different subspecies and are well marked as wrinkles even in the giraffe embryo.

GIRAFFE FETUS

Not many giraffe fetuses have been described in detail, but those that have been show several interesting features (Beddard, 1906; Broman, 1938b). Broman studied three giraffe embryos, two males over three months of 28-cm body length each and a female over four months of 60 cm in length. In the smaller fetuses no hair was macroscopically visible even at the tail tip, although low skin mounds on the lips indicated the future position of vibrissae there. The main horns were indicated by mounds about 8 mm wide and 5 mm high above the skull. The testes were already descended into the scrotal sacs. In the 60-cm fetus, bristles or hairs were apparent on both lips, on the upper eyelids, beside the ears, below the eyes, and on the tip of the tail where the hairs were 1.4 mm long. The main horn anlagen were 2 cm wide and 5 mm high, and at the anterior horn position there was a minute bump. The incisors and canines were visible through the gums. The four teats were papillae 3–4 mm high and 1.5 mm thick.

Beddard (1906) found the most striking feature of a two-thirds developed fetus of eight months gestation was its nearly uniform color and complete lack of spots. The body was covered with whitish hairs so fine that many were invisible to the naked eye. The hair on the trunk was slightly longer, and the horn hairs, eye lashes, tail tuft, and mane hairs were prominent, with whorls on the face already distinct. The horn cartilages could be felt through the skin above the skull.

NEWBORN GIRAFFE

The newborn giraffe has a relatively longer neck than the earlier embryo, but the neck is still relatively shorter than in the adult giraffe. The young carries its neck in a more erect manner than does the adult, in which the spinous tendons have stretched somewhat with age. The coat pattern of the young giraffe does not change with age, though the spots may become darker. There is often a black stripe running down the anterior of each lower front leg. This distinctive mark pales as the animal matures, until it is barely visible in the adult. The newborn's hair is soft, slightly woolly, and short. The position of the main horns is marked by tufts of black hair. The horn cartilages lie flat under the skin when the giraffe is born (Naaktgeboren, 1969), but they stand upright soon after birth—two hours (Benchley, 1946), on the second day (Lang, 1955a), after several days (Gijzen, 1958), or by the fourth week (Sigel, 1886). Later they become ossified and fused to the skull. (The horns of adults are discussed in Appendix C). The anterior horn may be represented as a small nasal bump. The hooves are soft, to facilitate parturition, but they harden quickly after birth.

Various authors have recorded anatomical measurements of fetal and newborn giraffe (Owen, 1849; Sigel, 1886; Müller-Liebenwalde, 1896; Beddard, 1906; Broman, 1938a; Patten, 1940; Paulus, 1943; Pournelle, 1955; Wilson, 1969). Others have noted newborn heights and weights (see Chapter 10).

GROWTH RATES OF GIRAFFE

Measurements taken of captive young giraffe show how incredibly fast they grow (Figs. 6–1 and 6–2). During the first month of a giraffe's life it may grow as much as 23 cm in height in one week (Patten, 1940). Much of this increase is centered in the neck region (Backhaus, 1961). During the first six months of

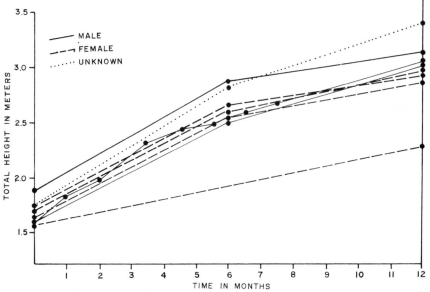

Fig. 6–1 Growth rates of captive giraffe during their first year.

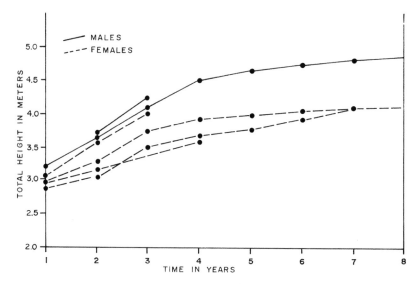

Fig. 6–2 Growth rates of captive giraffe after their first year.

life some giraffe shoot up as much as 100 cm, adding another 25 cm or so during the rest of the year. Other individuals grow more steadily, adding anywhere from 7 to 13 cm each month during their first year of life (Owen, 1849; Patten, 1940). In Nairobi Park the young are about 1.9 meters tall at birth. They grow about 75 cm in the first six months and 110 cm in the first year.

The growth rate slows to a rate of perhaps 2 cm a month during the second year, decreasing further in subsequent years. Even so, one female grew over 45 cm from her fourth to her seventh year (Paulus, 1943). The males grow more quickly than the females, attaining a greater final height.

MEASUREMENTS OF ADULT GIRAFFE

Many hunters and zoologists have recorded the heights of wild adult giraffe, but it is difficult to compare these figures. Some denote the height of the giraffe from the ground to the top of the skull; others are measured from the ground to the top of the horns. Some of the giraffe were standing, some lying, some living, some dead, some stuffed, some straight-necked, and some sloped-necked. Usually the author does not mention under which conditions the animal was measured. In the heights of 36 individuals recorded from 13 different sources, including the record giraffe of trophy hunters, the tallest giraffe, from Kenya and undoubtedly a male, measured 5.88 meters (19'3"—Caswell's giraffe in Shortridge, 1934); the largest female, from the northern Kalahari, measured 5.17 meters (16'10"—McSpadden, 1917). The average giraffe heights were much less—a male averaging about 5.3 meters and a female perhaps 4.3 meters. Thus it seems that estimated heights of 6.0 meters or more for wild giraffe are exaggerated. Captive giraffe are seldom over 5.0 meters tall, probably because of the artificial diets and unnatural climates. The shoulder height of a captive adult male is about 3.3 meters.

A giraffe's height is important in enabling it to reach high branches. To do so it raises its head and extends its prehensile tongue. A large male will be able to just touch the bottom of the browse line, which, in the case of Nairobi Park, is about 5.6 meters. Since a large male in the Park is about 4.5 meters high in a normal standing posture, it can add about 1.1 meters to its height with maximum extension.

The giraffe is so large that few people have been industrious enough to weigh a dead one whole, or well-organized enough to weigh one in parts. Black (1915a) recorded a two-month-old male of 149 kg and an adult of 524 kg; Schneider (1951) gave the weight of a ten-year-old tubercular male as 885 kg; Crile (1941) weighed an old male at 1220 kg, Talbot and Talbot (1961) a female at 800 kg, and Wilson (1968) a male at 1271 kg and a female at 1128 kg. Bourlière and Verschuren (1960) gave a mean weight of 1200 kg for adult giraffe. Lamprey (1964) used 770 kg as an average of all ages of giraffe in a population for the purpose of determining their biomass per unit area. Stewart and Zaphiro (1963) used 800 kg for this purpose, and Mentis (1970) 682 kg.

Other common adult male measurements in cm are (Owen, 1841; Farini, 1886; Stanley, 1890; Rothschild and Neuville, 1911; Meinertzhagen, 1938; Crile, 1941; Anon, 1951b; Schneider, 1951; Brink, 1954; Blancou, 1961):

	Number of giraffe examined (all males)	Average, cm	Range, cm
Ear length	7	22.9	15.2- 26.7
Tail length minus 1 m tassel	8	86.3	78.7-104.1
Hind foot	5	121.9	101.6-134.6
Head and body length	7	396.2	381.0-472.4

SCENT OF GIRAFFE BULLS

The peculiar scent of adult bull giraffe has often been noted (Cumming, 1850; Baldwin, 1894; Bryden, quoted in Sclater, 1900; FitzSimons, 1920; Percival, 1924). It has been compared to the smell of camels and described as being like "musk" or "like a hive of heather honey in September." It is said to frighten a horse or repel a lion. One writer believed that the odor was especially pungent in the mating season; another claimed that both male and female giraffe exuded an odor strong enough to permeate an area after the animals themselves had gone away.

Strangely, we followed wild giraffe for many months without ever detecting any special giraffe odor. Nor are captive giraffe particularly smelly. Giraffe do not possess specialized scent glands; therefore why some smell and others do not, and whether the smell is connected with reproduction or possibly with diet remains unknown.

GIRAFFE SPOOR

An adult male hoofprint may measure up to 31 by 23 cms (see below, Fig. 8–4). The prints of cows and young bulls are narrower, and those of old males, where the hoof halves are spread, are perhaps even broader (Jaegar, 1948; Hesse, 1958). The front hooves tend to be wider than the hind.

Giraffe droppings resemble large acorns up to 4 cm long, with one end of the pellet flattened. When fresh, a dropping is olive green in color. When it dries out it shrinks, turning yellow brown with a dark brown brittle skin that cracks into a network of tiny squares.

7 Individual Activities

FEEDING

Feeding is the most time-consuming of giraffe activities. In the Transvaal, Dagg noted that some giraffe browsed during every hour of the day (Fig. 7–1). At dawn about three-quarters of the giraffe on the ranch were tearing leaves and twigs off the bushes and trees. By noon, although a minimum of giraffe were eating, this was more than half of them. At dusk almost 90% were browsing. In Nairobi Foster also found the main feeding periods for giraffe were early morning and late afternoon, with least browsing activity just after midday when ruminating was at its peak.

Much of the night may be spent in feeding too. At Fleur de Lys in the Transvaal Dagg could hear giraffe browsing after dark, and at Nairobi Park Foster noted that they fed on and off throughout the nights of full moon when they could be observed. Usually Foster found that the giraffe began to ruminate at dusk, while either lying or standing. Not until after about two hours of ruminating did the first animal begin to feed again. By the third hour of darkness, half of the giraffe were feeding, and this continued intermittently until and after dawn (Fig. 7–2).

From early accounts of giraffe, one might assume that they browsed only on acacia trees or bushes, since these are usually mentioned as the main source of food. Giraffe probably eat more acacia leaves than any other kind, but they are far from being restricted to them. In the Tsavo National Park, where the most

74

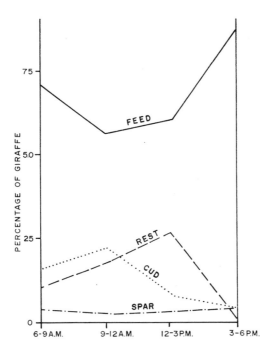

Fig. 7–1   Activities of giraffe at Fleur de Lys, Transvaal, during the day, based on 6,392 observations.

extensive observational study of food habits of giraffe has been carried out, Leuthold and Leuthold (1971, 1972) found that giraffe browsed on a total of 66 plant species. They fed at all the common large shrubs and trees, on a few vines and creepers, but not on herbs or grasses. There was a marked seasonal variation in their diet. In the rainy months the leaves of deciduous trees, shrubs, and vines were dominant in their diet; in the dry season they foraged largely on evergreen plants which grew in part in the riverine forest.

In analyzing their 4,025 observations of giraffe browsing, the Leutholds found that giraffe utilized the upper vegetational layers where these were available, but about half the time they browsed below a height 2 meters above the ground in competition with other mammals. The giraffe mainly ate leaves and small twigs, but also some bark, flowers, and fruit. They did not select, as lesser kudu and gerenuk do, chiefly young and tender shoots.

As in Tsavo Park, at Fleur de Lys more species of food plants (32) were taken in the dry season than in the green season (15) when the selection of foods was greater. In the dry season when few plants remained green, the giraffe visited many trees in succession, sampling a few dead leaves here and some dry twigs there. They browsed for longer periods each day during the dry season (Fig. 7–3), which Wyatt found was not true at Nairobi.

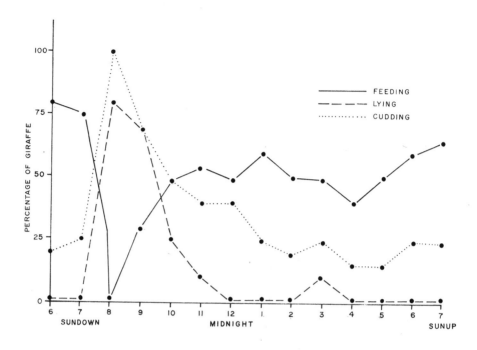

Fig. 7-2 Night activities of giraffe at Nairobi National Park based on 20 observations.

At Nairobi, especially, the trees that giraffe preferred showed a browse line at about 5 meters above the ground. One could deduce the giraffe's tastes by studying the shape of the trees. If the branches were bare below 5 meters but in full leaf above that height, the tree had been completely utilized by giraffe. A browsed bush of 2 meters or less, however, could have been cropped by antelope as well as by giraffe, especially those only a month or two old. Foster was able to determine preferred foods of giraffe by watching giraffe eat and by examining the vegetation for evidence of eaten twigs and leaves at levels above 2 meters, which only giraffe could reach (Fig. 7–4). Foster's 34 plant species taken by giraffe near Nairobi were almost entirely different from those listed for Tsavo where the vegetation is also different. Other food studies in East Africa have been done by Apfelbach (1970), Brahmachary (1969), and Nesbit Evans (1970). Nesbit Evans listed 21 food plants eaten by giraffe near Soy, Kenya, and 42 eaten by giraffe from the same Rothschild's population after they had been transported to Maralal. Often a plant that had been eaten at Soy was ignored at Maralal, perhaps because there was less choice of food at Soy. Similarly a tree common at Fleur de Lys but not eaten by giraffe was *Trichilia emetica,* a species however utilized in the nearby Kruger National Park. It seems, therefore, that not only are many different plants eaten, but that some are eaten in some places and not in others.

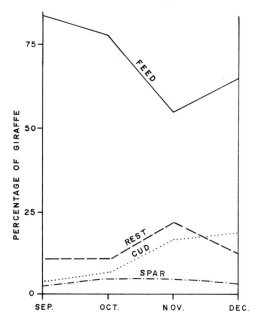

Fig. 7-3 Activities of giraffe at Fleur de Lys, Transvaal, from September (winter) to December (summer) based on 6,392 observations.

Fig. 7-4 Giraffe browse line on trees *Acokanthera schimperi,* near Nairobi National Park.

The only food study based on stomach contents has been done by Hall-Martin (1974b) at the Timbavati Private Nature Reserve of South Africa. He collected the rumen contents of at least three giraffe each month for a year. With the help of diagnostic keys which identified small plant parts, he classified 8,000 fragments which giraffe had eaten. His final results were similar to those obtained at Fleur de Lys: giraffe ate mainly a wide variety of leaves, but also fruit, flowers, and twigs depending on the season; and their choice of leaves varied with the season, depending on what plant species were in leaf.

Food studies of giraffe in other parts of Africa include those of Backhaus (1961) and Verschuren (1958b) in Zaire (17 spp); Berry (1973) and Klasen (1963) for the Luangwa Valley in Zambia (27 spp); Wilson (1969) in the Matopos National Park, Rhodesia (20 spp); and Van der Schijff (1959) and Brynard and Pienaar (1960) for the Kruger National Park (43 spp). These last studies noted the giraffe's use of leaves, branches, pods, and fruits.

It is not easy to assess the order of preference of plants, since a species' abundance is also related to the browsing pressure placed upon it; some species can withstand heavy browsing far better than others. Even within a species some plants seem to be favored over others by giraffe. Obviously the most common heavily browsed species is most important to the giraffe. Although all acacias but one (*Acacia stuhlmannii*) were heavily browsed in Nairobi Park, the small whistling thorn (*Acacia drepanolobium*) was the most important, not only because it was so abundant but because the leaves were always within reach, at less than about 2 meters high. Wyatt found that in his area 61% of all browsing was on this one species. The effect of such heavy browsing was dramatic. In comparing the whistling thorn trees on both sides of the fence near the Nairobi Park East Gate, Foster found that outside the park, where there had been no giraffe for about six years, the trees averaged 120 cm high, while inside the park they averaged 67 cm (Table 7–1). However, on the inside of the park there were far more young whistling thorns.

TABLE 7–1 COMPARISON OF WHISTLING THORNS *ACACIA DREPANO-LOBIUM* ON EITHER SIDE OF THE FENCE NEAR THE EAST GATE OF NAIROBI NATIONAL PARK

	Inside park	*Outside park*
Mean height	67 cm	120 cm
Number per hectare	1440	690
Giraffe	present	absent
Fire	rare	regular

Fire was another reason for the above discrepancy. While grass fires had been excluded from the park for the previous three years, on the outside such fires regularly had burned back the young plants. Indeed, in one area fire had killed both the young trees and the older ones which had been weakened by heavy browsing. A similar situation has occurred in the Tsavo National Park where elephants and fire are turning bush into grassland. To manage the giraffe habitat wisely, very hot, damaging fires, which result when the grass is long and dry, must be controlled. A grass fire after a long period of no fires is most damaging, since then the combustible material is most abundant.

The present trend in Nairobi Park is for the whistling thorns to become smaller (because of giraffe) but more numerous (because of the absence of fires). The low canopy resulting from the heavy browsing could be called an "inverse browse line" in contrast to the high browse line on the large trees. Giraffe are obviously adapted for reaching high rather than low. Hence an increase in the tendency to feed near the ground might be an indication that the favored food species are being overbrowsed (Fig. 7–5).

Fig. 7–5 Giraffe browsing near ground on whistling thorn bush, *Acacia drepanolobium.*

Two aspects of the evolution of typical African plants seem to have been directed by the giraffe and other large extinct browsers—the presence of thorns and spines on many plants and the characteristic flat-topped shape of the open country acacias.

Many of the common trees of the open woodlands of Africa are well armored with spines or hooks (Fig. 7–6)—*Acacia, Balanites, Scutia* are all plants which constitute favored foods of giraffe. Since they may be heavily browsed, one wonders whether the spines are of any protection for them from browsing animals. In fact, it seems probable that the spines have evolved as a result of the heavy browsing pressure by some of Africa's large mammals. First, in Australia, where there are more species of acacia than on any other continent, the trees are without thorns; and Australia is without any large browsing animals. Second, Foster and Dr. Paul Martin have found that the number and size of thorns on Africa's acacias rapidly diminish above about 5 meters—the height to which a giraffe can reach. This suggests that the thorns have evolved mainly as

Fig. 7–6 Giraffe browsing on thorny bush, *Balanites glabra.*

a reaction to giraffe and perhaps some of the equally large extinct browsers. No other living browser can reach above 2 meters except the elephant, and as they can knock down most trees in the open woodland, the 5-meter height is of no significance to them. Elephants, also, consume even mature thorns without concern; giraffe only rarely do. In dense forests, where giraffe seldom venture, the species of trees are generally poorly armed if at all.

The flat-topped acacias are the most characteristic trees on the plains of East Africa. This growth form has two possible advantages to the tree. First, a flat-topped canopy gives the minimum surface to drying wind and will throw the maximum amount of shade on the ground. This helps the soil at the base of the tree to retain moisture while the shade attracts ungulates during the heat of the day that will deposit manure. Under each acacia in open woodlands one finds a community of plants taking advantage of one or both of these factors. However, this explanation for the form of acacias is weakened by the fact that flat-topped trees are not characteristic of all arid countries in the world and the very flat-topped *Acacia lehai* is found in the cloud forest above 1,800 meters where moisture conservation is not a problem. A second possible explanation is that a tree, by being flat-topped, will confine browsing to its edges unless it is still very short. Again this factor is most important to the giraffe-acacia relationship, as an elephant can readily tear down the spreading branches of any acacia.

The acacias are not only well armed and often flat-topped, but they are also associated with stinging ants (*Crematogaster*). The acacias possess extra-floral nectaries in the form of a small pad at the base of each petiole. The nectaries have no function in pollination but do supply the ants with food. In some acacias, such as the whistling thorn, the plant also provides "galls" which serve as homes for the ants. Presumably the advantage to the plants in being so hospitable to these insects is that they will bite any browsing animal and deter some of the leaf-eating insects. Newborn giraffe occasionally shake their heads when they feed on these plants, but the adults, though their heads may be covered with ants, are less affected by their presence. However, the growing tips of the acacias are particularly rich in nectaries; therefore, the ants concentrate there. After a giraffe has taken a few mouthfuls from a whistling thorn, the ants are stirred up to great activity and the giraffe moves on to the next plant. Wyatt noted that two giraffe browsed only an average of 50 seconds and 100 seconds at whistling thorn bushes over one hour of observation. Consequently, the ants may in fact bother adult giraffe, thereby tending to spread the damage caused by giraffe throughout the tree population. Dr. M. G. Gwynne (personal communication) reports that the occasional mutant whistling thorn which has no galls is always heavily browsed, presumably because of its smaller population of ants. It is clear that the protections which the acacias have evolved are not perfect, but presumably the thorns and ants deter some of the browsers some of the time. (For more details on these relationships see Brown, 1960.)

Why giraffe like some leaves better than others remains a mystery. To determine if the amount of crude protein, crude fat, or ash content in the different leaves might explain their relative palatability, Dagg (1959) analyzed dried samples of 20 types of leaves that giraffe encounter in the wild. None of these constituents could be correlated with their preference by the giraffe. Fox (1938) also discussed briefly the chemical composition of acacia twigs and leaves, foods especially favored by giraffe, but he too could not decide why these foods were preferred.

When browsing, a giraffe usually reaches out with its long dark tongue, wraps the tip about a branch (often heavily thorned), and draws it gently in between its extended lips. Then it closes its mouth and pulls its head away, combing the leaves and small twigs into its mouth with its extra-wide row of lower front teeth. Twigs, leaves, pods, fruit, thorns, galls, and ants are all chewed together in the tough mouth.

Wyatt (1969) noted that twigs over half a meter long were discarded should they have been broken off by a giraffe; those of *Acacia drepanolobium* that were consumed averaged only 51 mm in length. Giraffe browsing on this species averaged 139 bites in 15-minute periods (range 105 to 217; $N = 12$). In each bite a single shoot was removed.

Sometimes only individual leaves, pods, or fruit are browsed, and then each is clipped off using the front lower incisors against the upper palate. Feeding is slower this way. Rogister (1957) reported that one young giraffe trying to reach some leaves planted its forefoot against a tree's trunk and pulled down foliage that would normally have been above it, much as goats and gerenuk do. Adult giraffe are probably too ungainly to emulate this feat.

Giraffe probably use both sight and smell to select a plant on which to browse. Dagg often watched a giraffe ambling along looking at bushes to find one it fancied. One female walked 30 meters across a grassy patch to feed at a small isolated thorn bush. Sometimes a giraffe sniffed at a bush before feeding on it. The sense of smell may be especially important at night, since Dagg has encountered giraffe eating avidly although it was so dark she could only tell what they were doing by listening to their munching. (Eating is a much noisier occupation than cudding; chewing is brisker, with the mouth usually open.)

Trial and error may also be important in selecting food, as some giraffe sample five or six bushes in rapid succession, taking no more than a few bites at each. Other giraffe eat steadily at a single bush or tree without glancing up for five minutes or more. Even a blind giraffe can survive, although it must choose its food by smell, taste, or feel. Schaller (personal communication) encountered such an animal in good condition in the Serengeti National Park. It was a three- or four-month-old juvenile, accompanied by an adult female. Schaller was able to walk upwind to within 2 meters of it, where he could see that both eyes were covered with a white film.

At times, feeding serves as a displacement reaction. One bull chewed momentarily on a branch while he continued a five-minute survey of Dagg's car, which stood nearby. Similarly when Dagg was parked close to other giraffe, one male paused in a head-hitting battle with a second male to grab several leaves, and another stopped chewing its cud briefly to snatch a mouthful of food.

Giraffe are allowed to remain on many ranches in South Africa because they do little harm. As they relish thorn shrubs and high leaves that cattle cannot reach, there is little competition for food between these two species. During six months of watching giraffe Dagg never saw one eat grass except at Whipsnade Zoo, although Pienaar (1963) saw them eating *Bothriochloa insculpta,* and Foster *Cyperus latifolius* (Fig. 7–7). Giraffe have upset farmers by walking through and raiding crops (Nesbit Evans, 1970); they have been specifically accused of nibbling the tops of sisal poles (Stott, 1950), of clipping cotton plants (Pitman, 1942), and of eating waterpumpkins and disturbing corn fields (Krumbiegel, 1939).

Various odd items in the diet of wild giraffe should be mentioned. Ogrizek (1954) reported that one giraffe consumed a hanging bird's nest which contained either eggs or young birds, while two others ate meat. The latter giraffe,

Fig. 7–7 Giraffe eating sedge, *Cyperus latifolius.*

which had been captured in the French Sudan, fed at dried or half-dried animal carcasses while en route to Dakar. They tore the meat from the bones with their teeth, ignoring the corn offered to them instead. Other writers have verified this habit by giraffe of scavenging the meat of oxen or antelope (Loveridge, 1945; Nesbit Evans, 1970; Western, 1971; Wyatt, 1971). However, meat is rarely left lying about on the plains where there are predators and scavengers to claim it. Both Foster and Wyatt have seen giraffe chewing on bones.

As giraffe, like other animals, need minerals, they often eat salt or salty soil in the wild (see Huxley, 1963) (Fig. 7-8). For this reason the warden in Nairobi Park regularly spread an unrefined mixture of salts from Lake Magadi for the game animals. This mixture included soda ash, sodium chloride, bicarbonate of soda, and sodium fluoride. However, in captivity the deaths of three giraffe, two belonging to William Randolph Hearst and one to the Tokyo Zoo, were attributed to eating earth (Koga, 1939).

DRINKING

There are two schools of thought on giraffe and their need to obtain water by drinking. The first is that if water is available, a giraffe will drink regularly, and

Fig. 7–8 Giraffe eating salt while lying down.

probably daily. This was true at Fleur de Lys, where giraffe were often seen drinking in the cattle trough, in small pools, at the dam, and in the Klaserie River. They drank throughout the day and also after dark. In the Wankie National Park where 339 giraffe were observed drinking water during dry weather, they also drank at all hours of the day and night, but there was a pronounced increase in evening drinking between the hours of four and eight o'clock (Weir and Davison, 1965). Berry often saw troops of giraffe drinking at the Luangwa River or at other lagoons, usually at the hottest hours of the day between mid-morning and early afternoon, but also at other times. Giraffe also drink frequently in captivity, where they may have less opportunity to eat fresh leaves which contain moisture. Cully (1958) gave the daily water requirement of a captive giraffe in 32°C weather as about 45 liters. In cooler weather giraffe drank about 12 liters a day of water. He does not mention what food these giraffe were given or how dry it was.

The second school claims that giraffe are independent of water, even if it is present. Backhaus, Apfelbach, Foster, and Wyatt seldom saw giraffe drinking. Schaller (personal communication), too, rarely saw giraffe go to water in the Serengeti. Vesey-Fitzgerald (1960) found that in Tanzania there was no evidence that giraffe needed to drink at all if green browse and shade were available. Certainly giraffe often live in arid regions where there is little drinking water. Bushmen have claimed that giraffe never drink at all, nor do they dig up and consume succulent roots in the Kalahari Desert as gemsbuck and Bushmen do (*Harmsworth,* 1910). In the northern Tsavo Park in the dry season giraffe have been found 80 km from the nearest known water (Simon, 1962); and Mason (1937) reported that three giraffe were seen near Wadi Hawar where the food supply was adequate but where the nearest wells, 170 km to the south, were always surrounded by men and livestock. The nearest open water was 500 km away. As it had not rained for three or four years, there was no possibility of water being held in pools.

There is an advantage in being able to survive in Africa on small amounts of water, since the animals that can will be more likely to survive in times of drought. Further, the less an animal visits a waterhole, the less chance there is that it will be attacked by lions which often await their prey near waterholes. Although giraffe live in hot regions throughout Africa, they never wallow in pools so that the evaporation of the water will keep them cool; and even when shade is nearby, they often settle down in full sunlight to ruminate or rest (Dagg, 1970a). Many mammals drink enough water to enable them to sweat in hot weather and be cooled as the sweat evaporates, but apparently giraffe can manage without much water.

The large size of the giraffe helps it survive in dry, hot areas. Since volume increases as the cube, and surface area only as the square, a large animal has relatively less surface area for dissipating heat. However, the long extremities of the giraffe greatly increase its surface area and therefore make the problem of losing heat far easier than for a buffalo, for example, of the same weight. Large mammals also generate relatively less heat, thereby making their survival in hot regions easier. In contrast small mammals in the desert must remain in the cool of their burrows during most of the day.

The water requirements of a giraffe have not been determined as yet. However, a few calculations using the most reasonable assumptions would seem to indicate that its diet of fresh browse could enable it to live for months without drinking. The water requirements have been determined for other pecorans (Taylor, 1968) and for the camel (Schmidt-Nielsen et al., 1956). By selecting a 250-kg giraffe, one can compare the water available to a giraffe through its food and metabolism with the water required by closely related species (see Appendix D).

Giraffe in the developed areas of Africa have become used to man-made changes. At Fleur de Lys they readily drank at the cattle troughs which wildebeest, impala, kudu, and zebra refused to approach. They often drank when Dagg's car was parked within 30 meters of the trough or when cattlemen were noisily rounding up cattle with whips at the adjacent paddock. At the Rusermi Farm nearby, Dr. Serfontein (personal communication) reported that giraffe liked to drink from a higher-placed open metal drum sunk into the bank of a stream rather than from the lower but naturally flowing water. In Rhodesia giraffe preferred to drink at the reservoirs where there was a firm floor of dried mud rather than in the river with its sandy bed (Dasmann, personal communication). Despite their large hooves, giraffe are unable to maneuver in soft ground and are wary of it. This is well shown at Whipsnade Zoo, where a water-filled ditch forms part of the bounds of their paddock. Since they first tested this barrier they have kept well away from it (L. Harrison Matthews, personal communication). Because of their great weight they could quickly become bogged down in quicksand or in swamps.

Shortridge (1934) found that giraffe tended to avoid large stretches of open water, perhaps because they are one of the few species of mammal which apparently cannot swim. In 1960 a giraffe that was being unloaded from a ship at the New York docks escaped from its crate, ran to the end of the pier, and fell into the water. The animal sank from sight almost at once without making any effective efforts to save itself (Crandall, 1964). C. S. Churcher (personal communication) encountered a giraffe that had either lain down or fallen into a muddy river in the Kruger National Park. It was unable to get up because it was unwilling to put its head under water to give it the balance it needed to regain its feet. It eventually drowned. However, in the Kruger National Park giraffe sometimes wade into the water to drink (Babich, 1964), despite the danger from crocodiles which have been known to catch and kill giraffe (Percival, 1924; Brynard and Pienaar, 1960).

Giraffe are cautious at watering places where lions may be hiding; a giraffe is a relatively easy prey once it has struggled down to a drinking position. If a number of them approach water together, several giraffe may remain erect, possibly acting as sentinels, while the others drink. Other game may be satisfied that there is no danger only when giraffe themselves are satisfied (Percival, 1913).

In the wild, giraffe usually attain a drinking position by bending their front "knees" forward (Fig. 7–9), by straddling their forelegs to either side, or by a combination of these methods. (Different methods used by captive giraffe are

Fig. 7–9 Giraffe bending its front "knees" forward to drink.

discussed in Chapter 8.) They often drink without pause from 20 seconds to a minute before they straighten up again. Two giraffe at the Taronga Zoo held their heads 5 cm above the water, lapping it into their mouths as dogs do. Like other mammals, a giraffe can swallow water even when its head is much lower than its stomach. An exception was a female at the Taronga Zoo that raised its head to an angle of 40° above the horizontal between each swallow, as if to let the water run down its neck. Dagg never saw it drink in any other way.

At one time it was supposed the giraffe must raise their heads slowly from drinking to give the circulatory system time to adapt to the change in blood pressure at the brain, but this is not so. Dagg has taken films which show the neck whipped from a drinking to a horizontal position in about half a second. There the arrested momentum of the neck helped them to shift their front legs more nearly under them. Then they lifted their heads again until their necks reached the nearly normal position of a 45° angle with the ground. This second movement lasted from one-half to one second. The mechanism used to keep the blood pressure at the brain relatively constant during rapid up and down movements of the head therefore acts quickly (see Appendix B).

Despite the effort involved in bending down and struggling erect again, Dagg saw giraffe do this as many as six times during one visit to the water. This may facilitate swallowing, the drinking stance may be too tiring to hold for long, or the giraffe may want to check for possible danger.

CUDDING

Rumination apparently evolved so that large browsing or grazing species could feed quickly in unprotected areas where they were vulnerable to attack by predators and rechew the vegetation in more sheltered regions at their leisure. Cudding not only results in the food being more thoroughly masticated, but it allows the microorganisms of the rumen more opportunity to aid in the breakdown of the food. Although the giraffe is less bothered by predators than most ruminants, it possesses this behavior nevertheless, spending much of the time when it is not eating in chewing its cud. Giraffe often ruminate for short periods too. Of 31 daytime observations Wyatt noted, 13 lasted less than 5 minutes although the longest lasted 75 minutes. A giraffe ruminates while lying, standing, or walking, allowing only a few seconds after swallowing one cud or bolus before regurgitating the next. Its throat bulges out noticeably as the bolus forges upward and again as it slips down. On one occasion a tick bird clinging to the front of a giraffe's neck gave a small jump of surprise as the cud slid past underneath it. On Fleur de Lys giraffe chewed each bolus about 40 seconds, at a rate of one chew a second. Wyatt (1969) found that boluses were chewed an average of 48 times in 50 seconds. Backhaus (1961), who timed several captive giraffe, reported a range of 29 to 81 chews per cud. The number of chews will depend on the size of the bolus and the type of food.

At Fleur de Lys giraffe chewed their cud frequently, especially in the middle of the day when the temperature might approach 37°C (Fig. 7–1). They cudded more in the daytime during November and December when the plants were in full leaf and less time had to be spent in foraging (Fig. 7–3). As mentioned earlier, the giraffe in the Nairobi Park usually ruminated for about two hours after the sun went down, while Apfelbach's three giraffe ruminated especially in the middle of the night.

REST AND SLEEP

If the day is hot, giraffe may stop cudding to rest or even doze, which they may do while lying or standing. At Fleur de Lys after noon especially many giraffe stood quietly, facing in various directions, their relaxed necks dropping downward, their tails motionless, their eyelids drooping (Fig. 7–1). Roosevelt (1910) encountered one dozing female that allowed a group of men to walk within 4 meters of her before she started and kicked out at them. Roberts (1951) claimed that giraffe could sleep while standing, but probably in real sleep the giraffe would not be able to maintain this position. Giraffe at Fleur de Lys often lay down to relax in the middle of the day. All of these kept their necks erect. They arranged themselves about 20 meters from each other, in the sun or shade, facing in any direction and gazing straight ahead of them, apparently as oblivious to possible danger as the standing giraffe. Of the giraffe Apfelbach (1970) noted resting, the longest lying period lasted 2 hrs 52 min and the shortest period 8 min.

A giraffe lies down by folding its forelegs under it and then bending its hind legs. To get up, it raises its forelegs slightly, then its hind legs and finally its forelegs again (see Chapter 8; Backhaus, 1961, and Zannier-Tanner, 1965). Young giraffe lie down more often than adult giraffe, perhaps because they find this operation less laborious. In Taronga Zoo, of 161 observations of lying giraffe, four were of the 11 adults, 32 of the three juvenile cows, and 125 of the four calves (Table 7–2). Each animal lay on its left or on its right side apparently indiscriminately with one leg stretched to the side (Fig. 7–8); none lay squarely on its hindquarters as a camel would.

Sleep in giraffe has been studied in zoos (Grzimek, 1956a, 1972; Immelmann, 1958; Hediger, 1959; Backhaus, 1961; and Immelmann and Gebbing, 1962), and the conclusions drawn from these observations doubtless apply to sleep in wild giraffe as well. While a giraffe is ruminating, resting, or dozing, a lying individual holds its head erect. When it wants to sleep more deeply, it bends its head back beside its body. In the young the head is tucked in beside the flank; in the adults, which have relatively longer necks, the head rests on the ground behind the tarsal joint of the outstretched hind leg, chin down. These positions are not held for long. Although a giraffe may lie down for most of the night, an adult only bends its neck back in deep sleep perhaps five separate times, each lasting from one to twelve but usually three or four minutes. The longest sleep

TABLE 7-2 NUMBER OF TIMES GIRAFFE LAY DOWN AT TARONGA ZOO DURING 80 HOURS OF OBSERVATION

| | | | Number of Times Observed | |
| | | | On left side with right hind leg stretched out | On right side with left hind leg stretched out |
Individual	Sex	Age (yr)		
Jan	m	25	(never seen lying by keepers)	
Clare	f	18		
Hazel	f	13		
Cheeky	f	11		
Parramatta	f	10		
Willoughby	f	10		
Oygle	m	8		1
Swinger	f	8	1	
Tiny	f	7		
Sydney	f	7		
Lumpy	m	5	2	
Cindy	f	2–3	1	7
Josie	f	2–3	10	6
Mosman	f	2–3	4	4
Frank	m	0.5	22	24
Reg	m	0.4	29	11
Helen	f	0.2	11	10
Marcia	f	0.2	11	7
			91	70

period Apfelbach noted in wild giraffe lasted 2 min 40 sec. A young animal may fall into deep sleep more often and for longer periods totaling an hour or more. Balch (1955) felt that ruminants in general do not sleep a great deal, although there is some controversy about this. As giraffe sleep with their eyes open (L. Harrison Matthews, personal communication), it is difficult to tell if one is asleep or not without measuring the brain activity. Ruminants not only must keep their trunks more or less vertical so that digestion in the reticulo-rumen, which is partly dependent on gravity, is not impeded, but they must spend a large part of their resting in rumination.

RUBBING AND SCRATCHING

These activities are common in wild giraffe. Despite their thick skin (up to about 15 mm on shoulder and rump and 8 mm on the neck), giraffe on Fleur de Lys were greatly bothered by ticks which were especially numerous in the lowveld during the rainy season. The giraffe relieved the irritated parts of its body by rubbing them. One giraffe scratched its lower abdomen, where ticks tended to congregate, by straddling a 2-meter bush and rocking back and forth over it. Another soothed its flanks or legs by backing in and out of a bush and its head or neck by rubbing it against a tree, along another giraffe, or on the ground. With its tongue or teeth it licked or nibbled at local areas on its body that it could reach. A young giraffe could lick its lower neck without trouble, but an adult with its longer neck was unable to reach this area, although one tried to swing its tongue over to it.

One Fleur de Lys female was bothered by an object in her nose. After sneezing several times, she rubbed her head on her flank. Later, still sneezing, she walked to a bush to rub her head in it. Sometimes giraffe lick inside their nostrils with their tongues or scratch this part carefully on a twig. When they are bothered by insects, giraffe are likely to jerk their heads and necks back and forth, but they rarely shake their skins as horses do, since the muscles attached to the skin are poorly developed. Their long tails can switch away flies from their hindquarters or even from their heads if they bend and lower them sufficiently.

Because of their short bodies and long legs, giraffe seem unable to scratch their heads with their hind hooves, as most ungulates can. Backhaus (1961), who watched a newborn holding its neck horizontally and trying to reach it unsuccessfully by swinging its hind leg forward, cited this attempt as an example of the principle "ontogeny recapitulates phylogeny." The young giraffe was unconsciously emulating more usual-shaped ancestors which would have been able to scratch their necks in this way. Backhaus discussed skin care in giraffe extensively.

VOCAL NOISE

Giraffe were believed for such a long time to be voiceless that recent observers (or rather listeners) have taken great care to record every vocal noise any giraffe emits. Because of this, giraffe are now credited with a large repertoire of sounds, even though each is rarely heard (Anon., 1943; Backhaus, 1961; Berry, 1973; Brown, 1947; Butler, 1912a; Crandall, 1964; Dagg, 1970b; Foran, 1946; Fox, 1938; Gatti, 1959; Gensch, 1969; Goodwin, 1956; Huxley and Koch, 1964; Huxley, 1963; Iles, 1960; Kettlitz, 1961; Loveridge, 1945; Maberly, 1947, 1955; MacMahon, 1947; Pocock, 1936; Rae, 1952; Selous, 1911; Shortridge, 1934; Sigel, 1887; Stanton, 1955; Stephan, 1925; White, 1948; Zellmer, 1960).

Many of their vocal sounds are loud and aggressive. Giraffe sometimes grunt or snort when they are alarmed, annoyed, or hungry; a male may cough during mating; captive giraffe may bellow when they are hungry; and a giraffe is reported to have screamed like a wounded hare, although this is not usual. Hart (1966) taped the bleating cry of a darted giraffe which sounded bovine and unmusical.

Other giraffe noises are more gentle. For example a captive female that had arthritis and was unable to stand up gave a gentle moo when men tried to help her rise. The young may moo or bleat when they are lonely, and females may call their young with a whistling sound. Stanton (1955) heard a giraffe snore while it was sleeping.

During 80 hours of observation at the Taronga Zoo, Dagg heard giraffe make only a few kinds of vocal noises. On three occasions when a female was being suckled by two or three juveniles, the dominant male cantered over to the group and snorted or growled at it, chasing the sucklers away. Another time a lactating female growled softly at three calves that were sucking at another female. Possibly in each of these cases the giraffe making the noise was "jealous" of the attention being paid to another adult. The other examples of noises made at the Zoo were a female that sneezed twice and coughed once while nosing the dominant male, the growling of this male as he sniffed at a female's genitalia, and the repeated snorting of a female as she galloped about the paddock, occasionally rubbing her head on other giraffe.

Usually giraffe do not communicate alarm to each other vocally, although Berry (1973) four times heard a single adult give a low-pitched "pe-rrr" sound which seemed to be an alarm call for the rest of the herd. If one member of a herd at Fleur de Lys saw something suspicious, such as a biologist sitting under a tree, it stared at the person intently. Other giraffe, gradually noticing its preoccupation, began to stare in the same direction, but it was as long as five minutes before all the giraffe were aware of this possible danger. Finally one giraffe snorted at the object; this perhaps was a threat or a noise to startle it into explaining itself, rather than a means of communicating its presence to the others. If a giraffe senses real danger, it dashes off immediately. The other giraffe stampede after it without taking the time to assess the danger for themselves. A herd of giraffe may also be stampeded by other species of animals running past. Apparently giraffe only communicate danger by posture, by retreat, and rarely by a vocal noise, although there is always the possibility that olfaction is used.

8 *Locomotion and Movements of Individual Giraffe*

THE WALK

Because of the unusual shape of the giraffe, it walks and runs in an unusual fashion. Its peculiar "pacing" walk was discussed by scholars as early as the fourth century (Mongez, 1827), while its gallop was one of the first to be analyzed in detail of that of any mammal (Bourdelle, 1934).

In its walk, the giraffe swings the two legs on one side of the body forward more nearly together than do most other quadrupeds. The right front leg leaves the ground soon after the right hind has begun its swing forward. This walk can be illustrated as in Fig. 8–1, although it must be remembered that the pattern of supports varies somewhat with the speed of the walk (Fig. 8–2).

From Table 8–1 it is clear that the walk pattern of the adult giraffe is similar to that of the young. The figures were obtained by calculating the number of frames in a moving-picture sequence of an animal walking that were spent on each combination of supporting legs. The patterns for the young and adult giraffe were similar (X^2 test), while those of the adult giraffe, okapi, and white-tailed deer were significantly different from each other ($p < .01$) (Dagg and De Vos, 1968a). Giraffe spend a large percentage of each stride on lateral legs—either the two right or the two left legs. The legs in both young and old are about 1.8 times as long as the trunk length, and in both the forelegs are slightly longer than the hind legs, so perhaps this similarity in patterns is not surprising. The okapi,

RH   RF

Fig. 8–1 The walk of the giraffe, showing sequence of supporting legs. Legs are represented by vertical lines. R-right; H-hind; F-front.

which has relatively slightly shorter forelegs, uses lateral legs somewhat less to support itself during a walking stride. The legs of each species swing forward somewhat faster than a cylindrical pendulum of the same length would; the time for one stride is therefore proportional to the length of an animal's leg (Table 8–1).

The extremeness of the giraffe's walk is underlined when it is compared with that of a woodland animal like the white-tailed deer *(Odocoileus virginianus)* or indeed any cervid. The white-tailed deer spends a large part of each walking stride on diagonal legs, a combination that giraffe normally never use at all (Fig. 8–3). It spends very little or no time balanced on all four legs, but then it is a much lighter animal than is a giraffe. If one watches a deer walking, it *seems* that the hind leg will strike the foreleg as it terminates its swing forward. The foreleg begins to move only fractionally before the hind leg on that side is set down on the ground. This timing is quite different from that in the giraffe.

The shape of an animal does not entirely explain its pattern of walking. The impala, kob, gazelles, waterbuck, and so on have shapes not unlike that of deer, with the hind legs longer than the forelegs, and yet all of these open-country antelope have walk patterns more like giraffe than cervids. They use lateral legs for a considerable part of each stride (all ungulates use them for some period of each stride, since it is only during their use that the hind hoof on the opposite side of the body can be placed down roughly on the spot which the forehoof is leaving), diagonal legs less commonly, and four legs for short periods or not at all.

It is possible to postulate what these differences mean. Large animals need more support, such as four legs on the ground at once, than do small animals, unless the latter are walking slowly. The faster an animal walks, the less time it is supported by each leg during a stride and the more time each leg has to swing forward (Fig. 8–2). All quadrupeds use at least two supporting legs during a walking stride, but as we have seen these can be predominately lateral legs (as in the giraffe) or predominately diagonal legs (as in the deer). The use of diagonal legs is the more primitive, since amphibians and reptiles, the earliest quadrupeds, generally employ them. So do very young quadrupeds. Diagonal supporting legs offer a better balance than do lateral supporting legs, which explains why a trotting horse (which uses diagonal legs together) is better able to maneuver over rough ground and less likely to fall than is a pacing horse (which uses lateral legs together). In woodland quadrupeds, diagonal supporting legs are important,

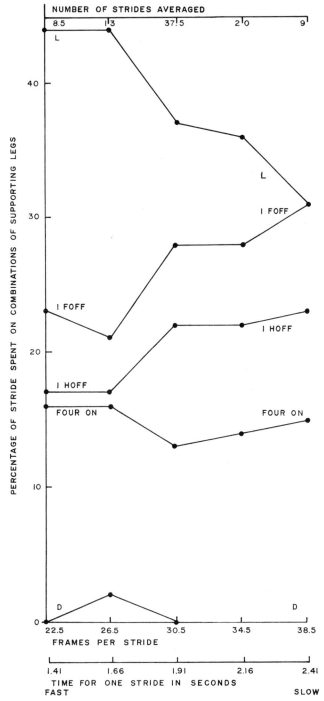

Fig. 8–2 Walking patterns of adult giraffe at varying speeds. H-hind leg; F-front leg; L-lateral legs; D-diagonal legs.

TABLE 8–1   THE PERCENTAGE-TIME DURING A WALKING STRIDE THAT EACH OF THE COMBINATIONS OF SUPPORTING LEGS IS USED BY FOUR TYPES OF PECORAN SPECIES

	Lateral legs on ground	Diagonal legs on ground	One hind leg off ground	One front leg off ground	Four legs on ground	Time of average stride (sec.)	Number of strides examined
Adult giraffe	40	0	20	25	15	1.94	92
Young giraffe	43	0	18	25	14	1.69	46
Adult okapi	28	0	33	32	7	1.68	18
Adult white-tailed deer	5	18	38	39	0	1.34	212

Fig. 8–3   The walk of the white-tailed deer, showing sequence of supporting legs. Legs are represented by vertical lines. R-right; L-left; H-hind; F-front.

since with them animals can not only stop and balance immediately if they sense danger, but they can bound off from this stable position if the danger is real. Since they live where they are unable to see far, their walk pattern is a definite asset to quadrupeds that inhabit densely vegetated areas.

Mammals that live in more open areas make greater use of lateral legs, which give them less stability, but such animals are not likely to be surprised by a predator at close quarters. The lack of stability in their "pacing" walk is offset by three advantages:

a.   the greater length of strides that may be obtained when the hind leg is not impeded as it swings forward by the forefoot planted on the ground in front of it;

b.   the greater facility with which the trunk musculature can fit in with that of the legs, if those on one side of the body are used more or less together;

c.   the impossibility of the hind leg ever hitting the foreleg during the walking strides, as it could conceivably do in a stride where diagonal supporting legs are used to a large extent. This is particularly important in a long-legged, short-bodied animal like the giraffe whose proportions could be deduced from its hoof prints; the hind foot is not set down near the print left by the front foot on the same side as it is in most deer and antelope, but up to half a meter ahead of this print (Fig. 8–4).

These suggestions may explain the slightly greater speed of a pacing horse compared to that of a trotting horse.

The third possibility listed above may also explain why giraffe never normally trot, unlike other artiodactyls (although they appear to do so under the influence of the drug M99, when they have a short, fast, high step). Since their bodies are short in relation to their long legs, in a trot there would be a strong possibility of the hind legs striking the forelegs. It is against this eventuality that the longer-bodied trotting horse is provided by its master with bandages to protect its legs.

At present, no one knows if the okapi can trot. The Brookfield Zoo in Chicago and the London Zoo, both of which own okapi, have never seen them trot (personal communications), but only walk or gallop.

THE GALLOP

One might expect the giraffe, with its long legs, to outrun the other plains animals, but it cannot; the record for an individual is only 56 km/hr (35 mi/hr) (Arbuthnot, 1954). Speed becomes increasingly difficult with increased size, mainly because of inertia and because larger muscles contract more slowly than smaller ones (Hildebrand, 1960). Most antelope can run faster than the giraffe, despite their smaller size. However, the giraffe has little need of excessive speed, since the only predator in Africa that relies on great speed to catch its prey is the cheetah, an animal that rarely attacks giraffe.

The giraffe's gallop has been called both ungainly and graceful, the latter adjective applying especially to the young, which run faster than the adults; if a family group is stampeded, the young animals soon sprint ahead of their elders. Their speed is illustrated in Figures 8–5 and 8–6 and Table 8–2, where the galloping strides of a young giraffe under 3 meters tall and of adult giraffe are analyzed (also see Dagg and De Vos, 1968b). The faster an animal runs, the less time it spends with its feet on the ground. During the time in which a quadruped is in the air, it can have its legs tucked under it following a push-off with the front legs (a flexed suspension as in the horse's gallop) or it can have the legs spread fore and aft following a push-off with the hind legs (an extended suspension as in the horse's jump). The young giraffe can have both types of suspension in its gallop, totaling 17% of the time of the stride (Table 8–2). This pattern is the fastest known for quadrupeds; it is that used by cheetah, pronghorn, and gazelles, for example, when they run at 100 km/hr. The front and hind legs work separately, each pushing the animal forward into the air in turn.

The adult giraffe is probably too heavy to hoist itself into the air so that no feet are on the ground at one time—at least none of the animals left the ground in the 18 strides examined (Table 8–2). The adults spent 29% of the stride with diagonal or lateral legs on the ground and 14% with three legs on the ground, both combinations of supporting legs that the young giraffe did not use at all. Except when it is changing leads, so that the major impetus of the gallop changes from one side to the other, the galloping giraffe sets its feet down in a rotary manner—left hind, right hind, right front, left front, or vice versa. This is evident in Figs. 8–5 and 8–6.

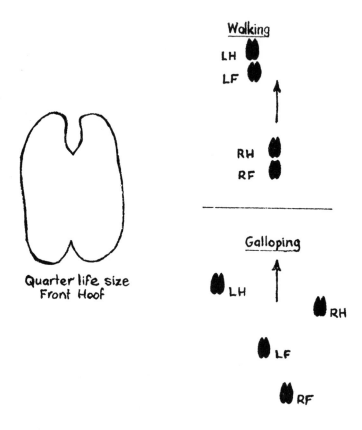

Fig. 8–4   Spoor of giraffe. L-left; R-right; H-hind; F-front.

Fig. 8–5   The galloping stride of a young giraffe, with the percentage-time of the stride that it spends on each combination of supporting legs. Legs are represented by vertical lines.

Fig. 8–6   The galloping stride of an adult bull giraffe, with the percentage-time of each stride that it spends on each combination of supporting legs. Legs are represented by vertical lines.

TABLE 8–2 PERCENTAGE-TIME SPENT ON COMBINATIONS OF SUP-
PORTING LEGS OF ADULT AND YOUNG GALLOPING
GIRAFFE

Combinations of supporting legs, not necessarily in the order in which they occur	Adults, percentage-time of stride	Young giraffe, percentage-time of stride
One foreleg on ground (not lead leg)	4	12
Both forelegs on ground	19	8
Lead foreleg on ground	16	22
Flexed suspension	0	10
One hind leg on ground (not lead leg)	3	22
Both hind legs on ground	14	10
Lead hind leg on ground	1	9
Extended suspension	0	7
Fore and hind legs on ground—2 legs	29	0
Fore and hind legs on ground—3 legs	14	0
Number of strides averaged	18	2

When a giraffe runs, it twists its tail over its back, perhaps to keep the tail out of the way of its legs (Fig. 8–7). One occasionally sees giraffe and other African ungulates without their tails, probably because the tail is the handiest thing for a predator to grasp in a near miss.

IMPORTANCE OF THE NECK

The giraffe is obviously a convenient animal in which to consider the role that the neck plays in its various movements (Dagg, 1962b, d). This has been done by tracing giraffe silhouettes from moving picture films. In both the walk and the gallop the neck moves back and forth during each stride. If the angle that the neck makes with the back is calculated for the walk, it is evident that the neck moves forward with the swing forward of the legs (Fig. 8–8). Just before the legs are set down at the end of a half stride, the neck begins its backward swing, halting the forward momentum of the animal somewhat until the opposite legs have started their swing forward. The neck therefore moves back and forth twice during each walking stride, pulling the center of gravity forward as the legs themselves move forward.

Because it is a more forceful gait, the neck-back angle is larger (to 174°) and has a greater amplitude (65°) in the gallop (Fig. 8–9) than in the walk. When the legs of the galloping giraffe are bunched together under it during a stride, the neck has been pressed back and is beginning to stretch forward. When the legs of the giraffe are spread out, as in the young giraffe between leaving the ground and regaining it, the neck reaches its farthest point forward and begins to be drawn back again. Therefore, in the gallop as in the walk the neck arches

A. Left foreleg on ground

C. Right foreleg on ground

Fig. 8–7 Four phases in the gallop of a giraffe

B.   Right foreleg nearing ground

D.   Legs bunched together as right hind leg approaches ground

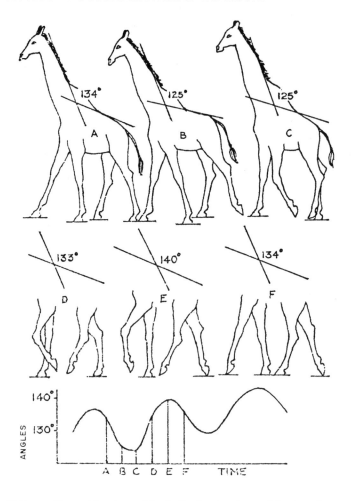

Fig. 8–8 Half a walking stride of an adult giraffe showing the neck-back angles at equal time intervals. (After Dagg, 1962b)

backward and forward between each forward lunge, with the neck momentum slightly preceding that of the body in each instance. The power and weight of the giraffe are more in its forequarters than in its hindquarters, so that the main propulsion for each stride comes from the forelegs. By pressing forward at the beginning of each stride, the neck moves into line with the power stroke. The neck facilitates the movement by shifting the center of gravity of the giraffe's body forward and more nearly over the forelegs. At the end of each stride or leg swing, as the hooves touch the ground again, the neck moves backward in order to slow down the forward momentum of the body and enable the giraffe to keep its balance.

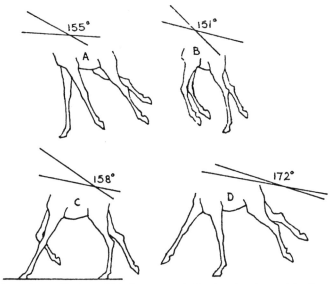

Fig. 8–9 Phases in a galloping stride of a young giraffe showing the neck-back angles at four intervals. (After Dagg, 1962b)

Because of its size, the giraffe has more trouble lying down and getting up again than most mammals have. By swinging back and forth at critical instants, the neck greatly assists an individual in getting up (Fig. 8–10). From the resting posture (Fig. 8–10*A*), this male throws its neck backward for impetus and hoists itself to its foreknees *(B–C)*, following which its neck swings forward again *(D)*. The giraffe maintains this ungainly position for a second, and then swings its neck backward slightly *(E)* and then forward again in order to lift its hind legs onto its feet *(F)*. It holds this pose for nearly a second. Then it draws its neck back again, and with it the weight of the body, and changes from kneeling on the forelegs to standing on them *(G–I)*. This sequence lasts about four seconds.

The giraffe also uses its neck to help it jump fences (Fig. 8–11). After looking at the fence (Fig. 8–11*A*), the adult swings its neck back until it is nearly perpendicular to the ground and all its weight is on its hind legs before it hops its two forelegs over the fence *(B–F)*. Then it moves forward with the fence under its belly *(G)*, swings its neck far forward so that its weight is balanced on its forelegs, and hops its hind legs over the fence together *(H–J)*. The neck therefore acts as a useful structure to pull the center of gravity first over the hindquarters and then over the forequarters.

Movements and positions of the neck, as well as of the head, also enable the giraffe to express emotions (Backhaus, 1961). In the standing animal, the angle of the back of the neck to the horizontal is usually about 50 to 60° in the adult and up to 70° in the calves. When the animals are resting and cudding, the neck may sink below this level, especially in the females. If a giraffe wants to threaten another giraffe or a person, it lowers its neck and head until they are nearly

Fig. 8–10 Sequences of an adult giraffe getting to its feet, giving angles of the neck to the ground. (After Dagg, 1962b)

horizontal with the ground. It may begin a sparring match in this position. If one giraffe submits to a stronger one, it holds its neck high with its nose pointing upward. If a giraffe is alert and nervous at the approach of something or someone that might prove dangerous, it holds its head more nearly perpendicular than usual, with its mouth pointing to the ground and its nostrils wide open. If it is preparing for flight, it turns its body at an angle to the disturbance. When it shakes its head, the giraffe holds its neck about 45° from the horizontal. In the young lying giraffe, the neck often assumes an S shape that may at first glance make the animal seem deformed.

BENDING TO THE GROUND

Although it looks awkward for giraffe to bend their heads down to the ground, they do so in the wild to drink and to obtain salts and in captivity to sniff the

Fig. 8–11 Sequences of an adult bull jumping a 1.5-meter fence, giving angles of the neck to the ground. (After Dagg, 1962b)

ground, pick up a branch or eat feces. At the Taronga Zoo Dagg kept a record of which giraffe bent to the ground and in what manner they accomplished this feat. One individual can bend down in a variety of ways although it tends to prefer one way (Table 8–3) (Fig. 8–12). The most common method was with all the legs straight, while the neck and head leaned to left or right over one shoulder. Most giraffe could not reach the ground that way unless they strained so far forward and down with their necks that one hind leg left the ground and swung free. If the giraffe leaned over its right shoulder, its left hind leg swung free and vice versa. In this stance the forelegs were somewhat apart; rarely, one foreleg was planted ahead of the other. A less common stance was that with the forelegs spread apart and bent forward. Two adults and the four calves preferred it. In the wild, giraffe often spread their straight forelegs far apart, so that the head and neck could reach between them, twisting neither to the left nor to the right. This position was exceedingly rare in captivity, perhaps because of the cement floor; since the front hooves could not sink into the ground to gain a purchase, they would likely slip too far sideways for the animal easily to regain its upright position.

TABLE 8–3   BENDING TO THE GROUND OF THE 18 TARONGA GIRAFFE

Giraffe, in order of age	Sex	Age (yr)	Forelegs somewhat apart and bent	Forelegs straight and spread far apart	Number of Times Observed				Total
					Forelegs straight and slightly apart—usually leans over one shoulder	Forelegs straight and slightly apart—leans over right shoulder with left hind hoof off ground	Forelegs straight and slightly apart—leans over left shoulder with right hind hoof off ground	One foreleg straight and one bent	
Jan	m	25							0
Clare	f	18	13		2				15
Hazel	f	13			4		15		19
Cheeky	f	11							0
Parramatta	f	10			8	5	22		35
Willoughby	f	10			2				2
Oygle	m	8	11						11
Swinger	f	8			1		1		2
Tiny	f	7			1				1
Sydney	f	7	1		2		45		48
Lumpy	m	5					12		12
Cindy	f	2–3			7				7
Josie	f	2–3							0
Mosman	f	2–3			6		1	1	8
Frank	m	0.5	5	1	2				8
Reg	m	0.4	7						7
Helen	f	0.2	5		1				6
Marcia	f	0.2	7		2				9
Total			49	1	38	5	96	1	190
Percentage Totals			26%	1%	20%	3%	49%	1%	100%

Fig. 8–12   Giraffe bending to the ground.

OTHER MOVEMENTS

Various other movements have been noted in giraffe. Occasionally at Taronga a giraffe stamped its forefoot while standing still or while walking—rather like a goosestep. In the wild, the former action seems a threat, at least if it is directed toward a person. St. Hilaire (1827) noted this action too in the first giraffe to enter France; it pawed the ground as if ready to kick when someone approached or irritated it.

Some Taronga giraffe made a habit of pointing their noses high into the air as they walked, so that their heads made an angle of more than 180° with their necks. Schaller (personal communication) has noticed the same action in the wild occurring as a result of dominance interactions.

The Taronga giraffe almost always stood with their legs straight, each bearing part of the animal's weight. On only three occasions did a giraffe stand with one leg slightly bent so that its weight was carried by three legs, something that horses often do.

⑨ *Social Groupings and Activities*

Backhaus (1961) defined a herd as a number of the same kind of animals that move together and are usually engaged in the same activity at any one time— such as eating, drinking, resting, walking, or running. By this definition giraffe form looser herds or groups than most game species; it is common for one member of a group to wander off over a hill while the others remain behind, or for one to chew its cud while the others forage for food. (In this book single giraffe are also classed as a "herd" for convenience.) Members of a herd may be so spread out—as much as a kilometer between individuals—that even though they are engaged in the same activity, usually eating, they may not seem to belong together. Month-old calves in the Nairobi National Park have been separated from their mothers by more than 2 km and for days without either calf or mother showing alarm at the separation; apparently the calves can manage without milk at this early age.

The number of giraffe in a group is usually small, although large herds have been seen (Table 9–1). The very large groups like those recorded by Baker in 1868 that included 76, 154, 103, and 100 giraffe were observed when giraffe were more plentiful or less disturbed than they are today.

Although plains game animals in general tend to congregate in large herds, so that there is a greater chance of one individual's spotting danger and being able to warn the others of it, most giraffe survive without this protection of large numbers. One reason may be that many giraffe spend time in relatively forested

TABLE 9–1   PERCENTAGE-TIME EACH SIZE OF HERD WAS SEEN IN THE WILD

Herd size	Nairobi National Park (Foster)	Eastern Transvaal (Dagg)	Serengeti (Foster)	Other East African herds (Foster and in literature)	Total for all herds
1	23.0%	44.4	16.3	24.0	25.9
2	17.1	13.2	10.9	13.3	15.0
3	13.7	8.6	8.9	9.3	11.5
4	10.7	1.0	10.2	16.0	11.0
5	9.8	8.6	8.9	6.7	9.1
6	7.1	6.6	8.9	2.7	6.9
7	4.5	2.6	0.7	6.7	3.7
8	4.5	2.0	2.0	2.7	3.4
9	1.9	1.3	6.1	6.7	3.0
10	1.9	0.7	3.4	1.3	1.8
11	1.6	0.7	—	—	1.0
12	0.7	—	2.7	1.3	1.0
13	1.0	—	2.7	1.3	1.1
14	0.4	—	0.7	—	0.4
15	1.4	1.3	3.4	—	1.6
16	0.4	—	0.7	2.7	0.6
17	0.2	—	—	—	0.1
18	0.2	—	0.7	—	0.2
19	—	—	2.0	—	0.4
20	—	—	1.4	—	0.2
21	—	—	1.4	—	0.2
22	—	—	1.4	1.3	0.4
23	—	—	—	—	—
24	—	—	—	—	—
25	—	—	0.7	1.3	0.2
26	—	—	0.7	—	0.1
27	—	—	0.7	—	0.1
28	—	—	1.4	—	0.2
29	—	—	—	—	—
30	—	—	2.0	—	0.4
31	—	—	—	—	—
32	—	—	—	—	—
33	—	—	—	1.3	0.1
34	—	—	—	—	—
35	—	—	0.7	—	0.1
≈					
45	—	—	—	1.3	0.1
46	—	—	—	—	—
47	—	—	0.7	—	0.1
N	439	151	147	75	812

areas where there is less advantage in large herds. Also, the giraffe is less subject to predation than the smaller game species. Many of these, like the giraffe, have solitary males in their populations, and many of them also, unlike the giraffe, have many more females than males among their number, implying greater predation on the males (Foster and Kearney, 1967). In any case the observation that giraffe apparently rarely communicate with each other negates some of the usefulness of herd relationships. There is less advantage in being in a herd if another member, aware of danger, fails to warn others of it.

Foster's data on 439 herds were analyzed to see if herd size could be correlated with the season, but there was no evidence that large or small herds were encountered in one month more than in another (Table 9–2).

The number of giraffe observed in a herd may be smaller than the actual number present if the herd is in a wooded area. Animals some distance from the rest may be missed, as may individuals that are particularly well camouflaged among large shrubs and trees. If one is noting the size and sex of each animal in such areas, the chances of a mistake are even greater. Such sources of error are the fault of the observer, but the giraffe themselves apparently have different habits in different areas, which makes it difficult to generalize about the species as a whole. For example, the proportion of adult males in the population was far higher at Fleur de Lys than in the Nairobi National Park. The Fleur de Lys data could not be applied to other herds; indeed, the sexual imbalance fostered homosexual behavioral patterns which are usually rare among giraffe. Similarly at the Nairobi National Park, although the numbers of either sex were similar, their habits were not; more males kept to the forested region where they were less likely to be observed than did the females (Fig. 9–1). To see if male giraffe were more inclined to stay in bush areas and females in plains areas in other districts, Foster noted the habitat of giraffe seen while on trips from Nairobi to the Serengeti Plains. He could find no such correlation there.

In summary, then, the following data describe the giraffe populations studied in detail by the authors, but they may not be true for other giraffe in Africa. Of more interest than the size of the giraffe herds are the kind of giraffe that make them up. Some information can be garnered from authors who have casually encountered giraffe in the wild (Table 9–3), but most of the information here is based on our own studies.

LONE GIRAFFE

It is evident from Table 9–4, where the percentage occurrences of all the herd sizes from one to three animals in four areas are listed, that lone giraffe are by far the most common type, from 44% to 16% of all sightings, depending on the area. In every area the number of times adult bulls were seen alone was significantly greater than the number of times lone adult cows were seen; and for the two areas with the most data, lone cows were seen significantly more often than single young, which are defined as animals less than two years old and under

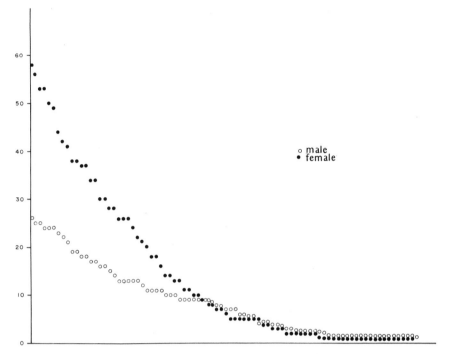

Fig. 9–1 Number of times individual giraffe were seen in the Nairobi National Park, in decreasing order. Giraffe dead, or presumed dead, are not included.

half the adult size. Four-month-old to subadult giraffe of either sex were virtually never seen alone in the Nairobi Park. The lone males were generally striding steadily along, perhaps looking for a receptive female; the lone females, at least in the Nairobi National Park, were often heavily pregnant and gave birth within a few days. The adaptive advantage of leaving the herd to give birth is not clear, but it happens also in other ungulates (Schenkel, 1966). Foster once saw a Coke's hartebeest giving birth, with the head of the young appearing from under its mother's tail. The other females in the herd chased the mother relentlessly until finally she left the herd to give birth alone.

The data in Table 9–4 underline the impossibility of referring to a *typical* pattern of giraffe herd composition. Each of the areas discussed has its own peculiar distribution of animals, based on such things as the amount of forested area and the ratio of male, female, and young giraffe.

GROUPS OF TWO OR THREE

Such small groups are common in each of the four areas analyzed in Table 9–4, with two giraffe present in 10.7% to 16.5% of all sightings and three present in 8.6% to 12.6% of them. When two animals were present, they were

TABLE 9-2 MONTHLY SIZES OF GIRAFFE HERDS IN NAIROBI NATIONAL PARK, IN PERCENTAGES[a]

	Number of Giraffe in Herds Sighted																		
Months	1	2	3	4	5	6	7	8	9	10	11	12	13	14	15	16	17	18	Actual total
January	17	39	11	11	11	—	6	—	5	—	—	—	—	—	—	—	—	—	18
February	32	7	21	11	4	—	11	14	—	—	—	—	—	—	—	—	—	—	28
March	19	31	13	8	5	8	5	5	2	2	—	—	—	—	1	—	—	1	62
April	21	14	21	7	10	10	—	4	4	3	—	—	—	3	3	—	—	—	29
May	36	14	7	22	—	7	—	—	7	—	7	—	—	—	—	—	—	—	14
June	29	6	—	6	24	—	6	23	—	—	—	6	—	—	—	—	—	—	17
July	30	17	4	13	15	4	2	—	2	7	2	—	—	—	—	4	—	—	47
August	31	15	23	6	6	11	5	—	—	—	—	—	2	—	1	—	—	—	65
September	11	22	13	13	13	16	3	—	—	—	—	3	—	3	—	—	3	—	37
October	19	13	10	13	13	2	10	6	6	2	4	—	—	—	2	—	—	—	52
November	16	7	21	11	9	5	5	9	—	5	5	—	7	—	—	—	—	—	43
December	22	15	4	15	11	15	—	4	—	—	4	3	—	—	7	—	—	—	27
Actual total	101	75	60	47	43	31	20	20	8	8	7	3	4	2	6	2	1	1	439

[a] After Foster and Dagg (1972).

often two adult bulls (especially at Fleur de Lys where bulls formed an unusually large part of the population) or two adult females. A male and a female or a female and a young were not uncommon, but two young together or a bull and a young were rarely seen in any area.

When three animals formed a herd, they were most often three bulls, three cows, two cows and a young, or a bull, a cow and a young. However, all possible combinations of the three categories were seen together at least once. Most rarely seen were three young together and two young plus a bull.

LARGE GROUPS

Herds of four or more giraffe were of such varied composition that the data cannot be presented in a concise table. The groups of males, females, and young and of females and young without males were by far the most common in the Nairobi Park (15.0% each of all herds sighted). Cows, bulls, and no young were present in 4.8% of the herds sighted (significantly less ($p < .01$) than the previous two categories), and males and young alone in 0.9% of the groups (again significantly less than the other three categories, $p < .01$).

At Fleur de Lys where there were comparatively fewer females and young, this difference was also reflected in these large herds. There were more herds with males, females, and young in them than any other kind (11.3% of all herds sighted), but only six nonmale herds (4.0%, $p < .01$). The number of herds with only males and young (6.0%) was far higher proportionately than at Nairobi. The number of herds with adults and no young was 7.3%.

TABLE 9–3 COMPOSITION OF GIRAFFE HERDS ENCOUNTERED BY VARIOUS AUTHORS IN AFRICA

Number in herd	Male	Adult Female	Unsexed	Young	Reference
12			7	5	Akeley, 1929
10		1		9	Stott, 1950
9	1	8			Thomas, 1959
9	1	4		4	Schillings, 1907
9			5	4	Brynard and Pienaar, 1960
8	1	5		2	"Countryman," 1954
7		2		5	Johnson, 1928
7	1	4		2	Roosevelt and Heller, 1914
7	1	4		2	Selous, 1907
7			4	3	Lönnberg, 1912
7		7			Babich, 1964
6		2		4	Grzimek, 1960a
5	1	3		1	Bryden, 1893
5	3	2			Brynard and Pienaar, 1960
4	1	2		1	Stott, 1950
4	1	1		2	Wells, 1931
4	1	2		1	Wood, 1894
4	4				Babich, 1964
3			2	1	Rogister, 1957
3		2		1	Lönnberg, 1912
3	2	1			Lönnberg, 1912
3	3				Brynard and Pienaar, 1960
3	2	1			Babich, 1964
3	1	1		1	Mahuzier, 1956
3	1	2			Bronson, 1910
2	1	1			Selous, 1907
2	1	1			Wood, 1894
2	2				Brynard and Pienaar, 1960
1		1			Roosevelt and Heller, 1914
1	1				Roosevelt and Heller, 1914
1	1				Stevenson-Hamilton, 1947
1	1				Farini, 1886
1	1				Babich, 1964
1	1				Rogister, 1957

TABLE 9-4   FOR EACH AREA, THE PERCENTAGE OF GROUPS SEEN OF THE TOTAL OF ALL HERDS SEEN[a]

	Fleur de Lys, Transvaal	Nairobi National Park	Serengeti National Park	Other areas in Africa reported in the literature
Number of sightings	151	439	147	75
Lone animals	44.4%	23.4%	16.3%	24.0%
1 m	**⟋35.1%	**⟋13.9%	**⟨13.6%	**⟨22.7%
1 f	**⟩ 9.3	**⟩ 7.7	2.0	1.3
1 y	⟍ 0	⟍ 1.8	0.7	0
Two animals	10.7%	16.5%	10.8%	13.3%
m–m	7.3%	2.1%	5.4%	2.7%
f–f	1.3	4.6	2.7	5.3
y–y	0	0.2	0	0
m–f	0.7	1.6	0	4.0
f–y	0.7	7.5	2.7	1.3
m–y	0.7	0.5	0	0
Three animals	8.6%	12.6%	8.9%	9.3%
m–m–m	2.6%	1.6%	2.0%	2.7%
f– f –f	1.3	3.2	1.4	0
y– y –y	0	0.5	0	0
m–m–f	2.0	0	0.7	2.7
m–m–y	0.7	0.9	0	0
m– f –y	1.3	0.5	0.7	1.3
f– f –m	0.7	2.7	2.0	1.3
f– f –y	0	1.1	0.7	1.3
y– y –m	0	0.5	0	0
y–y–f	0	1.6	1.4	0

[a] After Foster and Dagg, 1972.
Abbreviations: m—adult male, f—adult female, y—young.
**$p < .01$, χ^2 test.

The foregoing discussion indicates that some categories of giraffe are more likely to be together than are others; for example the adults are more often together than are several young, or bulls and young. To analyze this phenomenon further, the Nairobi data for giraffe in each herd were analyzed in pairs; for example, a group of three cows, one bull, and two young would give the following results:

Pairs	Number of pairs
Female–female	3
Male–male	0
Young–young	1
Female–male	3
Male–young	2
Female–young	6

For a total of 20,112 pairs calculated from the Nairobi data, the likelihood of members of the three categories being together worked out as follows, after a correction was made for the numbers of bulls, cows and young present in the park:

Pairs	Percentage of pairs present
Female–female	20
Male–male	9
Young–young	17
Female–male	13
Male–young	12
Female–young	29
	100

Thus the chance of a female and a young being in the same herd was high, while that of two males being together was low. The only values that were not significantly different ($p < .01$) were those for female–male and male–young pairs. This supports the hypothesis suggested by the large number of bulls seen walking alone, that they travel from group to group, perhaps in search of receptive females. Many herds included one bull, but at any one time there was less likelihood of two or more males being present at once than there was of other types of pairs being present.

INDIVIDUAL RELATIONSHIPS

For most species, collected data seldom allow further analyses of herd structure. For giraffe too this was true until 1965. In the two studies of wild giraffe before that time, only the few individuals that were recognizable could be traced from day to day and from herd to herd. At Fleur de Lys Dagg recognized only about 15 individuals by their color, their coat pattern, their size, or their horns. For example, Star was an immense bull with broken spots resembling stars; Retic was an equally big male, but with a coat pattern resembling that of a northern reticulated giraffe; Limpy was a male that limped because of a wire snare that was still tight around one foot; and Pom-Pom was a medium-sized female with perky tufts of black hair sprouting above her horns.

Backhaus (1961), who also recognized a few individuals in his study in Zaire, felt that some of the distinctive characteristics were inherited. In one of his groups the animals all lacked dark spots between their forelegs, in another the horns were small and bent inwards, and in a third the horns were especially well developed. He claimed these characteristics indicated a close relationship within each group.

More recently Foster used the varied spotting of the giraffe to identify them. In fact, he chose the giraffe as a subject for study for the very reason that each animal has a unique pattern of blotches on its body and can therefore be individually recognized. While the same is true of zebra (Klingel, 1965) and cheetah, the former is so common that the task of identifying an individual from its markings would be very laborious, while the latter is so rare or cryptic that too much time would be spent in looking for it.

The advantage in studying a self-marked animal is of course that the difficult and sometimes damaging task of marking animals by branding, collaring, or ear-tagging is unnecessary. And only by knowing the individuals in a population can gestation period, rate of calving, survival of the young and adults, precise movements, herd associations, and many other behavioral features be studied in wild animals.

Foster's method of identifying individuals involved photographing the neck of each giraffe from the left side. The photographs were then sorted first into adult male, adult female, and young (half size or less), then further subdivided by coat markings—those with regular, irregular, and highly irregular patterns. Foster carried a file of all his photographs into the field with him and, with practice, was soon able to identify any giraffe within a few seconds (Fig. 9–2). After three years he was able to recognize 241 giraffe that had been seen at some time within the park. Since only about 80 giraffe were present in the park at any one time, there must have been considerable movement to and from the Kitengela Conservation Area to the south of the park.

Even at Fleur de Lys, where the companions of only the few known individuals could be recorded accurately, Dagg suspected that associations of giraffe were remarkably loose. On many occasions, Star or Pom-Pom, for example, would be seen with certain giraffe one day, with others the following day, and with still others a week later. Few if any giraffe formed lasting attachments with other individuals.

Foster's data underlined this lack of close ties between individuals, which can be portrayed in two ways—either by delineating the companions with which an individual is seen during several years' study, or by noting the changes in the various herd compositions, again over a period of time.

To illustrate the first possibility, the associates of the five bulls, five cows, and five young for which there were the most sightings were analyzed to determine

Fig. 9–2 Foster identifying individual giraffe in the field.

how often various individuals were seen together. For each of these individuals the sightings extended over a period of from 18 to 29 months. Although the numbers of males and females in the Nairobi Park are relatively equal, the females and the young were seen much more often than the males ($p < .01$).

The data for the individual with the most sightings (F13) are given in Table 9–5, and the results for all the individuals in Table 9–6. From this latter compilation it is evident that:

1. The adult bulls were loners, never staying long with other male, females, or young. In fact the most that a male was seen with another individual was seven times; on an average, if one of two individuals were male, the two were seen together less than two times in the 20 or more months of observations.
2. Two females were seen together over twice as often on the average as a male was seen with any other individual; but even so, the females too were constantly changing their associates. In Table 9–5 it is clear that even

TABLE 9–5 THE ASSOCIATION OF GIRAFFE F13 WITH ADULT FE-MALE, ADULT MALE, AND YOUNG GIRAFFE IN NAIROBI NATIONAL PARK[a]

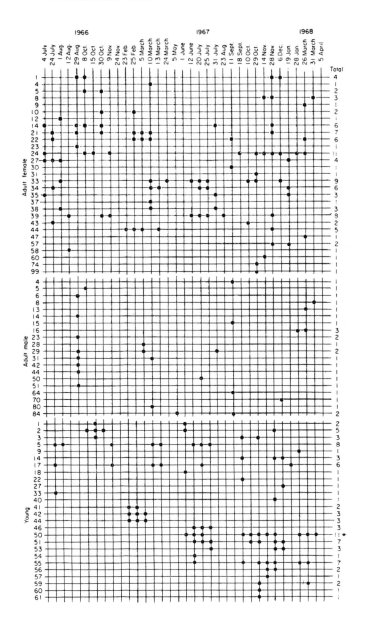

[a] After Foster and Dagg, 1972. (For adult females, the range of associate-days was 1–11, average 3.3; for adult males, the range was 1–3, average 1.3; for young, the range was 1–8, average 2.4.)

*Indicates own young (omitted from average and range).

118

TABLE 9-6 GIRAFFE SEEN WITH MOST COMMONLY SIGHTED INDIVIDUALS DURING THE STUDY AT NAIROBI NATIONAL PARK[a]

Commonly seen giraffe	No. of months between first and last sightings	No. of times seen	No. of individuals seen with			Range of times seen with any one individual			Average times seen with any one individual			Averages of times seen for all individuals in each category		
			f	m	y	f	m	y	f	m	y	f	m	y
Adult females														
F12	20	34	32	11	10	1–14	1–3	1–5	3.6	1.5	2.2			
F13	21	36	30	20	26	1–11	1–3	1–8	3.3	1.3	2.4			
F34	20	31	25	12	9	1–15	1–4	1–18	3.7	1.8	3.9	3.4	1.5	2.7
F35	20	30	28	12	10	1–10	1–3	1–6	3.7	1.4	2.2			
F39	25	34	37	9	19	1–8	1–3	1–8	2.8	1.7	2.8			
Adult males														
M3	20	12	6	22	11	1–4	1–5	1–4	1.8	2.2	2.3			
M10	20	17	13	21	10	1–2	1–4	1–2	1.1	1.9	1.2			
M13	20	14	23	12	8	1–2	1–3	1–2	1.2	1.2	1.1	1.5	1.7	1.7
M26	20	16	14	26	12	1–3	1–5	1–2	1.5	2.0	1.4			
M46 (=T4)	29	21	26	13	15	1–5	1–2	1–7	2.0	1.2	2.4			
Young														
T3 m	21	27	37	18	30	1–6	1–2	1–4	2.2	1.2	1.7			
T5 f	21	30	27	7	13	1–18	1–2	1–19	4.1	1.3	3.4			
T14 m	20	28	30	24	25	1–9	1–3	1–6	2.5	1.3	2.1	2.9	1.3	2.7
T17 m	26	32	25	11	8	1–12	1–3	1–19	3.8	1.6	4.1			
T27 f	18	34	25	18	15	1–9	1–2	1–12	1.9	1.3	2.2			

[a] After Foster and Dagg, 1972.

119

when two individuals were seen together a number of times, these associations were usually not successive; instead the animals drifted apart and came together again at irregular intervals. This was true for the associations of all of the 15 individuals analyzed. On an average, a female was seen with another female 3.4 times during the study. Only two of the four parturient females were alone to any extent before the day of birth of their young.

3. Female and young giraffe or two young animals were seen together about 2.8 times during the study, less often than two females but more often than a male was seen with any other animal. (Values for mothers and their own young are not included in the averages and will be considered later.) The mothers tended to associate with more young after their own young were born than before. However, groups of young individuals that stay together for extended periods while they were growing up were not a trait of the giraffe at Nairobi, although Mejia noted them at Serengeti.

The second way to portray the herd patterns is to analyze the changes in the groups over a period of time. To do this, the animals with which each individual was sighted were listed in chronological order under each animal's file. Under each list individuals were noted as "present" or "not present" for those herds sighted a week later than the previous herd but within a month's time. Thus, if the animals F3, F9, F14, M60, T1, and T54 were seen one day, and F3, F15, T1, and T54 eight days later, the relationship between the herds was noted as:

Females	(F)	1 present and 2 not present
Males	(M)	0 present and 1 not present
Young	(T)	2 present and 0 not present

When all of the groups were analyzed in this way, the 3,493 notations gave the following results:

	Present	*Not present*
Females	23%	77%
Males	13%	87%
Young	30%	70%

In general then, of all the herds encountered in the field, the members were the same one to four weeks later less than one-third of the time. The young were most likely to be with the same animals during the month, and the females were the next most constant. The males were very changeable. The differences between each of these three groups were statistically significant ($p < .01$, X^2 test).

MOTHER-YOUNG RELATIONSHIPS

The Nairobi data indicated that the newborn and young giraffe were not constantly with their mothers. For the animals analyzed in Table 9–6, during the one to two years of the observation periods, F13 was seen with her own young (T50) 11 out of 17 sightings, F34 with her young (T17) 27 out of 31 sightings, and F39 with her young (T46) 9 out of 14 sightings. These young (in Table 9–6) apparently remained with their mothers for their first six weeks, including T17, whose life history is given in Table 9–7; but they drifted away occasionally after that. Table 9–8 shows that T17 was more frequently seen with its mother than were most young giraffe. T9, for example, vanished (presumably to the south of the park) for 29 months, during which time its mother was seen regularly. This table indicates that there is no obvious relationship between strength of the mother–young bond and the chances for survival. This is as expected. Had the results shown that a close mother–young bond favored survival, selection would have made the bond stronger than it is. The bond may be so loose in the Nairobi Park that it is difficult to establish which giraffe is the mother of a given young.

In captivity young may nibble on leaves when they are only three weeks old, and such precocity occurred in the wild as well. Young were seldom seen sucking. Occasionally a young giraffe tried to suck a female other than its mother, but it was always rejected by the female, which butted it away or whisked her tail in its face. This behavior was also common at the Taronga Zoo.

LEADERSHIP

As might be expected in a species with such loose relationships between individuals, leadership tended to be arbitrary. When a mother and her young were alone, it was the mother that decided when she and her young would move and where they would go. The onus was on the young to keep up with her. At Fleur de Lys on one occasion a female jumped over a fence with the other adults in her group, leaving behind her baby, which was too small to follow her. The mother did not wander off from the fence with the adults, but stayed to pace up and down while her calf paced opposite her. The mother seemed concerned about this separation from her calf by the fence, but she apparently did not know what to do about it. The next morning the mother had rejoined the other adults in the paddock, but her baby was never seen again.

If bulls and cows were present in a herd, it was impossible to say which adult was the leader. Sometimes a cow and sometimes a bull would lead the way to a new feeding area. Nor was it possible to denote one member of a herd as a sentinel for the group. The giraffe might take turns watching and drinking at a waterhole, but in herds that were feeding or resting no individual seemed to keep watch for danger more than any other.

TABLE 9–7 LIFE HISTORY OF GIRAFFE T17 (MALE), BORN NOVEMBER 1965 TO F34 IN NAIROBI NATIONAL PARK

Date	Female adults present	Male adults present	Other young	Remarks
20.11.65	F34	—	—	Height ca. 2 m; horns 1 cm, umbilicus
11. 1 .66	F34	—	—	Suckling, horns 4 cm
18. 1 .66	F34	—	T3, 5	Browsing tender tips
2. 2 .66	F1, 38	—	T19, 20	Umbilicus gone; horns 5 cm
18. 2 .66	—	—	T19, 20	F34 300 m away
10. 3 .66	F1, 34, 38	—	T19, 20	Browsing; horns 5 cm
12. 3 .66	F1, 34, 38	—	T19, 20	Browsing regularly
30. 3 .66	F34	—	T5	T5 may be calf of F34
7. 4 .66	F12, 16, 27, 33–39	M5, 58	T3, 4, 5	
12. 4 .66	F6, 12, 13, 14, 24, 27, 33–39, 43, 44, 57	M5, 21, 38, 58, 59	T5	
30. 5 .66	F27, 34	—	T5	
2. 7 .66	F34, 43	—	T5, 33	
24. 7 .66	F13, 21, 22, 27, 34, 43	—	T5, 33	
13. 9 .66	F34, 35, 37	M48	—	
25. 9 .66	F34, 37, 57	—	T3, 5	
7.10.66	F18, 34	—	T5	
4.11.66	F33, 34, 57	—	—	
8.11.66	F34, 39, 47	—	T5	
9.11.66	F13, 24, 39	—	T5	Plus 4 unidentified
17.11.66	F27, 34, 57	—	T5	
22.11.66	F33, 34, 36, 38, 39, 43, 57, 75	M57, 70	T3, 5	Height about 3 m
12.12.66	F27, 33, 34, 36, 39, 43, 73, 81	M46, 70	T3, 40	
22. 1 .67	F34, 44	—	T44	
25. 1 .67	F34	—	—	
4. 2 .67	F6, 27, 34, 38	M28, 75	—	
15. 2 .67	F34	M10	T5	
20. 2 .67	F34, 36, 37, 57, 93	—	T5	
23. 2 .67	F12, 34–7, 57, 93	M16	T5	
10. 3 .67	F4, 13, 33, 34, 37, 38	M28	T5	
13. 3 .67	F13, 34, 44	M80	T5	
30. 3 .67	F34, 57	—	T5	Height about 3 m
28. 4 .67	F12, 34, 43, 57	M21		
11. 5 .67	F12, 27, 33–5, 37, 38, 43	M21, 58	T3	
17. 5 .67	F34	M21, 58		
25. 7 .67	F13, 33, 34, 39	M50	T5, 46, 50, 51	Height ca. 3.2 m; horns ca. 8 cm
31. 7 .67	F13, 33, 34, 39, 81	—	T5, 46, 50, 51	
12. 8 .67	F34, 57	—	T5	
29. 9 .67	F12, 14	—	T5	Plus 1
27.11.67	F4, 6, 12, 14, 37, 38	—	T46	
8.12.67	F4, 6, 35, 37, 43	M58, 70	T5	Plus others but not F34
28. 1 .68	F13, 27, 34, 35, 57	—	—	Plus others
18. 2 .68	F34, 57	—	—	
21. 2 .68	F34, 57	—	—	

TABLE 9–8 RELATION BETWEEN MOTHER–YOUNG BOND AND SURVIVAL[a]

Young	Age in months (Mar. 1968)	Status at end of study	No. of times seen with mother	No. of times seen without mother	No. of times mother seen without young
T9	31	alive	3	0	49
T10	3	dead	2	2	2
T11	14	dead	5	2	1
T12	1	dead	2	0	0
T17 m	27	alive*	37	4	1
T18 f	27	alive*	12	9	4
T20	4	dead	3	1	2
T29 m	16	dead	12	1	2
T31 m	15	dead	3	2	1
T33 f	4	dead	3	0	0
T35 f	16	dead	6	5	3
T36 f	2	dead	5	0	2
T44 m	9	dead	16	4	5
T46 f	10	probably dead	10	7	7
T47 f	3	dead	3	1	2

*Seen alive in November 1970.
[a] After Foster and Dagg, 1972.

NECKING AND SPARRING

Dagg originally defined necking as the gentle rubbing of one male's head or neck against the body of a second male, but Coe (1967) broadened the term to include serious fighting with the neck as well. In the wild, necking only occurs in males. At Fleur de Lys, where males made up about 70% of the population, gentle necking or sparring matches occurred during all times of the day and in every season, with about 5% of the giraffe participating at any one time (Fig. 7–3). Usually two bulls stood side by side facing in the same direction or in opposite directions, or circled slowly about. Every few minutes one male swung his head at the other, perhaps grazing his horns on the other's trunk or perhaps missing altogether (Fig. 9–3). The other retaliated with an equally unpunishing blow. Such bouts generally occurred between two adult or subadult bulls, but occasionally included a third bull or a very young male calf (Fig. 9–4). The combatants were never hurt in these encounters, which took place regardless of the presence of any females. Often the giraffe rested for long periods between exchanges; sometimes they decided to go off to eat together rather than to spar longer; sometimes the necking changed into sexual behavior, with a male rubbing his neck gently along the other's or one bull mounting the second (Fig. 9–5). Mejia felt prolonged bouts of "necking" established a dominance hierarchy among males; when bouts were followed by mounting, the mounting was an

Fig. 9-3   Two male giraffe sparring.

expression of dominance. These homosexual encounters were much rarer in populations where there were more females in proportion to males; in Nairobi National Park where there were slightly more females than males, Foster saw such behavior only three times in 400 hours of observation.

Males also sparred during all months in Nairobi Park. Coe (1967) observed that the sexually related types of sparring occurred in the head-to-tail position. The matches were initiated by a challenger that, on approaching a second male, assumed a "proud" posturing movement with the shoulders directed toward the opponent and the legs and erect neck held rigid. If the opponent assumed a similar "proud" posture, after a short interval both giraffe straddled their stiff legs

Fig. 9–4 Two male calves necking.

to obtain a firm stance and curved their necks away from each other prior to the first blows.

Serious sparring matches in which one member is perhaps injured are rare and were not seen at all by Coe nor Foster. Two such matches took place within a two-month period at Fleur de Lys, however, one of which was seen by Dagg. The two bulls Star and Cream approached each other with heads held high until they stood side by side, head to tail, close together, each with his legs spread apart under him for balance. Suddenly Star lowered his head and whipped it horns foremost at Cream's trunk, connecting with an impact that was heard easily from 40 meters away. Cream lurched sideways, collected himself and returned the blow with his head, striking Star on the neck. Star then aimed at Cream's front legs and knocked them out from under him with a blow of his head. Cream, struggling not to fall, missed Star entirely with his return blow. Both were so intent on the battle that they ignored an African fence repairman who walked past within 10 meters of them. Their swings, counter-blows, agile escapes, nimble footwork, and complete misses continued for 10 minutes. Then

Fig. 9–5 One male mounting another male following a necking match.

Cream turned and cantered off. Star followed him for a short distance before stopping to watch him retreat. Seven giraffe watching in the distance returned to their browsing.

The losing giraffe in such a struggle does not always escape so easily. His head may be gashed during a fight or he may be knocked to the ground unconscious, as one was at Rusermi in South Africa (in film of Dr. Serfontein). In such a contest in the Kruger National Park one of the contestants was killed. He had a large hole immediately behind one ear where his top neck vertebra had been splintered by a blow; part of the splinter had pierced the spinal cord (Clerck, 1965).

No matter how badly a fight is going, the loser never resorts to kicking—a method by which a giraffe fights predators—nor to biting, as some deer do. However, injury from sparring is rare. As Harrison Matthews (1964) has pointed out, those animals which have evolved weapons for intraspecific combat have also often evolved behavioral or morphological adaptations to keep the punishment minimal. Thus, the male giraffe's horns are blunt and that part of the hide which is usually hit is up to 15 mm thick.

The function of necking or sparring is conjectural. Mejia (1971–72) believed true fighting occurs to decide what male has the right to mount a female in heat, but there were no females in evidence during one of the matches at Fleur de Lys. Unlike the males of many African ungulates, the male giraffe does not defend an area of ground, a territory, from other male giraffe. Male gazelles, gnu, and hartebeest, for example, live either in bachelor herds, mixed herds, or alone, defending a territory from other males of the same species and attempting to court and retain any females that happen to pass nearby. Male giraffe also live in these kinds of herds, but when alone they are almost always found traveling, apparently in quest of females in heat rather in the manner of male gaur (Schaller, 1967).

Coe (1967), who also studied giraffe in Nairobi Park, felt that the function of necking was that of a "sexuo-social bonding mechanism." He believed that in a bachelor group a hierarchy of sexual and physical dominance was set up by the activity of necking, and the combined effect of both these forms of social contact was the basis of social cohesion in the giraffe community. Geist (1966) also suggested that necking helped to maintain a stable hierarchy in giraffe groups. Foster's data, analyzed since these works, indicate that bachelor groups comprised of the same individuals are virtually nonexistent in the Nairobi giraffe. However the building-up of a hierarchy if individuals associate with each other for some period of time is possible.

FLEHMEN IN THE WILD

Because of the dearth of females, Fleur de Lys was not a good place to observe heterosexual behavior. Even so, Dagg was able to watch giraffe flehmen, or urine-test, many times and mate once (see Chapter 11 for flehmen behavior in captivity). To test the urine of a female, a bull walked up to her and licked her tail, grasped her tail between his lips, or nuzzled her flank with his head. This behavior stimulated the female to urinate. As she did so, the bull lowered his head and collected some of the urine in his mouth or on his tongue (Fig. 9–6). Then he raised his head, closed his mouth, and curled back his lips in a charac- teristic fashion known as "flehmen" (Dagg and Taub, 1971) (Fig. 9–7). Some- times he ejected the urine from his mouth in a long thin stream, licking his lips momentarily before beginning to browse or ruminate. If there were other un- tested females present, the male generally made his way to the closest to repeat the performance. Sometimes, presumably when the flavor was right, the male followed the female for hours, obtaining successive samples of urine.

The whole performance was calm and sedate. Sometimes a bull collected urine from a female that was urinating spontaneously. On one occasion Dagg saw three males collect urine from a single female at one time. There was no

Fig. 9–6 Bull giraffe collecting urine from a urinating female.

jostling among these males. Backhaus (1961), however, observed in the Garamba National Park that the larger and stronger males chased the more inferior bulls away if they tried to collect urine from a female. The behavior of testing urine has sexual significance, as a male collected only a female's urine in the wild. Presumably the male can determine by the composition of the urine whether the female is in heat or approaching this condition. An example lends some weight to this supposition. Foster had been observing a herd of five female giraffe in Nairobi Park, as usual trying to determine if any were pregnant. (This is not an easy task in giraffe, whose bodies are so short compared with their size that the bellies, even of males, always look round.) In this group one female was definitely heavily pregnant. Soon a large male appeared from across the plains to join the female group. As expected he went to each female in turn, nudged her rump to make her urinate, sampled the urine, and flehmened. He did this to all of the females except the pregnant one. Perhaps the male also recognized that she was pregnant and therefore that it was useless to determine whether she was in heat.

Fig. 9–7 Male flehmening female's urine.

MATING

Dagg did not see if urine-testing preceded the single mating that she witnessed at Fleur de Lys in which Star mounted a female at least three times. (In a species with a gestation period of 15 months, mating is not common.) Between each mounting the two animals walked about restlessly while a second male walked about with them. Star followed closely behind the female until she stood still. Then, after standing motionless behind her for a minute in the erect posture, he lifted his forelegs up and slid them forward along the sides of her flanks. In each case the female ran forward several seconds after being mounted. The second male moved closer and closer to the pair until, after the third mounting, Star chased him away by charging toward him. Then the male circled around Star to approach the female from the other side. The last that was seen of them, the animals were galloping away in a trio behind some bushes. This mating, like the two witnessed by Morris Gosling (personal communication) in the Nairobi National Park, took place in the late afternoon. Backhaus (1961) reported that in the Garamba National Park when a female was in heat, she stayed near the bulls, sometimes approaching one to rest or rub her head on him. Her advances usually stimulated the male to mate with her.

Dagg also watched the dominant male mount a receptive cow three times during a three-hour period at the Taronga Zoo. The bull prepared to mount her more often, but the cow refused to remain standing still. His preparation consisted of nosing her, rubbing against her with his head, smelling her vulva, flehmening her urine, lining himself up behind her, edging her into position with his foreleg, bowing his head down over her, unsheathing his penis, and moving his hind legs closer to his forelegs to give himself a better thrust. After each mating he sniffed the cow's vulva. On this occasion a second adult bull flehmened the cow's urine twice and sniffed her genitalia five times—all activities which the dominant male ignored—but the second bull did not mount her.

10 *Reproduction and Population Structure*

REPRODUCTION

A female giraffe comes in heat for one day about every two weeks. Since she allows, if not encourages, a male to mount her at these times but at no other times, these periods are easy to detect in captivity. For example, Lang (1955a) noticed that a female mated at the following intervals—12, 13, 1, 13, 15, 13, 15, 30, and 40 days—after which time she became pregnant and avoided further advances by the male.

This female was slow in conceiving. Other captive females which were in heat three weeks after parturition (Nouvel, 1958) and every two weeks after that, became pregnant two, three, and seven months after the birth of their calves, in each case while they were still nursing their earlier calves (Schlott, 1952; Gijzen, 1958). These females were always enclosed with a male. (In many zoos the male is separated from the female during parturition and for some time afterwards, so that data of lengths between successive births at these zoos are meaningless.) On Fleur de Lys too it was noticed that the bulls showed especial interest in cows whose calves were several months old. One bull followed such a female for days, collecting her urine at intervals.

A female giraffe can reproduce until she is at least 20 years old (Ried, 1958). She produces her first calf when she is about five years old (Gijzen, 1958; Anon., 1960a; Backhaus, 1961; Reuther, 1961; Crandall, 1964), so that in her lifetime she could bear up to ten young if one was born every 18 months. (Males too become sexually mature when they are about three and a half years old.) This potential could probably be reached in the wild, since in Nairobi Park second offspring have been born 17 months after the previous one. Giraffe twins have been reported for wild giraffe (Percival, 1924; Shortridge, 1934), but as the actual births were not seen, this evidence is of doubtful validity. The mother–young bond is remarkably weak in giraffe, and Foster has often noted a female together with more than one newborn, none of which was necessarily hers. As far as is known, only two sets of twins have been born in captivity. The stillborn twins, born at the San Francisco Zoo in 1943, together weighed only 41 kg (Reuther, personal communication). Those born at the Parc Safari Africain at Hemmingford, Quebec, in May 1975 are thriving.

The gestation period of giraffe in captivity is about 15 months (Backhaus, 1961, cites records for over 35 pregnancies in captivity), although young have been born 394 days (a premature animal that died shortly after birth; Lang, 1955a) and 488 days (Robinson *et al.,* 1965) after the last mating of the mother. First pregnancies seem to be slightly longer than subsequent ones, and perhaps all are longer than pregnancies of wild giraffe, which have never been timed; for deer at least it has been postulated that captive females, with their necessarily reduced exercise, carry their young longer than wild deer (Haugen and Davenport, 1950).

Backhaus (1961), who noted the dates of calvings of 53 females in captivity, found that they occurred in all months of the year. This lack of a breeding season was confirmed by Reuther and Doherty (1968). In wild giraffe it would seem advantageous if calves were born only at the beginning of the growing season. Then they would be able to take advantage of the new vegetation, either directly or through their mother's milk. In these animals too, however, calves may be born throughout the year. At Fleur de Lys Dagg did not notice that calves were born at one season more than at another. Calving peaks have been reported from the Kruger National Park nearby, but since these peaks have been cited from October to January (Stevenson-Hamilton, 1947), from February to April (Brynard and Pienaar, 1960), and for September–October (Pienaar, 1963), they are not very decisive. Most recently Fairall (1968) reported two calving peaks for the giraffe in this park—February and March and August to October, although newborn giraffe have been recorded in every month but January and June.

Ansell (1960) found no definite calving seasons for giraffe in Zambia, although he recorded that October and March have been mentioned by other authors. In nearby Rhodesia, Dasmann and Mossman (1962) reported that most births occurred in May during the dry season. Fig. 10–1 illustrates the months in which Foster noted calvings in Nairobi Park over a three-year period. In summary, giraffe breed throughout the year, but different calving peaks may occur in different areas.

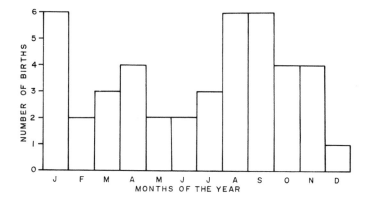

Fig. 10–1 Months of calving in the Nairobi National Park.

Even in captivity where a female is under constant observation, it may be difficult to determine if she is pregnant, although her appetite often increases, and she no longer comes in heat. Several months before the birth her abdomen may reveal fetal movements; a month or less before parturition the udder may swell to such an extent that milk secretions leak out. The sacral muscles above the tail usually relax about one week before the birth, and about this time, too, occasional muscle contractions of the uterus may be visible.

One would suppose that the best time for parturition would be at dawn so that the calf would have maximum strength by nightfall when most predators are active. The calf would also be most effectively imprinted by seeing its mother clearly (Backhaus, 1960). Of 27 calvings in captivity, 78% occurred in the daytime, although these timings may have been influenced by the presence of human observers (Backhaus, 1961).

Parturition and the newborn giraffe have been described in so many zoological garden reports that only a summary of their contents need be given (Anon., 1907, 1908b, 1951c; Benchley, 1946; Bigalke, 1939; Bridges, 1948; Calcaterra, 1972; Clarke, 1970, 1972; Crandall, 1964; Davis, 1949; Doorn, 1967; Erk *et al.*, 1967; Fitzinger, 1858; Germanos, 1907; Gijzen, 1958; Hediger, 1950, 1955; Iles, 1957; Koga, 1939; Lang, 1955a, b; Nakaegawa and Nakagawa, 1957; Owen, 1839, 1849, 1868; Patten, 1940; Pillai, 1957; Pournelle, 1955; Rensenbrink, 1968; Schlott, 1952; Sigel, 1886; Slijper, 1958). Some females about to give birth pace about restlessly; others lie down; most eat little. After the fetal membranes have been ruptured, either spontaneously or on being rubbed by the giraffe against a wall (Slijper, 1958), the forelegs of the fetus appear and then the head of the calf resting between or beside them (Fig. 10–2). Even though the head is born some time before the hindquarters, the young makes no attempt to breathe before the umbilical cord is broken. During the labor contractions which force the calf outward, the mother remains standing

Fig. 10–2 Giraffe giving birth to young; only calf's feet can be seen.

with her hind legs spread apart and her head extended forward as she strains. Between contractions she may eat some hay, ruminate, or pace about.

The calving lasts about one or two hours; Gijzen (1958) recorded four parturition times of 20 minutes, 2 hours, 2¾ hours, and 3½ hours. The presence of observers may delay the birth for many hours—even once the feet have appeared—if the giraffe is bothered by them (Backhaus, 1961). If the birth lasts longer than several hours, keepers may interfere by pulling the young outward with a rope. The female may stoop slightly to lessen her young's drop to the ground. The umbilical cord breaks during the fall, about 30 cm of the cord remaining hanging from the calf for up to five months (Savoy, 1966). The umbilical cord remained attached for two or three months in the Nairobi Park. The mother licks her calf free of the fetal membranes (occasionally they hang in rags in captive giraffe; Backhaus, 1961), but she may or may not eat the afterbirth, which is expelled any time up to nine hours later.

Fig. 10–3 Newborn calf sucking.

Normally the young struggles to its feet about an hour after birth, and shortly after this, sometimes with prodding by its mother, it locates her teats and begins to suck (Fig. 10–3). The precocity of a number of newborn giraffe is given in Tables 10–1 and 10–2. The mother's maternal instincts are released by the calf's successful efforts to help itself, so that the ablest young are more likely to survive than the weaker ones. If the young is born prematurely, often the mother loses interest in it and may exhibit no maternal behavior. In captivity one premature calf only 1.2 meters high was too small to reach its mother's udder. The mother seemed suspicious of her offspring. She licked it only perfunctorily before carelessly stepping on and breaking its leg (Steinemann, 1963). The 394-day calf mentioned earlier was too weak to stand following its birth. The mother shied away from her struggling infant, kicking it with her foreleg. When it had still not

TABLE 10-1   PRECOCITY OF NEWBORN CAPTIVE GIRAFFE

First stood	First walked	First ran	First suckled	First defecated (meconium)	First urinated	Reference
10 min						Matthews, L. H., pers. comm.
10 min	25 min		10 min			Gijzen, 1958
30 min						Pournelle, 1955
30 min		11 hr	42.5 hr	46.5 hr		Koga, 1939
35 min						Robinson et al., 1965
37 min			50 min	55 min		Gijzen, 1958
39 min	47 min		ca. 32 hr			Clarke, 1970
46 min			11.8 hr			Backhaus, 1961
48 min			98 min			Lang, 1955a
49 min	69 min		90 min			Clarke, 1972
50 min						Backhaus, 1961
55 min						Gensch, 1969
60 min						Robinson et al., 1965
60 min						Owen, 1868
60 min			60 min			Calcaterra, 1972
60 min						Anon., 1907
60 min			60 min			Hediger, 1950
60 min		9 hr	9.0 hr			Schlott, 1952
65 min			115 min			Davis, 1949
72 min			5.9 hr			Backhaus, 1961
80 min				73 hr	23 hr	Zellmer, 1960
86 min			94 min			Robinson, et al., 1965
90 min			120 min			Sigel, 1886
90 min						Schlott, 1952
120 min						Patten, 1940
120 min						Owen, 1839
126 min			8.3 hr			Backhaus, 1961
			8.5 hr			Grzimek, 1972
			10 hr			Fitzinger, 1858
			12 hr			Owen, 1849
		18 hr				Owen, 1849
		36 hr				Sigel, 1886

risen after five hours the mother stepped on it accidentally, also breaking its leg. It died soon afterward.

However even full-term young may be in trouble. One mother ignored her newborn after she had stepped on and broken its leg (Hediger, 1955). Another calf, unable to stand because its thigh muscles were damaged during birth, was also abandoned by its mother (Pournelle, 1955). A third primapara mother was so nervous that she paced continuously before, during, and after her young was

TABLE 10–2   FEEDING BEHAVIOR OF YOUNG CAPTIVE GIRAFFE

Tasted solid food	Ate solids regularly —ruminated	Drank water	Weaned	Reference
7 days			8 or 10 mo	Benchley, 1946
17 days	24 days			Sigel, 1886
19 days	20 days			Koga, 1939
21 days	4 mo			Anon., 1908b
21 days				Fitzinger, 1858
21 days	35 days	7½ mo, bottle-fed		Zellmer, 1960
39 days		2½ mo	1 year	Schlott, 1952
3 mo	4 mo		1 year	Patten, 1940
	19 days			Schlott, 1952
	4 mo			Krumbiegel, 1937
			10 mo	Gijzen, 1958

born. She stepped on its belly, neck, and mouth, crushing its lower jaw (Gensch, 1969). A fourth mother refused to let her calf suck, despite her full udder, when it did not stand until it was four days old (Lang, 1955a). If the mother refuses to let her young suck, zoo keepers usually try to raise it on a bottle, with occasional success (Zellmer, 1960; Savoy, 1966).

Even if the calf is normally precocious, the mother may have such poor maternal drives that she will try to strike or trample her calf whenever it approaches her, as did a female giraffe at the Cincinnati Zoo (Stephan, 1925). Another female at the Columbus Zoo trampled her first young to death as soon as it was born (Savoy, 1966). Nor are maternal aberrations confined to animals in zoos. In Kenya, Schaller (personal communication) reported seeing a lactating female killing a very young giraffe by blows with her front feet. The calf could have belonged to another female. It would be interesting to know the proportion of young that experience such maternal neglect or antipathy and the number of cases in which this animal is the first born of the mother.

In the Kruger National Park a giraffe giving birth to a calf was surrounded by nine other giraffe, apparently all females. These "midwives" all nuzzled the calf when it was strong enough to run. Three male giraffe and two hyenas watched the proceedings from a distance (Anon., 1965). In this same park another mother gave birth to her young entirely alone. The mother remained calm during the process although she was standing only 20 meters from the road (Anon., 1966). In Nairobi Park the female usually left the herd and remained alone for at least a few days before and after the birth of her young. One such female apparently died in childbirth (Grjimek, 1972).

Mejia (1971–72) observed mother–calf relationships in the Serengeti. The mother left the other giraffe for the birth and avoided contact with them for the first few days; when the pair joined the other giraffe again, the mother attacked any females that "nosed" her calf. (At the Taronga Zoo the mother allowed all other giraffe to nose her somewhat older young when they first saw it.) The "nosing" behavior by the mother is an invitation to the calf to follow and suckle, and is thought to be important in establishing an early mother–calf bond. Despite our earlier data, Mejia felt that "Calf subgroups" were one of the most characteristic features of giraffe society. In the Serengeti, calves stayed together and alone during the day, usually on a hill top where they were relatively safe from predators, while the mothers fed in nearby dense vegetation. Older calves formed separate subgroups which fed at the edge of the vegetation. Later still the calves mingled with the adults, and their subgroup disappeared. The calves left their mothers finally at about 16 months of age, after a short period in which mother and calf stayed in different neighboring groups. The separation was not precipitated by aggression on the part of the mother, but some evidence suggested that males courting her may have played a part in the process.

The newborn are about two meters tall at birth, not only because they must be able to keep up with their mothers in the wild but because they must be able to reach her udder. Table 10–3 gives the weights and heights of giraffe born in captivity. These young, like the young of most herbivores, are able to look after themselves soon after birth. They may suck for up to two years, but they supplement the milk with solids at about one month. Perhaps they need relatively little milk because of the high nutritional value of the acacia tips that they eat.

In the Taronga Zoo Dagg watched the four calves suck 18, 12, 8, and 5 times respectively during 50 hours of observations, mostly during the mornings. This sucking was often elicited by the mother nosing or licking her young's body. No mother was ever sucked initially by any but her own calf, as in the wild, although other giraffe up to three years old tried to suck. Once her own calf started sucking though, almost invariably other giraffe hurried over to suck too. Sometimes four giraffe including adults sucked at once from one mother, but few females allowed this number to suck for any length of time. Even with fewer participants no giraffe sucked for longer than a few minutes at a time. On four occasions sucking sessions were broken up by either male or female adults that approached and hit the sucking giraffe lightly or growled at them.

Ben Shaul (1962), who analyzed giraffe's milk before and after the tenth day of lactation, found that the earlier milk had a very high fat content and therefore also a high satiety value. She correlated this with the mother's habit of leaving her young in a secluded place and returning to nurse it at widely spaced intervals. However, such behavior would seem to be the exception rather than the rule. The later milk, according to Ben Shaul, had much less fat and was more dilute. She correlated this with the high maternal attentiveness of the giraffe mother after her young was 10 days old; after that time she assumed it sucked frequently from its mother. However her values for this milk are unlike those of Aschaffenburg et al. (1962) and Greed (1960), who showed high fat values in

TABLE 10-3 HEIGHTS AND WEIGHTS OF NEWBORN GIRAFFE

Height (cm)	Weight (kg)	Sex	Reference	Comment
122	30	f	Lang, 1955a	premature—died
134		m	Swope Pk. Zoo, clipping June 1965	
144			Fitzinger, 1858	
151		m	Sigel, 1886	died
152			Crandon Pk. Zoo, clipping March 1965	
155		f	Sigel, 1886	died
156		m	Gensch, 1969	
157		f	Schlott, 1952	
157		m	Zellmer, 1960	
161	43.5		Stephan, 1925	
165		f	Sigel, 1886	
168		f	Gijzen, 1958	
168		f	Crandall, 1964	
168	51		San Francisco Zoo, clipping January 1965	
169		m	London Zoo, pers. comm., 1957	
170		m	Crandall, 1964	
172	50		Bridges, 1948	
ca. 172	72	f	Gijzen, 1958	
172			Crandall, 1964	
174		m	Gensch, 1969	
175			Crandall, 1964	
178	50–55	m	Lang, 1955a	
178			Crandall, 1964	
180			Brookfield Zoo, clipping September 1961	
180	ca. 59		Clarke, 1970	
181		m	Gijzen, 1958	
182	60.5		Bigalke, 1956, pers. comm.	
184		m	Gijzen, 1958	
208			Fitzinger, 1858	
214	81		Benchley, 1946	born dead
	31		Hediger, 1955	first-born
	39.5	m	Crandall, 1964	died at one day
	48.5	f	Savoy, 1966	
	50.5	m	Savoy, 1966	
	53.5 at 3 days		Reventlow, 1949	
	63.5	f	Savoy, 1966	
	63.5		Patten, 1940	

TABLE 10-3   (continued)

Height (cm)	Weight (kg)	Sex	Reference	Comment
	67.5		Reventlow, 1949	
	67.5	m	Savoy, 1966	
	73 at 5 days	m	Backhaus, 1961	
	73		Pournelle, 1955	
	77		Wilson, 1969	wild

milk collected as late as the 150th day of lactation (Table 10–4). Aschaffenburg and his colleagues noted, as well as the high fat content of this giraffe's milk, similar to that of deer and antelope, the high casein and sodium content compared to that of an average cow's milk and the lower lactose and potassium contents. They carried out electrophoresis of the soluble protein fraction of the giraffe's milk and found a pattern of complexity not unlike that of cow's milk, with both globulins and albumins present. In their analysis of vitamin content of giraffe's milk, these workers found the content of calcium pantothenate, riboflavin, thiamine, and vitamin B_6 to be similar to that in good-quality cow's milk. The contents of biotin and α-tocopherol were lower than in cow's milk, and those of nicotinic acid, vitamin B_{12} and vitamin A were higher. Glass et al. (1969) analyzed the triglyceride composition of the milk fats of giraffe.

Recently medicines have been used with success on captive giraffe that refused to suckle their newborn calves. One such mother, whose udder was swollen and painful, allowed her young to nurse 24 hours after she had been treated with a tranquillizer to soothe her and a diuretic to relieve the engorgement of the udder (Gandal, 1961).

Of 117 giraffe born in captivity, 61.5% were males (Bourlière, 1961). This value is statistically significant ($p < .05$), so the ratio may be the result of an excessive intrauterine mortality of female embryos. Of 31 newborn giraffe in Nairobi Park, 16 were males.

POPULATION DYNAMICS

In Nairobi Park Foster accumulated data on the population dynamics of giraffe. Twelve giraffe gave birth to second offspring, with the birth dates known for all 24 young. In five cases the first young disappeared within a month of birth and the second young was born 17 months after the first. In four instances the first young lived for about three months and 21–22 months elapsed before the second birth. In three cases the young survived and a second young was born 23, 23, and 24 months after the first. If one assumes that there were about 32 resident females in the park and that they gave birth every 20 months, then

TABLE 10–4a COMPOSITION OF GIRAFFE'S MILK—GRAMS PER 100 GRAMS OF MILK

	On 150th day of lactation (Aschaffenburg et al., 1962)	Comparison	
		Guernsey cow (Skinner, 1966)	Human milk
Fat	12.50	4.65	4.62
Solids, nonfat	10.44	9.10	8.97
Lactose	3.41	4.70	6.94
Protein (total N x 6.38)	5.76	3.65	1.23
Casein (N x 6.38)	4.80		
Soluble protein (N x 6.38)	0.80		
Nonprotein nitrogen	0.023		
Ash	0.90		
Calcium	0.154	0.13	0.03
Phosphorus	0.104		
Sodium	0.100		
Potassium	0.100		
Chloride	0.134		
Magnesium	0.008		
Iron	0.00016		

TABLE 10–4b COMPOSITION OF GIRAFFE'S COLOSTRUM

1. A sample from a 14-year-old female taken two days after calving contained 17% butterfat, 37% total solids, 20% solids not fat, 17% protein, and 1% ash (School of Veterinary Studies, University of Edinburgh, pers. comm.).
2. A sample from the Cincinnati Zoo, which had a specific gravity of 1.066, contained in each 100 cc: 2.60 gm fat, 3.70 gm sugar, 25.41 gm casein and albumin, and 1.60 gm of mineral matter only (Stephan, 1925).

about 19 young should be born a year. In the first year of study 15 newborn were discovered; nine were recorded alive after two months and six after one year. Therefore, the mortality rate was highest in the first months of life, and over 50% of the discovered young died in their first year. If one assumes that 19 young were born (but four not found), the mortality rate was about 68% in the first year. In the second year of the study 10 newborn giraffe were discovered, but only five of these were still alive after two months. It is likely that other newborn vanish before they are discovered. Thus, well over half of the newborn giraffe die in their first year. Such a high mortality rate is usual among plains game in East Africa, and may be much higher; in the wildebeest up to 80% of the animals may die in their first year (Talbot and Talbot, 1963).

The causes of death in young giraffe are difficult to determine since a predator leaves no trace of a small kill after a few hours. Lions, which were known to kill two calves in Nairobi Park and one juvenile at Fleur de Lys, probably account for most deaths. Those newborn which occasionally live separately from their mothers are presumably more vulnerable to predation, and one would imagine that there would have been a strong selection for those giraffe displaying a closer mother–young bond. Apparently there has been no such selection.

In an attempt to determine how long adult giraffe might live in the wild, Foster has collected old photographs taken of giraffe in Nairobi Park (Fig. 10–4). Among these pictures he looks for the neck patterns of animals still living. Table 10–5 summarizes the results. As it is safe to assume that every giraffe has been photographed in the park by visitors each year for the last 20 years, the search for old photographs continues.

Foster's researches show that a number of the giraffe in Nairobi Park are at least 20 years old. A minimum figure was set when the animal was an adult in the photograph, using the assumption that it takes five years for a female and seven for a male to reach full size (Backhaus, 1961). For example, an adult male in a photograph taken in 1954 was at least $14 + 7 = 21$ years old in 1968. However, if there is some sort of scale in the photograph which shows that the giraffe is not fully grown, then the actual age in years may be approximated. In

Fig. 10–4 Photograph of giraffe taken in Nairobi Park about 1960, by permission of Pegas Studios Ltd., Nairobi.

TABLE 10-5 THE RESULTS OF LOOKING AT OLD PHOTOGRAPHS FOR THE NECK PATTERNS OF GIRAFFE LIVING IN NAIROBI NATIONAL PARK IN 1968

Year photo taken	Not Known Now, Presumably Dead		Now Known		Minimum Age in 1968	
	male	female	male	female	male	female
1948	6	3	1	2	27	25
1949	4	5	1	—	26	24
1950	2	6	1	—	25	23
1951	5	—	—	—	—	—
1952	2	—	—	—	—	—
1953	—	—	—	—	—	—
1954	1	—	2	—	21	—
1955	1	—	2	—	20	—
1956	2	—	2	—	19	—
1957	2	2	3	1	18	16
1958	—	—	—	1	—	15
1959	2	—	—	1	—	14
1960	1	2	—	4	—	13
1961	—	2	—	1	—	12
1962	—	—	1	2	13	11
1963	—	1	6	1	12	10

this way some of the adults have been aged. For example, F60 (Fig. 10–4) was about two years old in 1960 and therefore about ten years old in 1968.

C. A. W. Guggisberg has supplied photographs of giraffe taken in Nairobi Park as early as 1948. In studying these pictures, Foster has been able to identify various individuals still alive at the end of his study (April, 1968). One male that was three-quarters grown in 1948 was about 25 years old in 1968. Four other males were over 26, about 25, 23, and 21 years old. Two females were each over 25 years old.

It was possible for Foster to determine the growth rates of known-aged giraffe in Nairobi Park and then to use these figures to calculate the age of subadult giraffe whose birth dates were not known. The simplest way to measure the height of a very small giraffe was by comparing its height to its mother's; the newborn's height is generally the same as the height of the base of the mother's tail (about 2 meters) (Fig. 10–5). However, after it was a few weeks old, the young rarely stood next to an adult giraffe, and another method was used. The animal was photographed from the side while standing erect; then a measured pole, placed exactly where the animal had been standing, was also photographed. From the two pictures Foster was able to measure the giraffe's dimensions. The resulting growth rates were apparently slower than those determined by Backhaus (1961) for giraffe in captivity (Fig. 10–6). In Nairobi Park a female reached about 4 meters during her fifth year and a male 4.5 meters in his seventh year.

In studying his giraffe populations in Wankie National Park, Dasmann (personal communication) estimated that about 30% consisted of immature animals, over 20% of which were calves. A similar population structure was observed in the Garamba National Park by Backhaus (1961). In contrast, at Fleur de Lys with its fewer females only 12% of the population was immature, and half of these were recently born calves.

In September 1967 the resident giraffe population of Nairobi Park consisted of the following groups:

31% adult female
25% adult male
14% young in their first year (5% less than three months old)
10% in their second year
8% in their third year
12% in their fourth and fifth years

These figures are approximate since it was difficult to know what constituted a resident animal—in two and a half years the number of observations varied from

Fig. 10–5 Newborn calf beside mother as placenta is expelled.

one to 58 for different animals. Also the aging technique was only approximate. The population structure of giraffe remained stable in Nairobi Park for seven years and the above percentages of each age class are probably characteristic of a stable, unchanging giraffe population.

An age distribution for this population may be hypothesized using the following assumptions:

a. The population is constant.
b. The numbers for 1967 (from newly born to five years) are typical for any year.
c. Giraffe over 25 years of age are not uncommon.
d. Probably no giraffe reaches 30 years of age. (The captive longevity record is 28 years.)
e. The death rate is fairly constant for the adult animals.

From these data it seems that (1) about 13% of the giraffe die annually, which roughly balances the 14% that are born each year; (2) most of the mortality is of young giraffe; and (3) the average life span of a giraffe in the Nairobi Park is about six years. These data probably hold as true for males as for females; although the numbers of male and female adults in the park were not the same, the fact that the males lived more in the forest may account for this discrepancy. Equal numbers of males and females were born in the park and no differential mortality has been indicated.

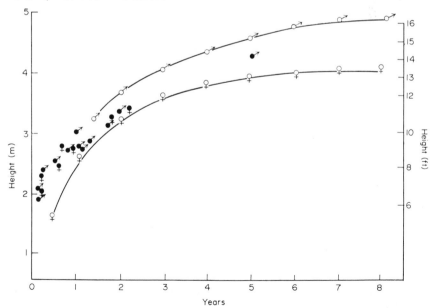

Fig. 10–6 Growth rates of six wild and two captive giraffe. Wild individuals are noted as solid circles.

11 Giraffe
In Captivity*

Giraffe are expensive to keep in captivity because they eat large amounts of food. One adult needs about 15 kg a day of hay, grains, vegetables such as carrots, onions, beans, and cabbages and, if possible, fresh leaves suspended high in the air. Care must be taken that the giraffe receive enough calcium and vitamin D so that they do not suffer from rickets and have to be destroyed (Iles, 1957).

Giraffe breed well in zoos, although rarely a mother refuses to suckle her young. If there is sufficient room, the male giraffe need not be separated from a mother and young. However, males are often hypersexual in captivity as are many zoo animals that have few diversions. One female learned when she was harried by a male giraffe to go into her stall, turn around, and shut the lower half of the door behind her so that the male could not follow (Iles, 1960). Sometimes the males have flehmened the urine of other species such as zebra and eland, although when the eland was in heat, the giraffe showed no especial interest (Backhaus, 1961).

In general, giraffe have a good viability in zoos. They breed readily and live up to 28 years (King, 1947). Grzimek (1956b) reported that 35 captive giraffe lived an average of 14 years, four of them surviving past age 20. In a recent

*The following references include descriptions of the pens, care, and diet of giraffe in various zoos: Stephan, 1925; Fox, 1938; Patten, 1940; Hediger, 1950; Street, 1956; Grzimek, 1956b; Schomberg, 1957; Hagenbeck, 1960; Wackernagel, 1960; Crandall, 1964; Ewert, 1965; Jarboe, 1965; Clarke, 1968; Dittrich, 1968; Freiheit, 1970; Poglayen-Neuwall, 1970.

146

longevity survey, of 22 captive giraffe born, 45% died when less than a year old (Anon., 1960b). Of those surviving, the average life span was 10 years, and the maximum life span nearly 23 years. Earlier at the London Zoo Mitchell (1911) found that 10 giraffe lived an average of 8½ years.

Giraffe are usually friendly or at least docile in captivity. At the Ceylon Zoo (Weinman, personal correspondence) they answered to their names, cantering across their paddock when called to receive a tidbit. Some giraffe dislike certain keepers, however, for no apparent reason. A giraffe may recognize this enemy even in a crowded room, displaying anger by dilating its nostrils, opening its mouth, and pressing back its ears. One giraffe attacked its keeper with its horns at the London Zoo, leaving a dent 1 cm deep in the wooden supporting beam of its pen. Another hit his keeper in the face with his horns, breaking his cheek bone (Anon., 1951a). A giraffe may also kick a keeper unconscious (Laufer, 1928).

Giraffe in northern climates are usually kept inside during the winter, but they do not seem to mind. One female in the Manchester Zoo remained indoors by choice for 3½ years (Iles, 1957). At the Bronx Zoo a new arrival which was unloaded in the outside paddock immediately developed a fear of the dark stall adjoining the paddock and refused to enter it (Ditmars and Bridges, 1937). After several weeks the giraffe was forcibly pushed indoors for the night, but for years afterwards it crossed the doorway in a rush. The keepers at the Bronx Zoo unloaded the next new giraffe directly into its stall. This individual was then afraid to enter the bright outdoor yard for three weeks, although other giraffe walked in and out during that time. Giraffe are often upset by small changes in their pens or in their keeper's attire (King, 1947).

Giraffe have been captured in Africa and shipped to zoos throughout the world for over 150 years. Originally the mother giraffe was killed so that her calf could be caught. More recently young giraffe have been chased and lassoed by men on horseback or in trucks, or have been captured in a stockade (Ogrizek, 1954; Webb, 1954; Stanton, 1955). Today a giraffe can be immobilized and thus captured with a dart filled with drugs (see Chapter 3).

Formerly giraffe were transported on litters or on trains; now they are generally moved in trucks, although wires and bridges crossing the road are a hazard. A blindfolded giraffe is led by a halter up a ramp into a narrow topless crate on the vehicle, where a leather strap is fastened under the animal's belly so that it cannot lie down. Penicillin is injected into the giraffe to prevent possible infection (Kettlitz, 1962). At the nearest seaport the giraffe are shipped to the zoos that requested them. At present there are hundreds of giraffe in North American zoos and game parks, a large increase over the fifty giraffe Cully estimated were here in 1958.

A wide variety of ailments have been identified in captive giraffe. In the Philadelphia Zoo for example, Fox (1938) listed gastritis (fatal), gastroenteritis (fatal), fracture of the pelvis and shock (fatal), obstruction of the pylorus by the condensation of food (fatal), anemia, congenital cystic disease of the kidneys,

Bright's disease and fibrosis of the liver, pneumonia, and tuberculosis. Improper diet caused scurvy, rickets, osteomalacia, brain diseases, and hoof injuries including spreading, mold growth, splitting, and ulceration.

Giraffe are highly susceptible to shock. One captive died of a heart attack when its hooves were pared (Hediger, 1950); another died of heart failure when a sheep was introduced into its pen (Cobbold, 1860); several died of shock during severe thunderstorms (Stephan, 1925; Weinman, personal correspondence, 1960); a young giraffe died of exhaustion from running around its enclosure when it was frightened by a bomb that landed near it at Whipsnade Zoo (Spinage, 1962b); and a female died of a thrombosis following calving (Iles, 1960).

In captivity giraffe seem especially prone to lung infections such as tuberculosis and pneumonia (Anon., 1906; Krumbiegel, 1937; Paulus, 1943; Anon., 1951b; Rai and Chandrasekharan, 1958; Iles, 1960), to kidney diseases (Crisp, 1864a; Mann, 1944; Ried, 1958; Chaffee, 1968), and to bone diseases. Different individuals have suffered from arthritis (Crandall, 1964), rickets (Iles, 1960), and osteoporosis (Fiennes, 1960). Many bones are so long in giraffe that they are easily broken (Anon., 1899; Beddard, 1902a; Anon., 1902; King, 1947; Scheidegger and Wendnagel, 1949; Gijzen, 1958; Iles, 1960). Finally, in a unique misfortune, a male giraffe butted a pregnant female so hard in the side that the fetus and subsequently the mother herself died (Iles, 1960). Internal parasites of captive giraffe are given in Table 11–1.

BEHAVIOR OF GIRAFFE AT TARONGA ZOO

At the Taronga Zoo in Sydney, Australia, Dagg (1970b) studied the social behavior of the 18 members of the giraffe herd. It is virtually impossible to study interactions of sight or smell that may exist between individuals, but it is possible to record all tactile encounters that occur. This was done during 66 days over a four-month period. The herd included one 24-year-old bull, Jan Smuts, formerly the dominant male and sire of most of the other giraffe in the herd, but latterly with little contact with the other animals; two sexually active bulls—Oygle, at seven years of age the dominant animal, and Lumpy, four years old; eight adult females, four of which were lactating and only one of which was barren—Cheeky; three subadult females two or three years old; and four calves, each under six months of age.

An "encounter" usually lasted for a very short period, with one giraffe touching or licking another briefly before walking away; rarely a giraffe licked or rubbed against another for several minutes continuously, but this too was counted as a single encounter.

Nosing occurred when a giraffe touched another briefly and lightly with its nose. Since the nosing giraffe used the upper end of its rostrum where its nostrils are situated, it was probably smelling the other giraffe rather than just touching

TABLE 11-1 DISEASES AND INTERNAL PARASITES OF CAPTIVE GIRAFFE

	Location	Reference	Zoo
Monodontella sp.		Fox, 1938	Philadelphia
Trichocephalus sp.	colon	Fox, 1938	Philadelphia
Whipworms	caecum	Fox, 1938	Philadelphia
Strongyloid worms	bile duct	Fox, 1938	Philadelphia
Cestodes	ileum	Fox, 1938	Philadelphia
Cysts	liver	Fox, 1938	Philadelphia
Hookworms	—	Fox, 1923	?
Haemonchus sp.		Sloan, 1965	Whipsnade
Trichostrongylus colubriformis		Sloan, 1965	Whipsnade
Trichuris sp.		Sloan, 1965	Whipsnade
Trichocephalus gracilis	caecum	Cobbold, 1860	London
Cysticerci	liver	Cobbold, 1860	London
Cysts	tongue, bile duct	Cobbold, 1854	London
Fasciola sp.	bile duct	Cobbold, 1854	London
Fasciola gigantea	—	Cobbold, 1855	London
Cercaria	liver	Cobbold, 1855	London
Taenia echinococcus	—	Crisp, 1864a	London
Cyst	spleen	Crisp, 1864a	London
Uncinaria smithi	liver	Weidman, 1918	Philadelphia?
Trichostrongylid infection	feces	Patten, 1940	Sydney, Australia?

it. Typically a giraffe nosed the trunk, neck, or head of the other. *Licking* usually lasted longer than nosing, but seldom more than one minute. Generally one giraffe licked the trunk, neck, mane, or horns of the second giraffe; sometimes two giraffe licked each other's eyes at the same time. Occasionally a giraffe rubbed with its head against another's trunk or neck. This, plus the occasional rubbing of one's leg against the back of a giraffe that was lying down, or the pushing of one animal against another, were included in the *rubbing* category. The *hitting and necking matches* were less common than the foregoing encounters. In the *necking matches* two giraffe hit each other at length, occasionally breaking off to lick or rub each other. (This licking and rubbing was not included under those separate headings when it occurred in a necking match.) For the *hitting* category the encounters were entirely one-sided, with only one giraffe delivering the blows. The blows, dealt by the head, were usually aimed at the trunk or neck of the opponent. They were delivered upward, downward, or sideways, the head often obtaining considerable momentum because of the length of the neck. The fifth category, that of *sniffing the genitalia,* was usually done by the males to the females, likely to see if the female was in heat. The males nosed at the base of a female's tail. Rarely a giraffe of either sex nosed the penis of a male. The activity of a male in nosing about her tail often caused the female to urinate. When she did so the male usually flehmened, collecting some of the urine in his mouth. He then raised his head and curled back his upper lip for a moment in a characteristic pose, as if testing the urine. Male and female giraffe might also flehmen when a female urinated spontaneously. More rarely a giraffe collected the urine in its mouth and licked its lips, rather than raising its head and curling its lip back. This was called *urine-licking*.

The frequency with which each of the basic types of encounters occurred is given in Table 11–2.

Nosing and *licking,* the most ubiquitous and common encounters between giraffe, probably acted as bonding mechanisms between individuals (Tables 11–3 and 11–4). In these tables and the five following, the individuals listed at the left of the table are those that carried out the activity, and the individuals

TABLE 11–2   FREQUENCIES OF DIFFERENT TYPES OF ENCOUNTERS BETWEEN THE TARONGA GIRAFFE[a]

Encounter	Number of encounters	Percentage of encounters
Nosing	424	29%
Licking	362	25%
Rubbing	223	16%
Hitting	202	14%
Necking matches	16	1%
Sniffing genitalia	127	9%
Flehmening	78	5%
Urine-licking	15	1%
	1447	100%

[a] After Dagg, 1970b.

TABLE 11–3   NOSING ENCOUNTERS AMONG TARONGA GIRAFFE—PERCENTAGE OF AVERAGE NOSINGS PER INDIVIDUAL[a,b]

Active Giraffe	Passive Giraffe				
	Jan	Males	Females	Calves	Total
Jan	—	0	4	0	4
Males	5 — * — 27	10	6	48
Females	4	7 **	4	15	30
Calves	1	0	1	16	18
Total	10 —*— 34	19	37	100

[a] After Dagg, 1970b.
[b] In this and the following six tables, two values that are significantly different are marked ** ($p < .01$) and * ($p < .05$).

TABLE 11–4 LICKING ENCOUNTERS AMONG TARONGA GIRAFFE—
PERCENTAGE OF AVERAGE LICKINGS PER INDIVIDUAL[a]

Active Giraffe   *Passive Giraffe*

	Jan	*Males*	*Females*	*Calves*	*Total*
Jan	—	0	0	0	0
Males	12	26	6	2	46
Females	2	3	4	10	19
Calves	0	1	2	32	35
Total	14	30	12	44	100

[a] After Dagg, 1970b.

listed at the top of the table are those on which the activity was carried out. For example, in Table 11–3 it is evident that 27% of all nosings were carried out by the two sexually active males on each other, while no calf ever nosed one of these bulls. This difference was significant ($p < .01$). Nosing and licking had some sexual significance, since the sexually active males were particularly keen participants. The dominant male, Oygle, both nosed and licked all the other adults at least once during the observation periods of this study. In return, the other giraffe nosed him more than the other adults. The mothers also often nosed or licked their own young, sometimes to elicit suckling in the calf. The calves were often nosed or licked by adults, but they took little active part in such activities, unless to nose or lick each other. That nosing also acts as a kind of introduction was evident from the number of giraffe that nosed the newborn calves on the days when they first joined the herd.

Rubbing was an adult activity, almost never including the four calves (Table 11–5). When two mothers that had been locked in separate barns with their newborn calves for weeks were liberated for one hour each day with each other and Oygle, the cows each rubbed against Oygle many times, but they seldom rubbed against each other. When these females were reunited with the herd, they paid almost no attention to the bulls, however. Oygle and Lumpy rubbed against a number of females, but they rubbed against each other most often, even on days when a cow was in heat. Such absence of rivalry between breeding males is unusual in social ruminants, but it is confirmed by observations on wild giraffe. Unlike those in the Fleur de Lys herd, where the number of adult males was large, the rubbings of the two captive bulls never led to sexual behavior between them.

In the wild, *necking matches* are male prerogatives. During six months of daily observations in the wild, Dagg never observed necking that involved a female, nor did Foster or Coe (1967) during their extensive research. Curiously, therefore, in the 16 necking matches observed in the Taronga herd, all of them included the barren nine-year-old cow Cheeky (Table 11–6). Cheeky fought 15 times with Lumpy and once with Oygle. The matches often lasted for an hour or more, during which time Cheeky always received far more blows than she delivered. In one hour of a match Lumpy hit her body or neck with his head 142 times, while she retaliated 11 times; in other bouts with Lumpy the numbers of blows exchanged were 103 to 8, 58 to 2, 37 to 5, and 46 to 4. Despite this

TABLE 11–5 RUBBING ENCOUNTERS AMONG TARONGA GIRAFFE— PERCENTAGE OF AVERAGE RUBBINGS PER INDIVIDUAL[a]

Active Giraffe		Passive Giraffe			
	Jan	Males	Females	Calves	Total
Jan	—	8	2	0	10
Males	11	51	7	0	69
Females	6	6	4	1	17
Calves	0	1	2	1	4
Total	17	66	15	2	100

[a] After Dagg, 1970b.

TABLE 11–6 HITTING AND NECKING MATCHES (NM) AMONG TARONGA GIRAFFE—PERCENTAGE OF AVERAGE HITTINGS PER IN-DIVIDUAL[a]

Active Giraffe		Passive Giraffe				
	Jan	Males	Females	Cheeky	Calves	Total
Jan	—	4	0 (0.1%)	24**	0	28**
Males	1	3	0 (0.2%)	68** (16 NM)	0	72**
Females	0	0 (0.2%)	0 (0.1%)	0 (0.1%)	0	0
Cheeky	0	0 (16 NM)	0 (0.1%)	—	0	0
Calves	0	0	0	0	0	0
Total	1	7 (16 NM)	0	92** (16 NM)	0	100

[a] After Dagg, 1970b.
** Highly significant statistically compared to any other of the values in the same column.

imbalance, Cheeky followed Lumpy if he retired from a match and never re-treated herself. Lumpy and Cheeky stopped hitting each other frequently to rub heads together or to lick one another, as necking bulls do in the wild, but Lumpy never showed signs of being interested in Cheeky sexually other than flehmening her urine.

Although most *hitting* took place, like the necking, among Oygle, Lumpy, and Cheeky, Jan as well as several females occasionally hit other giraffe. There was no obvious reason for these random blows, which were generally light, with the exception of Oygle's blows at Cheeky. These were usually so hard that they were heard across the paddock. Once when Cheeky ducked as Oygle was swinging at her, he hit the pipe of the fence instead, cutting his head so that it bled profusely. Cheeky tried to avoid his blows sometimes by cantering among other giraffe. She was caught anyway when Oygle edged her into a corner or the feeding house so that he could clout her as she rushed out. These blows were delivered on a total of eight days, so that Cheeky was not perpetually persecuted by Oygle. On one of these days Oygle was mating with another female. Several times during the morning he broke off his activities to find Cheeky and pound her fiercely.

Sniffing genitalia was almost entirely an activity of the bulls to the cows, especially when a cow was in heat (Table 11–7). The three females whose genitalia were sniffed most often, notably by the bulls, were all nonpregnant females, each of them having recently given birth. Cheeky, the only cow that was barren, never had her genitalia sniffed. This type of encounter may also be used like nosing, in which one giraffe assessed another briefly. In this way the adult males were sniffed several times and the calves occasionally sniffed each other's genitalia.

TABLE 11–7   SNIFFING GENITALIA AMONG TARONGA GIRAFFE—PER-CENTAGE OF AVERAGE SNIFFINGS PER INDIVIDUAL[a]

Active Giraffe		Passive Giraffe			
	Jan	Males	Females	Calves	Total
Jan	—	6	6	0	12
Males	11	11	49	0	71
Females	0	2	2	0 (0.3%)	4
Calves	0	2	0	11	13
Total	11	21	57	11	100

[a] After Dagg, 1970b.

Flehmen or urine-testing also has sexual significance, as it was usually done by the bulls to the cows (Table 11–8). The following observations were made:

1. The sexually active males Oygle and Lumpy were by far the most ardent flehmeners.
2. The urine of the females was not tested by the males only when they were in heat or nearly in heat. For example, Oygle tested one nonpregnant female's urine during December on the seventh, eleventh, eighteenth, nineteenth, twentieth, and twenty-first days of that month.
3. Two nonpregnant females were not tested daily by Oygle during December when they were together for an hour each day. On some days he showed no interest in either of them, even though they urinated near him.
4. A female may be tested several times in a short period. One female was tested four times by Oygle and two times by Lumpy on December 28. Although she was not observed mating then, she may have been in heat, as she was mated 25 days later. Another cow had her urine tested twice by Lumpy and once by Oygle on the day that she was mated by Oygle.
5. The two bulls, and sometimes a female as well, together flehmened the urine of one urinating cow.
6. Females and calves are more likely to urine-lick than to flehmen, but both were done infrequently by them. The urine of the calves was never tested, and that of the males was only licked, never flehmened.

TABLE 11–8   FLEHMENING AND URINE-LICKING ( ) AMONG TARONGA GIRAFFE—PERCENTAGE OF THESE ENCOUNTERS PER INDIVIDUAL[a]

Active Giraffe		Passive Giraffe			
Jan	*Males*	*Females*	*Calves*	*Total*	
Jan	—	0	0	0	0
Males	0	0 (38)	80 (8)	0	80 (46)
Females	0	0 (13)	19 (13)	0	19 (26)
Calves	0	0 (25)	1 (3)	0	1 (28)
Total	0	0 (76)	100 (24)	0	100 (100)

[a] After Dagg, 1970b.

Large branches of *Eucalyptus* sp leaves were given to the giraffe each morning; but as those did not last long, continuous observations could not be made on the sharing of this food. When branches were available, one giraffe often held a branch in its mouth while pulling off the leaves with its tongue—a remarkable feat. Frequently one or more giraffe joined this individual, holding another part of the branch while consuming the leaves there. Such sharing occurred 191 times (Table 11–9). This asexual activity was virtually restricted to the adults, which is understandable since the calves were still suckling. In very few cases did a giraffe move away so that another that wanted to feed off its branch could not do so. They showed a notable tolerance for each other that is not found in all animals.

The evidence of hierarchy among these giraffe was small:

a. Oygle was dominant to Lumpy because only Oygle mounted the receptive cows;
b. Oygle was the most active individual in initiating encounters, especially those with sexual significance like sniffing genitalia and flehmening;
c. Oygle was dominant to a cow, because she cantered away from him when he emerged from her barn on one occasion;
d. this cow was dominant to a second which she chased away when she was rubbing against Oygle.

The tolerance of giraffe for each other contrasted greatly with the behavior of other ungulates at the Taronga Zoo. In the breeding season many of these males have to be separated. When this had not been done earlier, fighting had caused the death of both fallow and red deer bucks and injury in sitatunga, white-tailed deer, Père David's deer, and blackbuck. Elk, eland, and anoa males were also routinely separated to avoid such incidents. Even female ungulates were sometimes intolerant of each other; dominant females of red deer, Barbary sheep, and water buffalo have refused to allow subordinate individuals to have their share of the food. What an admirable example is set by the gentle giraffe.

TABLE 11–9 SHARING BRANCHES AMONG TARONGA GIRAFFE—PERCENTAGES PER INDIVIDUAL—FROM 382 NOTATIONS OF 191 SHARINGS

Active Giraffe		Passive Giraffe			
	Jan	Males	Females	Calves	Total
Jan	—	0	2	0	2
Males	0	32	17	1	50
Females	2	17	22	2	43
Calves	0	1	2	2	5
Total	2	50	43	5	100

Appendix A
Races
of the Giraffe

No extensive review of the taxonomy of giraffe has been undertaken other than Lydekker's report in 1904 and Krumbiegel's in 1939. However studies on specific races have necessitated updating of these works (Ansell, 1968). The ranges and brief descriptions of the races currently recognized are given here. Ranges are mapped in Fig. 4–1.

Giraffa camelopardalis reticulata

De Winton (1899) chose the type location for this race as the Loroghi Mountains in Kenya. The type specimen, now in the British Museum, was shot by Neuman. Lydekker (1904) elevated this race to a distinct species, although there is no reason to believe that it was ever isolated for any lengthy period from the other giraffe in northeast Africa.

The present range of *reticulata* covers a large arid area with the type location near the southwest boundary. It is bounded by the Loroghi Mountains, the Barta Steppes, and Lake Rudolph in the west, by the headwaters of the Webi Shebeli River and the mountains of Ethiopia in the north, by the coast of Africa on the east although much of the vast coastal country is too dry to support giraffe, and by the Tana River on the south.

The reticulated giraffe was regarded as a separate species until recently, although many transitional individuals between the reticulated and blotched giraffe have been recorded both in captivity and in the wild (see Krumbiegel, 1951). Some were even given new names: the *nigrescens* type specimen had smaller spots and wider interspaces (Lydekker, 1911), while the *hagenbecki* type had a reticulated neck and body but simple blotches on the hindquarters (Anon., 1910). The Rift Valley partially separates *rothschildi* from *reticulata,* and the Tana River *reticulata* from *tippelskirchi.* Mertens (1968a,b) noted that the subspecific name *reticulata* as used by Weinland in 1863 should be suppressed by the International Commission on Zoological Nomenclature, as the animal referred to belonged to the same population as *G. c. antiquorum* rather than to the reticulate race, *G. c. reticulata. Australis* is synonymous with *reticulata* (Ansell and Dagg, 1971).

The large, smooth-edged liver-colored spots are placed closely together with only a fine network of light color dividing them in the typical *reticulata* giraffe. Spotting may extend some distance below the hocks and may be very dark in old animals. Descriptions of giraffe belonging to this race were given by Wood (1894), Rothschild and Neuville (1911), and Krumbiegel (1951).

G. c. camelopardalis

The Nubian giraffe was first described by Linnaeus in 1758 from a captive giraffe seen by Belon in Cairo (Thomas, 1911). He gave the type location of his *Cervus camelopardalis* as "Sennar and Aethiopia" which is too large an area. Presumably the giraffe was from Upper Nubia in the Sudan, where early Arabs captured all the giraffe that were exhibited alive. In 1788 the giraffe's location was revised to "Sennar between Upper Egypt and Ethiopia."

The Nubian giraffe's range was believed to cover the east part of the Sudan south to 16° north latitude and north to 18° north latitude. In this century there are no records of giraffe east of the Nile or north of 16° north. At present the range is farther south. This subspecies is fairly common in the Eastern Sudan bordering Ethiopia.

The smooth-edged spots of the Nubian giraffe are more widely separated than in *reticulata*. The inner sides of the legs are unspotted, with the legs pure white below the hocks (Trouessart, 1908). The Nubian giraffe at the Taronga Zoo was noted for the large number of her spots and their small size.

G. c. antiquorum

This Kordofan race was first described by Jardine in 1835 with the type location given as "Sennar and Darfour" in the Sudan. This location is too vague, however, and overlaps that of *G. c. camelopardalis,* although the type specimens may well belong to the Nubian race. Harper (1940) claimed that the type should be a male in the Senckenberg Museum which was shot at Baggar el Homer, Kordofan, about 10° north and 28° east. The Kordofan giraffe, now quite rare in the Sudan, is believed to occupy the west and southwest areas of this country, while *G. c. camelopardalis* is restricted to the east and northeast (Setzer, 1956). Lydekker's *congoensis* race, now restricted to the Garamba National Park in Zaire, is synonymous with *antiquorum* (Ansell, 1968).

In this race the spots are somewhat more irregular and smaller than in the preceding races, so that the net pattern is less evident, especially at the throat. The inner sides of the legs are spotted, with spots sometimes extending below the hocks on the hind legs. Mitchell (1908) and Schouteden (1912) described in detail individuals of this race.

G. c. peralta

The Nigerian giraffe was first described by Thomas (1898) from the skin, skull, and cannon bone of a large female. This type specimen was shot near the junction of the Niger and Benue rivers in Nigeria—Happold (1969) believed north of the junction rather than southeast of it as Thomas originally stated. In any case giraffe have been extinct in this location for many years. Suitable vegetational conditions for giraffe and therefore the giraffe themselves are uncommon throughout Nigeria. The Nigerian race apparently had a large range encompassing much of the area of western Africa.

The spots of *peralta,* which are often coarsely divided or constricted, extend below the hocks. The ground color of the adults is yellowish-red (Mitchell, 1905a).

G. c. rothschildi

This giraffe was first discovered by Sir Harry Johnston on his expedition through Kenya in 1901 (Thomas, 1901). He emphasized the feature of five horns which the males often possess and sent the skin and skulls of two males and two females to the British Museum where Thomas described them (Thomas, 1901). It was named for Lionel Rothschild, second Lord Rothschild, who founded the Tring Museum and was an eminent zoologist (Dr. Miriam Rothschild, personal communication). The type for this race was shot by Major Powell Cotton on the Uasin Gishu Plateau east of Lake Baringo, but the type location should rather have been west of Lake Baringo (Lydekker, 1908). The *cottoni* race is now considered synonymous with this race.

The range of *G. c. rothschildi* is uncertain, as it is bounded on most sides by the ranges of neighboring races which intergrade with it, and it has decreased greatly in recent years. Roughly the range extended to Lake Rudolph, Lake Baringo, and the Loroghi Mountains in the east, at least as far south as 1° south latitude, to Mount Elgon where it is more numerous in the west, and north into southern Sudan. In 1962, Simon reported that 200 members of this race remained in the Soy area and Baringo and West Suk areas, and quoted Brooks in stating that 900 head survived in Uganda, mostly in what is now Kidepo Valley National Park.

The spots of Rothschild's giraffe are usually smooth-edged, but they may at times be fanlike, streaky, and diffused. The legs are often spotted well below the hocks but never all the way to the hooves. Further descriptions were given by Rothschild and Neuville (1911), Lönnberg (1912), and Granvik (1925).

G. c. tippelskirchi

Matschie described two giraffe groups in 1898 from southern East Africa as *G. tippelskirchi* and *G. schillingsi* from Lake Eyassi, Tanzania, and Taveta, Kenya, respectively. Lydekker (1904) combined these two in his race *G. c. tippelskirchi* with the type location the southeast shore of Lake Eyassi within 16 km of 3°40' south and 35°15' east. This race is well represented in Africa, largely in Tanzania.

The range of the Masai giraffe extends north through the Serengeti Plains and Masailand and to the south of Mount Kenya and Lake Nakuru, east to Mount Kilimanjaro and beyond to the coast, south to the Rufiji River, and west to Lake Rukwa and Lake Tanganyika. The Masai race is holding its own throughout most of its original range.

The spots are usually splintered, forming all shapes of sharply differentiated leaf or stellate designs, although some approach *reticulata* in design and color. The spots always continue down to the hooves. Rothschild and Neuville (1911), Lönnberg (1912) and Kollmann (1920) gave further descriptions of this distinct race.

G. c. thornicrofti

The type specimen of this race was first described by Lydekker (1911) from a giraffe shot by Mr. Thornicroft at Petauke in the Eastern Province of what was Northern Rhodesia. There were only one or two herds of giraffe in this whole region in the first part of this century, and these herds have been protected. The *thornicrofti* race is now represented by perhaps 300 individuals which live along the Luangwa River from 11°50' to 14° south latitude (Ansell, personal communication, 1974).

Ansell (in press) strongly feels that, in view of the isolation of the Luangwa Valley, the *thornicrofti* race is a recognizable subspecies, paralleled by the *cooksoni* race of the wildebeest which is also isolated in the Luangwa Valley. Three adult *thornicrofti* males have tri-lobed canines, and an unsexed giraffe has a tendency toward this. In contrast, six giraffe from Rhodesia have bi-lobed canines. This difference, noted by Ansell, may be a racial one.

The *thornicrofti* race has slightly stellate spots which become oblong on the neck. The neck is usually lighter in color than the body (Ansell, 1968), and the legs are fully spotted.

G. c. angolensis

The type specimen is a male, now in the Tring Museum, from the Cunene River 240 km southwest of Humbe in Angola. The *angolensis* race extends in sparse patches where the vegetation is suitable in southern Angola as far east as the Kwando River. There is no geographic barrier between *G. c. angolensis* and *G. c. giraffa* which ranges in the northern areas of Namibia. The 300 giraffe found in the Barotse area of Zambia between the Zambeze and Mashi rivers from 16°30' south to 17°30' south latitude, often classed as *G. c. infumata* (Noack, 1908), also belong to the *angolensis* race.

In this race the spots are well differentiated and slightly notched, appearing superficially to be uniformly rimmed. They disintegrate into small splashes high up at the throat and on the hind legs. All of the legs are fully spotted.

G. c. giraffa

The giraffe described for this race were encountered just north of the Orange River near Warmbad by Brink in 1761. This race is now considered to include *G. c. capensis* and *G. c. wardi* and may prove to be synonymous with *G. c. angolensis.*

The range of this race was once much wider than it is today, extending throughout Namibia, Botswana, eastern South Africa, southwest Mocambique, and the western parts of Rhodesia. The giraffe still inhabits these countries, but its range is reduced to the more arid and uncultivated areas.

In this race the spots, which extend down to the hoof, are more or less round, although they may have delicate needlelike extensions. The coloring may be very dark, as it was in the Taronga male, Jan, from South Africa.

Appendix B
Anatomy
and Physiology
of the Viscera

The internal systems of the giraffe are discussed here in general terms but with complete references to the pertinent literature. The few physiological experiments that have been carried out on the giraffe, because they *are* so rare and offer new insights, are given more space.

Digestive system

The giraffe grasps leaves with its supple tongue and long, prehensile lips, which are covered with dense hairs as a protection against thorns. The inner surfaces of the lips have large papillae that point inwards to help retain the leaves. The oral cavity is also so constructed that the internal callous processes direct all food to the area between the grinding cheek teeth. For example, the palate has 15 or 16 well-developed irregular transverse ridges, with the free edges turned backward. These ridges become less pronounced posteriorly, so that between the molars the palate is smooth. In addition a row of large obtuse papillae lies between the ridges, others are dotted closely on the soft palate, and still others are present on the inner cheek. These latter may measure up to 1.6 cm in length (Schneider, 1951).

The enamel ridges on the molariform teeth are arranged parallel with the length of the jaw; the movement of the jaw when cudding is lateral, or perpendicular to these ridges. This "wash-board effect" is most efficient when grinding food.

Sonntag (1922) claimed that the tongue of the giraffe possesses greater mechanical power than that of any other ungulate. It grows up to 54 cm in length (Schneider, 1951) and is about 8 cm wide in the molar region. For some time it seemed impossible that the mouth could encompass such a mass of material. Indeed, Home (1828) reported that the size of the tongue was dependent on the amount of blood filling the blood vessels in the organ. He said that the tongue could withdraw into the mouth only when the blood reservoirs were empty and the tongue of a reasonable size. A careful dissection of the tongue refuted this theory. Owen (1841) and later Burne (1917) showed that the muscles present were very similar to those found in other ruminants; to withdraw the tongue into the mouth, the transverse muscles relaxed while the longitudinal muscles retracted. The free end of the tongue, like the undersurface, is nearly black because of the dark pigment under the epithelium. It has been suggested that this pigment protects the tongue from the blistering effects of the sun. The giraffe tongue has about 50 papillae, more than in any other mammal (Sonntag, 1922). The anterior part has prominent obtuse papillae scattered over it, as well as many retroverted spines to help in gripping the leaves. The red back part of the tongue has large papillae and a thick layer of mucous glands.

The salivary glands are large as in all ruminants. Two main ducts drain each parotid gland, one from the anterior and one from the posterior region. These ducts join in front of the gland to form Wharton's duct, which opens behind the incisors (Burne, 1917).

The palatine tonsils occupy oval pits at the back of the throat. They are flattened and small, about 5 cm by 2.5 cm in area (Burne, 1917; Hett, 1928).

The long esophagus leading down the neck to the stomach is very muscular (Owen, 1868; Richiardi, 1880). Leaves can be swallowed and cud regurgitated with equal facility by the peristaltic action of the esophagus.

The stomach of the giraffe is divided into four parts as in the cow: rumen, reticulum, omasum, and abomasum (Cordier, 1894; Mitchell, 1905b; Hofmann, 1968a,b). These areas are modified for the diet of a "selective feeder" (Hofmann, 1968a). After the browse has been briefly chewed, it is swallowed and passed into the capacious rumen, which is composed of a dorsal and a ventral sac, plus two blind caudal sacs. The rumen epithelium is thick, supporting many large papillae which are more close-set in the young than in the adult, apparently because they are not regenerated or reproduced during an individual's lifetime (Hofmann, 1968b). The water that the animal drinks passes mainly to the drop-shaped reticulum or second stomach. Early authors like Owen (1841) and Home (1830) claimed that the reticulum cells of the giraffe were abnormally shallow, but Neuville and Derscheid (1929) reported that the reduction is not excessive. Fox (1938) concluded that, as in the camel, there are no special stomach cells for water retention. The reticulum cells support rows of long, pointed, horny papillae.

The food rotates in the rumen where it becomes thoroughly moistened by the gastric juices produced there, and partly fermented. When the animal is resting, the softened food is made into boluses which are shot up into the mouth, chewed thoroughly for a minute or so, and then reswallowed. Only three or four seconds elapse between the swallowing of one bolus and the regurgitating of the next. When the cud is swallowed, it bypasses the rumen and proceeds directly to the large omasum or psalterium. (In nursing young the milk goes there directly, the first and second stomachs being relatively small.) The omasum has rows of alternately broad and narrow cornified lamellae beset with short clawlike papillae. In this third stomach much of the superfluous alkaline fluid is absorbed before the less dilute food-mass passes into the abomasum.

The retort-shaped abomasum is judged, because of the specialized cells in its walls, to be the only one of the four stomachs that is truly homologous with the stomach of other mammals. This fourth stomach has a thin lining beset with fine villous processes scattered over about 25 longitudinally wavy folds. Digestive juices secreted here are mixed with the food. The strongly muscular pylorus guards the opening into the intestine with two projecting valvular protuberances.

The intestines are very long in the giraffe (Table B–1), increasing rapidly in length as the young grows up. These lengths seem incredibly large when one measures the intes-

TABLE B-1 LENGTHS OF THE ALIMENTARY TRACT IN GIRAFFE, IN METERS

Age	Sex	Esophagus	Stomach	Small Intestine	Cecum	Large Intestine Colon	Large Intestine Rectum	Total length of intestine	Reference
2 mo	—	—	—	—	—		—	32.9	Crisp, 1864a
2 mo	m	1.5	0.7	25.1	0.48		5.4	31.0	Murie, 1872
7 mo	m			27.6			10.1	37.6	Crisp, 1864b
3 yr	f			27.7	0.66		13.2	41.5	Owen, 1841
3 yr	m			26.8	0.61		13.1	40.5	Owen, 1841
4 yr	m			25.0	0.61		12.2	37.8	Owen, 1841
young	m							63.7	Crisp, 1864a
12 yr	f	1.9	1.8	39.8	0.53		24.8	65.1	Murie, 1872
—								64.3	Joly and Lavocat, 1843
18 yr	f							77.4	Crisp, 1864a
21 yr	m	2.5	2.0	40.4	0.46		27.7	68.6	Murie, 1872
adult	f			59.7	0.76		22.9	83.4	Beddard, 1902b
wild adult	f							85.3	Goetz and Budtz-Olsen, 1955
old				52.0	0.71	4.0	20.1	76.7	Richiardi, 1880
wild old	m			39.5	1.83		36.6	78.0	Innis, 1958
adult	f			59.7	0.79		22.9	83.4	Garrod, 1877

tines of a giraffe with a ruler as Dagg has done, but compared to the size of the giraffe, they are not excessive. In comparison, a 90-kg pig has an intestine of 24 meters, or 26.6 meters of intestine. For the giraffe there is only about 7.3 meters of intestine per 100 kg of animal. Murie (1870) compared the total intestine length of animals to the body length, which seems a less meaningful comparison. If this is done, the ratios of intestine lengths to body lengths of pigs and giraffe are more similar.

The small intestine of the giraffe is about 10 cm in circumference. At the junction of the small and large intestines is the cylindrical cecum, which is relatively short as in all artiodactyls with complex stomachs. It is about 15 cm in circumference, with small oblong glands opening along its inner walls.

Long ago, much academic attention was centered on this area with the discovery by Cobbold (1856, 1860) of large crypts near the iliocecal opening and other small cul-de-sacs scattered in the small intestine. Cobbold considered these crypts to be unique, and to be complications of Peyer's patches, then believed to be true digestive glands. Later Crisp (1864b) and Garrod (1877) found similar conditions in deer, antelope, elephants, and a jaguar. Neuville (1922), who dissected many different races and ages of giraffe, found crypts present in varying positions and of varying sizes, but always on the colon, emptying as far as 20 cm from the iliocecal junction. The largest crypts were 1 cm deep. By histological study he determined that only mucosa and submucosa formed the walls of the crypts, so that they were not related in any way to lymphoid tissue or Peyer's patches. The role of these crypts is perhaps to increase the amount of mucous surface and therefore the amount of mucous secretions at the beginning of the colon, to facilitate progression of food out of the cecum where much of the liquid has been absorbed (Derscheid and Neuville, 1924).

Digestion is completed in the small intestine and cecum, with only absorption of water occurring in the large intestine. The colon, which has an *ansa spiralis* with three coils (Borelli *et al.,* 1973) progresses by way of four distinct loops into the rectum (Mitchell, 1905b), which may or may not have inner longitudinal ridges (Crisp, 1864a,b). The rectum ends in the small anus, from which the feces are eliminated as pellets.

The liver

The weights and dimensions of this organ and other visceral organs are given by Cobbold, 1854; Crisp, 1864a; Murie, 1872; Stanley, 1890; Retterer and Neuville, 1916; Fox, 1938; Crile, 1941; Schneider, 1951; Anon. 1951b; and Goetz *et al.,* 1955. As might be expected in the liver, there is great individual variation in contours, volume, and position, although in general it resembles that of sheep (Wakuri and Hori, 1970). It shows such slight traces of lobulation that there is some doubt if the caudate and Spigelian lobes can be located on the dorsal surface (Neuville, 1914b). The right and left hepatic ducts unite into the wide choledochus or common bile duct, which joins the gut 15 to 20 cm beyond the pylorus. It runs intramurally about 10 to 15 cm farther on before opening on a low elongate papilla into the duodenum (Cave, 1950). The choledochal duct is therefore long, although it is longer in cows (about 75 cm) and in sheep and goats (about 40 cm). Occasionally the thinner pancreatic duct joins the choledochal duct, allowing the different digestive juices to mix before reaching the intestine (Neuville, 1914b). This also occurs in deer. More often, both ducts empty into the intestine separately as in the cow. During the embryological development it seems that the two ducts develop and approach each other at variable rates which determine if there will be some or no fusion.

Gall bladder

Cave (1950) recorded 19 dissections of giraffe, of which only two individuals possessed gall bladders. One of these was abnormal—a double organ 5 by 7.5 cm with a septum dividing it in two. Cave also dissected a fetus in which a minute vestigial gall bladder 8 by 4 mm with a 13-mm duct was present. He surmised that this gall bladder was in the process of regression and would not have been present in the adult if the animal had lived that long. This theory of early development and later degeneration of the gall bladder in giraffe has not been substantiated by Kobara and Kamiya (1965). In their dissections of two adult females they found a gall bladder in each, one over 11 cm long. Wakuri and Hori (1970) located a gall bladder 11 cm by 5 cm in an adult male. Perhaps gall bladders were also present but unrecognized in the earlier dissections of giraffe and are usual in the giraffe.

Respiratory system

The giraffe's trachea is the longest known, supported in the adult along its length by over 200 cartilaginous tracheal rings. The vocal cords are normally constructed, despite much controversy about the supposed muteness of the giraffe. They are of the simple form found in most ruminants (Burne, 1917). Because of the controversy on the giraffe's ability to make vocal noises, Chapman (1877) investigated the laryngeal nerve of a giraffe during an autopsy. He reported that the lower two-thirds of the recurrent laryngeal nerve was almost completely atrophied. Either Chapman was mistaken or his specimen was abnormal, because this nerve is functional in normal giraffe.

As in most ruminants, the left lung has two lobes and the right three plus an azygous lobe. Robin *et al.* (1960) have studied not only the microscopic structure of the lungs, but also the respiration of giraffe in order to compare it with that of normal men and of people with emphysema. The giraffe is similar to the latter; because of its long trachea it has a relatively large respiratory dead space where no exchanges of gas can take place. The dead space is nine times that present in a healthy man, but only five times that present in a person with emphysema. This dead space in the giraffe is partly balanced by the large total lung capacity of the species, which is eight times that of a normal human being and five times that of a person with emphysema. The giraffe maintains an adequate alveolar ventilation by breathing about eight to ten times a minute; this slow respiration rate reduces the number of times a minute the dead space (largely trachea) must be filled with air. The resting tidal volume of the giraffe is about 4 liters per breath (Patterson *et al.*, 1957) so that the giraffe, like the normal man, uses about one-tenth to one-twelfth of its total lung capacity under basal conditions.

Urinary system

The kidney of the giraffe is described at length by Wrobel (1965). The position of the kidneys is similar to that of other mammals, with the right kidney situated near the diaphragm and the left kidney placed farther back.

Reproductive system

The chromosomes of the giraffe can perhaps be included in this section. Wallace and Fairall (1965) gave the karyotypes of two individuals drugged in the Kruger National Park. Blood was taken from the ear or the sternum of these giraffe, so that dividing cells in metaphase could be examined microscopically. The modal number of chromosomes found in 31 chromosome counts was 30 chromosomes per cell. The Y-chromosome was metacentric, not acrocentric. The karyotype of the giraffe is similar to those of bovids, especially the sitatunga (Koulischer *et al.,* 1971).

Female. Murie (1872) measured the ovaries of an adult female giraffe at 7 by 2.5 by 2.5 cm each. The right ovary contained a dark corpus luteum 1.3 cm in diameter. The left contained another, plus the remains of a burst follicle. Kellas *et al.* (1958) studied the ovaries of two fetal and one new-born giraffe, while Kayanja and Blankenship (1973) described prenatal and postnatal ovaries of giraffe using histological and ultrastructural techniques. Gombe and Kayanja (1974) analyzed the progestins of the ovaries of giraffe of different ages.

The relatively wide horns of the uterus are about 35 cm long. The umbilical cord is about 1 meter long. Goetz and Budtz-Olsen (1955) tested the urine of a wild pregnant female and found the frog test and tests for protein and uric acid were negative, while tests for hippuric acid, creatinine, urea, and phosphates were positive. Wilkinson and de Fremery (1940), however, stated that a pregnant giraffe's urine does contain gonadotropic hormones.

The placenta of a female weighed nearly 8 kg and had many cotyledons, the largest measuring 23 by 5 cm, and the average 6.4 cm in diameter (Wilson, 1969). The placenta is described in detail by Owen (1868) and Ludwig (1962, 1968).

Male. The anatomy of the penis is described by Gerhardt (1905), Retterer and Neuville (1914), and Neuville (1935). As in other ruminants, the penis of the giraffe does not contain a bone. The giraffe has both Cowper's glands and prostate glands (Owen, 1868). The structure and function of the testis and epididymis are discussed by Glover (1973).

Glands

As in most ruminants, the thyroid glands are found in the angles between the esophagus, the posterior part of the larynx, and the trachea. They are composed of lateral lobes without any connection between them (Burne, 1917). The adrenal glands, as in most antelopes, are only about 20% larger than the thyroids (Crile, 1941). These glands were examined by electron microscope and described after they had been removed from six pregnant giraffe which had been chased for 30 minutes before being shot (Weyrauch, 1974). The giraffe lacks preorbital, inguinal, and interdigital glands (Pocock, 1910) which are often used by territorial mammals to mark their territories. The pituitary gland is bigger in the giraffe than in the elephant, although the body weight of the latter is three times as great as that of the giraffe. As in several very large mammals, the giraffe's pituitary has a neurohypophysis which is insignficant in size compared to that of the adenohypophysis. Kladetzky (1954) and Hanström (1953) examined the gross and microscopic structure of the giraffe's pituitary. Frank (1960) discussed the parathyroid and the thyroid glands of the giraffe, Kayanja (1973) the ultrastructure of the buccal glands, and Kayanja and Scholz (1974) the ultrastructure of the parotid gland.

Nervous system

The volume of the brain compared to the volume of the skull is lower among ungulates than among any other group of mammals, which probably explains the relatively low intelligence of this group. The small brain size may be a direct result of the grass and leaf diet of the group, with the necessary complicated dental mechanism developed at the expense of the cranium. Oboussier and Möller (1971) compared the brains of giraffe and bovids. While the total brain weight in comparison to body weight was higher in Giraffidae than in Bovidae, the development of the neocortex surface in relation to the brain weight was smaller. Considering the neocortical surface in relation to the body weight, the difference between these families was eliminated. The cerebellum is relatively strongly developed to facilitate agility in such a large animal (Godina, ca. 1970). The giraffe like the horse has a brain weight only one–eight hundredth of its total body weight. The brain of the young giraffe is relatively much larger than that of the adult (Black, 1915a; Fox, 1938).

The anatomy of the brain of the giraffe is detailed by Black (1915a), Friant (1952a, 1954), and Kato (1963). The brain of the giraffe is compared with that of the okapi by Black (1915b), Le Gros Clark (1939), Friant (1943), Munoz (1959), and Oboussier and Möller (1971). Friant (1952 a,b) described the brain of two fetal giraffe to elucidate the development of the giraffe brain.

Little work has been done on the nerves of the giraffe. The total length of the circuitry is immense, because of the size of the giraffe, but otherwise the nervous system is believed to be much as in other ungulates.

Muscular system

The musculature of the giraffe has been broadly described by Owen (1841), Joly and Lavocat (1843), and Murie (1872). More recently anatomists have studied small muscle groups in greater depth. Zuckerman and Kiss (1932) and later Willemse (1958) examined the shoulder muscles and their innervation in the giraffe; they refuted the previous claims that long-necked mammals lack the accessory nerve. In the giraffe as in other ungulates (but not the camel) the trapezius and other neighboring muscles are innervated by the spinal accessory nerve. Angermeyer (1966) continued this work, discussing the muscles and nerves of the neck as well as of the shoulder.

Bego (1960) reported on the innervation and blood supply of the foreleg muscles in the giraffe and other species, while Chaine (1902) discussed the muscles in the throat of the giraffe.

Heinze (1964, 1965) gave detailed descriptions of the muscles and ligaments of the hind leg of the giraffe, together with their blood and nerve supply. More recently he examined the internal structures of the masseter and peroneal musculature of the giraffe and other mammals (Heinze, 1969).

Rothschild and Neuville (1911) studied the omotrachelian muscle, which, in short-necked mammals, usually extends from the acromion of the scapula to the atlas. In the camel, whose neck is curved, this muscle is inserted at the fifth or sixth neck vertebra. In the giraffe this muscle extends to the sixth or seventh cervical. They also noted the often close correlation between muscle masses and whorls, feathering, and crests in the hair above these masses.

Finally Joly and Lavocat (1843) commented particularly on the absence of skin muscles in the giraffe. Instead the body is enveloped in a strong aponeurosis of fibrous sheet, fastened loosely to the skin and often confused with the yellow fibrous fat layer. The giraffe is thus less able to dislodge insects and other pests by shaking its coat than are other animals.

Vascular system

This system is the only one in which extensive physiological experiments have so far been carried out. The first of these was done by Goetz and Budtz-Olsen (1955), both medical doctors concerned with high blood pressure in human beings. The long neck of the giraffe interested them, because the giraffe has solved the problems arising from great changes in blood pressure which occur when the giraffe leans down to drink. The heart must pump blood up 2.5 meters to the brain when the giraffe is erect, then down 2.5

meters when the giraffe stoops to drink. The circulatory system must have some mechanism to prevent the blood from rushing too quickly back to the heart from the brain when the animal is erect or down to the brain when the animal's head is lowered. Armchair biologists have hypothesized that the giraffe raises its head slowly from a drinking position so that the blood system will have time to adjust to this change, but in reality the giraffe lifts its head in a rush after drinking.

To study the giraffe circulation, Goetz and Budtz-Olsen shot a wild adult near the Kruger National Park with a .303 cartridge in which had been embedded 200 mg of curare, a poison originally used by South American Indians on the tips of their weapons to paralyze their prey. The giraffe, which was paralyzed within 45 minutes, then had an adjustable scaffold built around it so it could stand upright when it was able to move again. While it was still immobilized, the doctors passed a catheter up the carotid artery into the base of the brain so that they could record the blood pressure at the brain when the giraffe lowered and raised its head. A small chip of radioactive cobalt was fastened to the tip of the catheter so that its exact position in the carotid artery could be located with a Geiger counter. When the giraffe was standing upright, they found that the pressure at the base of the brain was 200 mm Hg. When the giraffe lowered its head, and the experimenters took the new blood pressure, which they expected to be higher, they found instead that the pressure had dropped to 175 mm Hg. Goetz and Budtz-Olsen had expected that the viscosity of the giraffe's blood and its protein content would be high in order to prevent the blood from flowing too quickly. Instead, the viscosity of the blood was found to be the same as in man; and the protein content of the blood, which might have caused a high osmotic pressure, was low rather than high by human standards.

Several years later Goetz carried out further experiments, this time with four captive giraffe, each about two years old (Goetz and Keen, 1957; Goetz et al., 1960). The blood pressure and other hemodynamic measurements they obtained are probably not those of normal giraffe, since both drugs and anesthetics were used in operations lasting up to four hours. During one such marathon the subject giraffe died of hypotension. In general the blood pressures of these giraffe were high; even in a quiet giraffe the systolic pressure reached 353 mm Hg and the diastolic pressure 303 mm Hg. The cardiac output and the blood volumes of two individuals were similar to those of cattle of about the same weight; the former values ranged between 22 and 75 liters/minute in standing, unanesthetized animals, while the latter were 73 and 78 ml/kg body weight. The circulation times of two animals were 11 and 16 seconds. The lowest heart rates were 60 beats/minute for the four giraffe, but these rose rapidly to as high as 125 beats/minute when one struggled in its confining pen.

More recently, the blood pressure changes in freely ranging wild giraffe have been obtained (Van Citters et al., 1966; Warren, 1974). The experiments were carried out quickly on two adult bulls on the plains of Kenya. Within 90 seconds of having been lassoed from a truck, each giraffe was hobbled flat on the ground. Immediately a local anesthetic was injected in the upper neck and the skin of the giraffe cut open so that the trachea and carotid arteries were exposed. A small length of the right carotid artery was clamped off for 10 minutes while a transducer to measure blood pressure changes was introduced into the lumen of the artery. The artery was sewn up again around the wires leading from the transducer, and the muscle layers and skin were also returned to place. The wires were attached to a telemetry pack which was fastened to the animal's neck with adhesive tape. With this apparatus a continuous record of the blood pressure was radioed from the giraffe after it was allowed to rejoin its herd. While each was lying flat on the ground following the operation the blood pressure in the upper carotid was 280/150 mm Hg. When each had struggled to its feet, it was about 190/120. The blood pressures largely varied between 180/120 and 140/90 as the freed giraffe walked and browsed. When one was standing quietly, surrounded by other giraffe and apparently unconcerned, the carotid blood pressure fell as low as 150/105 mm Hg. The pulse rate also varied considerably; it was 90 beats per minute while the animals were flat on the ground and less than 60 beats per minute when they stood up. When one giraffe galloped, the rate reached 170 beats per minute with a peak blood pressure of 230/125 mm Hg.

Later the same day the giraffe were chased, recaptured, and again held on the ground so that the instruments could be removed and the incisions closed. During this operation, after the animals had lain on the ground for 10 minutes, the carotid blood pressure was 280/160 mm Hg and the heart rate 100 beats per minute. Both animals ran off apparently unharmed when the ordeal was over, suffering no serious aftereffects.

From these experiments, calculations have been made of the blood flow in the carotid artery (Van Citters *et al.,* 1968). The calculated blood flow in this artery ranged between 50 cm³/sec in the prone animal and 35 cm³/sec in the standing giraffe. The peak systolic blood velocity measured was 60 cm/sec; during diastole the velocity remained above 40 cm/sec. Jefferson (1971) gave electrocardiogram and phonocardiogram tracings of a female undergoing surgery, and Rossof (1972) a further electrocardiogram of an anesthetized female giraffe.

As in most ruminants, the blood reaches the brain from the heart via the common carotids and the external carotids. The two latter vessels divide just before each reaches the brain into many small vessels forming a tight network that is called the *rete mirabile,* a structure that is present near the brains of many if not all ungulates. The vessels of the giraffe's *rete* have elastic walls which can accommodate excess blood when the head is lowered so that the brain is not flooded. As a further safeguard for the brain while the giraffe is in this position, a connection between the carotid artery and the vertebral artery drains off a portion of the blood even before it reaches this network. The walls of the *rete mirabile* vessels are also elastic enough to retain sufficient blood when the head is raised so that the brain's supply is not depleted momentarily until the system has adjusted to the pressure changes (Lawrence and Rewell, 1948).

The blood pressure of a mammal is a function of cardiac output and of peripheral resistance. An increase in the blood pressure will be caused by an increase in either or both of these variables, and a decrease by a decrease in either or both of them. In most mammals, information on the actual blood pressure in the carotid arteries is forwarded by the two carotid sinuses to the vasomotor center in the brain. This center in turn regulates the heart beat and the diameter of the arterioles. In the giraffe the blood pressure must remain high at all times, to keep blood flowing to the brain. Perhaps because of this, the reflex activity related to changes in position of the giraffe appears to be at a low level. The relatively small changes in blood pressure and in heart rate with changes in the position of its head may also be correlated with the absence of a carotid sinus in the giraffe. Possibly the occipital sinus serves the same purpose as the carotid sinus does in other species (Goetz *et al.,* 1960).

Several other anatomical factors help the giraffe adapt to its normal blood pressure— probably the highest present in any animal—and to sudden changes in that pressure. These factors include the extensive presence of valves in the vessels, the structure and histology of the vessels, and their arrangement. All of the large veins, the splenic, the renal, the saphenous, the brachial, the axial, and the inferior vena cava, have valves which counteract the effects of gravity, preventing excess backflow in the blood returning to the heart from the long legs (Amoroso *et al.,* 1947). Even the jugular veins have valves which prevent a backflow of blood to the brain when the animal leans down to drink. These pocketlike cusps may be present singly or in groups. Five tricuspid valves are present on the thick walls of the jugular vein, and tricuspid, bicuspid, and simple cusps are found in the brachial and axillary veins. The tributaries emptying into the jugular veins also have valves which are able to withstand high pressures in the jugular vein even if there are negative pressures in the tributaries themselves (Goetz and Budtz-Olsen, 1955). In an experiment carried out on a preserved length of giraffe axillary vein complete with its serried valves, the valvular system enabled the vein to withstand pressures up to 200 mm Hg, a value far above that which would occur naturally there (Amoroso *et al.,* 1947).

The structure of the blood vessels also assists in regulating the circulatory system. The vessels in the legs, especially the veins, are very thick with tiny lumens. By contrast the jugular vein is also large, but the lumen diameter measures over 2.5 cm even at the base of the head. This vein is relatively collapsed when the head of the giraffe is upright, but when the head is down, it acts as a large reservoir that keeps the excess blood from flooding into the brain. Histologically, the aorta, pulmonary artery, and common carotid, as in the long-necked ostrich, consist mainly of elastic tissue in the well-developed middle layer of the vessel, with only a few scattered muscle fibers. The muscle fibers increase in prominence towards the head in the carotid (Franklin and Haynes, 1927). The entire wall of the aorta is 1.5 cm thick, that of the pulmonary 0.75 cm thick. In the limbs, the histology of the vessels is reversed. Here there is little elastic tissue and a thick layer of smooth muscle, largely situated in the huge *tunica media.* These leg vessels must withstand high hydrostatic pressures, which explains the necessity for their extensive muscularity.

The structure of a blood vessel may be determined to some extent postnatally. Goetz and Budtz-Olsen measured some blood vessel walls in a fetus and compared them with the adult vessels. The thickness of the metatarsal artery in the adult was 15 times as great as in the fetus, whereas the thickness of the carotid artery in the adult was only eight times as great. These figures indicate that the limb artery developed to a greater extent as the animal grew than did the neck artery, presumably as a response to greater gravitational stress in the legs. Goetz and Keen (1957) and Goetz *et al.* (1960) found in general that arteries from different parts of the body had wide variations in structure corresponding to the prevailing hydrostatic pressure. In a captive giraffe Williamson *et al.* (1971) found that there were significant increases in the muscle capillary basement membrane width in the direction of head to foot. These regional variations probably are also related to differences in venous hydrostatic pressure effective on the capillary bed. Sikes (1969) examined four giraffe for evidence of cardiovascular disease, but this was slight.

The rather pointed heart of a wild giraffe is much larger than that of a captive; the heart of the female killed by Goetz and Budtz-Olsen in their experiment weighed 12 kg, while the heart of a captive adult is more likely to weigh about 4.5 kg. Giraffe in the wild are used to spurts of running that increase the size of their heart muscle fibers. The right ventricle wall of the female's heart mentioned above was 2.5 cm thick, the left ventricle wall 7.5 cm thick. This great difference explains how the left ventricular rate of pressure ascent can be five times that of the right ventricular rate (Goetz *et al.,* 1960). The two auricles are relatively small. Crisp (1864b) gave the dimensions of the heart of a seven-month captive giraffe. This young animal had no heart bone, although this bone may be 2.5 cm long in old animals.

The histology of the heart does not differ greatly from that of other ruminants in most respects, although the atrioventricular node has a greater volume in giraffe than in most animals. Also, the Purkinje cells and fibers of the common atrioventricular bundle are particularly well developed in the giraffe (Castigli and Sacchi, 1941).

There are twice as many blood cells per cubic mm in the giraffe as in man. In this the giraffe is similar to the camel and the llama, both of which have a very efficient oxygen exchange system. As well as blood counts, Goetz and Budtz-Olsen (1955) gave the results of a number of tests made on the blood of their pregnant giraffe. Sikes (1969) also gave figures for blood serum analyses of giraffe.

The arrangements of the blood vessels in the giraffe follow the generalized mammalian plan, although there may be considerable variation in the local disposition of vessels. Although few giraffe have been dissected, at least three variations of the aortic arch have been recorded (Owen, 1841; Chapman, 1875, 1877; Neuville, 1914a). Owen reported as well (1841) that the common trunk of the carotids is very long, although in Neuville's giraffe (1914a) the common trunk is only about 5.8 cm long, with the right and left carotids extending the length of the neck.

Beauford (1928) stated that with a few exceptions the course of the blood vessels of the skin corresponds with the white background lines on the coat of the giraffe.

Goetz and Budtz-Olsen (1955) and Keen and Goetz (1957) reported on the fetal circulation of giraffe. The umbilical cord contains two arteries and two veins plus the allantoic duct. The *ductus arteriosus* is large and thick-walled, but the *ductus venosus* that bypasses the liver in the human fetus is not functional in the giraffe. It is represented only by a fibrous cord. The *foramen ovale* connecting the right and left atria is a finely fenestrated opening. About 60% of the postcaval blood uses this route through the heart, thus bypassing the right ventricle.

In situ, the spleen is shaped like a low dome with the concave face fitting the surface of the first stomach and the convex face adjacent to the diaphragm (Crisp, 1853; Lönnberg, 1900; Retterer and Neuville, 1916; Derscheid and Neuville, 1925). Because of its close contact with both the stomach and the diaphragm, the flow of splenic blood should be increased during both digestion and excessive respiration when the spleen is compressed frequently from without. The spleen itself is a contractile organ, but its rate of contraction is probably much less frequent and energetic than that imposed by the neighboring organs.

Body temperature

Recently radiotelemetric thermometry has been used to find the deep body temperature of giraffe. Bligh and Harthoorn (1965) experimented on a 400-kg female in Kenya. They implanted the battery-operated apparatus in its lower neck, where they left it for 46 hours. They found that when the ambient temperature was low, the giraffe was remarkably thermostable. Although the environmental temperatures and relative humidities varied respectively between 10.5°C and 21.5°C and 48% and 91%, the deep body temperature of the lower neck varied only between 37.75°C and 39.1°C. Two elands were almost as thermostable as the giraffe under similar conditions. This thermostability in the giraffe may break down at high ambient temperatures as it does in the eland (Taylor and Lyman, 1967).

Color vision

Although zoos offer ample opportunities to study various aspects of giraffe biology, with few exceptions these have not yet been exploited. One of these exceptions is the study done by Backhaus (1959) on color vision in a giraffe. He tested a male by offering it food in up to four containers, each marked by a different color. By teaching the giraffe to find food in the different containers, he was able to list the colors that he felt the giraffe could distinguish from other colors and from shades of gray of the same intensity. These were red, orange, yellow, yellow-green, and violet.

Appendix C
The Skeleton

The skull

The skull, because it is important in the taxonomy of mammals, has been measured by many zoologists (Cobbold, 1854; Thomas, 1898, 1901; Rothschild and Neuville, 1911; Lönnberg, 1912; Roosevelt and Heller, 1914; Kollmann, 1920; Granvik, 1925; Shortridge, 1934; Willemse, 1950; and Roberts, 1951). Unfortunately these measurements have not yet been used to quantify racial characteristics of giraffe.

The skull is large, with the part in front of the eyes considerably longer than that behind (Fig. C–1), a characteristic apparently correlated with a diet of arboreal vegetation (Godina, ca. 1970). The facial bones are flat, with a long narrow nasal opening. The bottom of the skull is flat too, with the base of the face and the base of the brain nearly in a straight line. As an individual grows into an adult, the area around the eyes and the upper nose becomes relatively wider than that farther forward (Singer and Boné, 1960). The nasal region is elevated into a boss even if a median horn as such, with a separate center of bone formation, is absent (see Rhumbler, 1932). The anterior lateral fontanels in this region are soon obliterated in the giraffe but not in the related okapi, which retains the more primitive condition (Rothschild and Neuville, 1911).

The eyes are situated laterally, giving the giraffe a better field of vision than have most mammals (Smythe, 1961). The eyes themselves are exceptionally large with active lacrimal glands; some giraffe at the Taronga Zoo have eyes which drip tears onto the ground. The bone structure around the orbits appears deep, but it is not excessively so. Those of various cervids and bovids are the same relative size (Rothschild and Neuville, 1911).

As an individual grows, the cerebrum becomes relatively larger in proportion to the brain case (Cobbold, 1860) and changes from a position above the level of the nasal

171

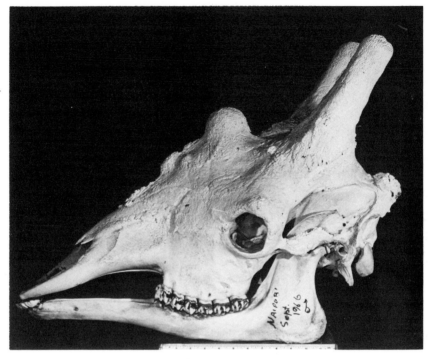

Fig. C–1 Skull of adult male giraffe.

passage to one approximately level with it. The auditory bullae are large in the young giraffe but relatively smaller in the adult (Colbert, 1938).

The occipito-parietal crest at the back of the skull is well developed even in very young giraffe. Below the crest where the strong neck muscles are inserted, there is a deep and irregular furrow. This is relatively deepest in moderately young giraffe (Rothschild and Neuville, 1911). The occipital condyles are prominent with rounded edges that allow free movement of the head on the neck for browsing and fighting. The articular surface extends up and down, enabling the giraffe to raise its head in a straight line with the neck or slightly beyond.

In their study of aging in giraffe, Singer and Boné (1960) have noted the time of closing of various sutures in the skull. When they are first formed, the skull bones are in contact with each other, but they do not fuse together until later in the animal's growth, the time depending somewhat on the individual. The interparietal suture on the top of the head closes first at about the time the giraffe is born. The parieto-occipital suture at the back closes soon afterwards. When the giraffe is about four years old, the occipital suture has fused, and soon after the fronto-sagittal suture is also closed. The fronto-parietal suture across the top of the head fuses at the end of the giraffe's growth period, when it is five or six years old. The temporo-occipital and palatal sutures close much later.

The skull sinuses are bounded and transected by fibrous connective tissue walls as well as by bony partitions, so that their structure should be studied in wet rather than in dry skulls where the tissue walls will have been destroyed (Anthony and Coupin, 1925). The paired small anterior nasal sinuses and the paired larger posterior nasal sinuses, rare in all but the largest land mammals such as elephants and rhinoceros, are present in both the giraffe and the okapi (Fig. C–2). The two sphenoid sinuses are well developed in the giraffe as are the large low-set superior maxillary sinuses. The frontal sinuses, common in ungulates, are vast in the adult giraffe (Saito, 1962). In the young giraffe the skull has only a single limited frontal sinus below the median horn area that has curved bony ridges projecting into it from the walls. This sinus increases in size during the growth of the giraffe, with the projecting ridges developing into numerous bony partitions which follow transverse or oblique wavy courses and so strengthen the sinus area (Owen, 1868). In the adult, the sinus has enlarged into the fronto-parietal sinus which extends from the center of the facial region to the back of the skull. Sinuses are extensive in both females and males; so their function is probably not to help prevent fracture of the skull during fights.

A unique feature of the giraffe's skull is the tendency to tumescence, a tendency found primarily in males. The bony exostoses or concretions that grow on the skull bones are very variable and usually asymmetrical, either sharp, round, or flat with compact or concreted surfaces. Sometimes the entire upper part of the skull and face is covered with these superficial growths so that the original profile is completely obliterated. The 70-cm skull of such an old male may weigh 13 kg, while that of a female (Fig. C–3) or a young male which has not yet developed exostoses weighs only about 4.5 kg (Dagg, 1965). For example one Cape giraffe's skull had large bony growths on each orbit, under the left zygomatic arch, and on the right jugal bone, with smaller bumps scattered over the skull surface. The main horns were considerably increased in volume because of this second-ary bone growth (Rothschild and Neuville, 1911). Lydekker (1904) described the orbital horn above the right eye of a bull giraffe from Kenya. The horn, which projected horizontally out from the middle of the frontal edge of the right orbit, had the capped appearance of a distinct epiphysis. Other individuals have similar horns above the left orbit. The tumescences often grow more profusely on one side of the skull than the other, perhaps indicating a "right-" or "left-headedness." Granvik (1925) noted such "right-headedness" in individuals of the *rothschildi* and *tippelskirchi* races. Series of exostoses in front of the median horn have been described as "supernumerary horns."

These bony growths may be a primitive mode of horn formation. They resemble the main horns in structure, but they differ in that true horns are epiphysial in nature, possessing their own centers of ossification and fusing secondarily to the skull bones. The

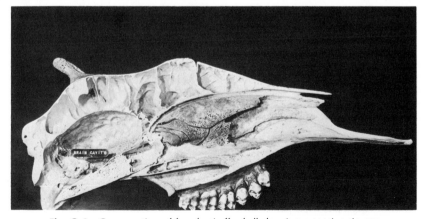

Fig. C–2 Cross section of female giraffe skull showing extensive sinuses.

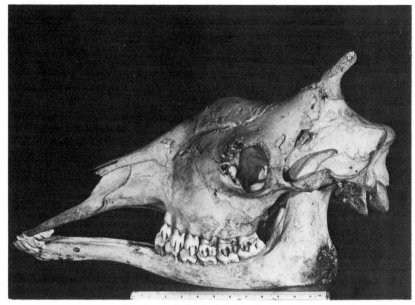

Fig. C–3 Skull of adult female giraffe.

secondary bone growth seems to be a secondary sexual phenomenon which may origi-
nate either from mechanical irritation or spontaneously (Krieg, 1944). In man, injuries
such as fractures may cause the appearance of neoplasms at the end of the fracture which
are similar in structure to those on the giraffe skull (Rothschild and Neuville, 1911). If
mechanical irritation is responsible, it is probably caused by the frequent head-hitting
battles of the males. However, female skulls occasionally also possess some secondary
bony growth (Urbain et al., 1944; Krumbiegel, 1965). In general the female and juvenile
skulls are smooth and thin while those of the males are rough and heavy. The female
giraffe, like okapis, has skull bones that are more fragile than those of most ungulates of
equal size. Apparently the male okapi does not develop the same large accretions of extra
bone as the bull giraffe, although it also can have small supernumerary growths.

Rothschild and Neuville (1911) believed there is a tendency for bony proliferation to
operate more diffusely but more strongly in the southern races of the giraffe. In northern
races, they felt, epiphysial horns and the orbital "horns" are particularly well developed,
while in southern giraffe the formation of rough scattered secondary growths are the
more important, especially on the frontal and nasal bones and on the occipito-parietal
crest. East African giraffe form a transitional stage between the more extreme north and
south types.

The giraffe is one of the few ruminants born with horns (Naaktgeboren, 1969). These
flat-lying cartilaginous cores are laterally compressed and of tough fibrotrabecular ele-
ments, attached by connective tissue to the periostium of the parietals (Beddard, 1906).
Ossification seems to begin at several small independent centers near the periphery of
the upper half of the cartilage tubercle (Owen, 1849). Eventually the horn becomes solid
bone attached to the skull in the adult over both the parietal and the frontal bones
(Spinage, 1968b). (In the okapi, Bovidae, and Cervidae the "horns" develop from or over
the frontals in what is regarded as the more primitive position.) The early core forms the
terminal part of the adult horn, which rests on the upgrowth of the frontal and parietal

bones. The horns of the male are larger than those of the female and may even meet at their base in the middle of the skull, thus obliterating the median suture. The main horns themselves are largely of compact bony tissue without axial differentiation, in this way resembling the simple bony growths which cover the skulls of old bulls. In both types of growth, epiphysial or secondary, the terminal parts may show a tendency to form bony lamellae which are oriented approximately parallel to the surface of the growth. Because of the frequent head-hitting matches of the males, their horn tips are smooth and round with the circle of black hair worn away. This hair remains in the more pointed horns of the cows.

The bases of the horns have extensive cancelli which join the great fronto-parietal sinus. As the frontal sinuses increase in size, the horn cores are forced away from their primitive position over the eyes towards the midline of the skull (Colbert, 1938). The main horns of the giraffe do not stand erect, nor are they usually symmetrical in any one individual (see chart in Rothschild and Neuville, 1911). The angle of the horns with the Frankfort plane is between 48° and 58° (Singer and Boné, 1960). The male horns measure from 10 to 25 cm in length, and the female horns slightly less. The left and right horns in one individual may differ in length by as much as 35%.

The number of horns in the giraffe has been a point of contention for many years (see Newman, 1862). Everyone agreed that the giraffe had two horns or perhaps three—the third being the median horn lying on the frontal and nasal bones in front of the main horns; but Johnston discovered a five-horned giraffe on Mount Elgon in 1901 (Thomas, 1901). The two new horns, situated at the very back of the skull, were referred to as the posterior, occipital, or mizzen horns. They serve for the attachment of tendons, ligaments, and muscles running down the back of the neck. They are not independent growths like the main horns, but rather outgrowths of the skull; Singer and Boné (1960) described them as a type of occipital crest condensed into two parallel projections. In the Taronga Zoo these were well developed in the three adult males and in the only female that took part in sparring matches; they were virtually absent in the other females and in the calves. There seems little doubt therefore that their presence and size is a function of the use of the neck muscles and that they are usually large in adult males and unnoticeable in the other giraffe. The male okapi possesses a thickened posterior crest on its skull which may be analogous with these posterior horns in the giraffe.

There is also controversy about the nature of the median horn. Some median horns have developed from their own center of ossification as have the main horns, although the median horn unites with the skull at a later period than do the main horns. This type of horn is more usual in males but may also occur in females (Rothschild and Neuville, 1911). Other median horns are only enlarged bosses, showing no evidence of a separate ossification center. At present no one is sure if two types of median horns exist or if one type is present indifferently in any one individual or subspecies. It is certain that these horns are used in the sparring matches, as the hair is worn off their apex in the two oldest bulls—those that have fought most often—at Taronga Zoo. The 11 cows at the zoo have small median bumps only.

The unusual horns of the giraffe have been regarded both as a primitive and incipient type of growth from which more complex horns have been developed in other families (Anthony, 1928–29; Colbert, 1935a), and as a degenerate type which were more fully developed in ancestral giraffids (Thomas, 1901). If the giraffe horn is a primitive type, we may assume that other ancestral forms also had free integumentary horns as in the giraffe. In other horned ruminants these horns perhaps united earlier and earlier with the skull until they appeared as an original growth of the skull.

If the giraffe horn is a degenerate type, the ancestral giraffids presumably possessed more developed horns. This is true of some early giraffids such as *Sivatherium* and

Bramatherium, but it is not true of others like the hornless *Helladotherium.* In all ancestral giraffids the horns of the female were either absent or less well developed than in the male, an indication that the horns had sexual significance and that their growth was perhaps proportional to their use. As the giraffe evolved and grew taller, the long neck would have been increasingly unable to support a heavy mass of horns. As in *Sivatherium* and the moose, a short massive neck is required to make effective use of such huge head weapons. It is impossible to tell how the ancestral giraffid horns developed, but possibly the same cartilage horn developed separately before ossifying and fusing with the skull, as in the giraffe. Alternately, the primitive giraffid might have possessed horns that grew out from the skull in the way that horns and antlers of the bovids and cervids do. In time, a separate ossification center might have developed in the horn, independent of the skull. If so, it is difficult to explain the presence of the median horn in the giraffe which has no forerunner in either of the other two families.

The dental formula of the giraffe is

$$\frac{0.0.3.3.}{3.1.3.3.}$$

the same as that of cervids, bovids, and pronghorn antelope. The cheek teeth are broad and low-crowned with a rough enamel coat (Fig. C–4). The upper molars lack the inner accessory column found in the cervids (Sclater, 1900). In the upper jaw the cheek teeth are nearly square in cross section, although the breadth of each tooth normally exceeds the length. (Cheek-teeth measurements for four southern giraffe are given by Roberts, 1951.) The diastema of the giraffe is long, but not much lengthened beyond the primitive ancestral condition (Colbert, 1938). Willemse (1950) found that the molar row of the giraffe became relatively shorter with increase in age. In an examination of 17 giraffe skulls, the posterior margin of the molar teeth row was shifted farther forward comparatively in the older specimens, while at the same time the anterior margin was shifted farther backward, increasing the length of the diastema.

The incisors and canines of the lower jaw of the giraffe are ranged in an open half-circle (Fig. C–5) unlike those in the bovids, which are nearly rectilinear, and those in the camelids, which form a more elongated half-ellipse. The incisors are all approximately the same breadth, but they decrease in width from the middle outward. The canine is extended into two or more lobes in order to extend the arc (Boué, 1970). The front teeth tend to meet the upper callous pad with their lingual faces, which gives the giraffe a less firm grip than if the incisors were completely vertical. The incisors and the canines each possess a single root, which slopes backwards horizontally. The lower cheek teeth each have two roots, one anterior and one posterior. All the upper teeth have three roots, two lateral and one medial.

Singer and Boné (1960) studied the growth and eruption of teeth in the giraffe. They found that the measurements of the last two milk molars in giraffe are fairly constant, while the measurements of the other milk teeth are often quite variable. All the milk teeth are longer than they are broad, and relatively longer than the corresponding permanent teeth. With both milk and permanent teeth, the upper teeth erupt slightly before the corresponding lower teeth. The milk dentition consists of six lower incisors, two lower canines, and 12 milk molars, the latter occupying the places of the future permanent premolars. These teeth appear before birth and during the first few months of life. In one female born four weeks prematurely no teeth had yet erupted (Lang, 1955a); in another individual all of its deciduous teeth were visible in its fourth month of postnatal life, and

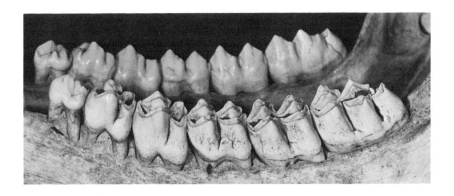

Fig. C–4 Lower cheek teeth of giraffe.

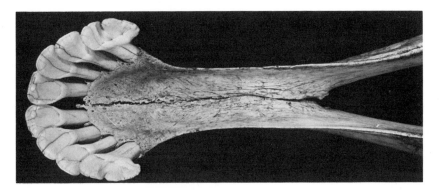

Fig. C–5 Incisor and canine teeth of giraffe.

these were fully grown and functional by the time the animal was nine months old (Owen, 1849). In this same individual, the four middle incisors and the two anterior milk molars were conspicuous at one month, and one month later all six incisors were evident. A second full-term baby had six incisor teeth present (Patten, 1940). In two others six incisors and one molar in each jaw were apparent at birth (Lang, 1955a; Backhaus, 1961). The first teeth to appear are the incisors, followed by the milk molars and finally by the canines. In the mandible the milk molars seem to erupt in a rather regular succession from the back to the front.

The permanent teeth do not begin to erupt until the giraffe is about three years old. In one individual the two middle incisors were shed when the giraffe was just over three years old. The second incisors were shed four months later, and the first milk molars seven months after that. One four-year-old male however, still possessed all his deciduous teeth (Owen, 1841). The first permanent teeth to appear are the molars, erupting in succession from the front to the back of the mouth. The premolars appear in variable order immediately after the eruption of the third molars. The permanent incisors appear at the same time as the cheek teeth, the first incisors erupting during the growth of the last molar, the second incisors erupting next after the full development of all the permanent cheek teeth, and the third incisors erupting next. The canines erupt last, when the giraffe may be over six years old.

Spinal vertebrae

Despite its length, the neck of the giraffe looks stiff rather than supple. The swan has evolved a long neck through an increase in the number of vertebrae present, but in the giraffe the number of cervical vertebrae is seven as in most mammals. The neck, therefore, has few joints, with each vertebra very long. To counteract this somewhat, the first vertebra in the dorsal or thoracic series resembles a cervical vertebra. The cervicals articulate with each other by lateral pairs of anterior and posterior articular facets, while the thoracics typically have median pairs. In the okapi and most other ruminants, the transition between the lateral and median facets occurs between the seventh cervical and the first thoracic vertebrae. In the long-necked giraffe, the transition takes place between the first and second thoracic vertebrae (Lankester, 1908).

The short neural spines of the cervical vertebrae are perpendicular to the vertebral bodies. All the cervicals have small superior transverse processes and small inferior transverse processes confined to the anterior portion of each vertebra. Short-necked ungulates including the okapi usually have larger and more varied individual transverse processes; so the uniformity of the cervicals in the giraffe indicates specialization. In an adult giraffe the length of the neck vertebrae was 129% as long as the trunk (thoracic and lumbar) vertebrae (Slijper, 1946).

At the London Zoo a young male giraffe was received whose neck had a permanent bend in it, the severity of which increased as the giraffe grew older (Beddard, 1902a). The bend was caused by excess growth on one side of the neck and no growth on the other side, so that the fourth and fifth cervicals were fused at right angles to each other. The second, third, and sixth vertebrae were bent the other way to help rectify the curvature.

There are 14 (rarely 13) thoracic vertebrae, each with a pair of ribs. The anterior dorsal spines increase in length as they go back, reaching their maximum size in thoracics four and five. The longest neural spine of the thoracic vertebrae was 22% and of the lumbar vertebrae 6% as long as the trunk length (Slijper, 1946). The large thoracic projections which form the hump in the upper back of the giraffe serve for the attachment of the large muscles and the ligamentum nuchae which support the neck and head. There are seven true ribs followed by seven false ribs, the former being so-named because they are joined directly to the sternum. The sternum, which narrows anteriorly, is composed of six bones.

The five lumbar and four-to-five fused sacral vertebrae are followed by 16 to 20 caudal bones. The pelvis is shorter than in most ruminants, with the upper ends of the ilia more expanded (Flower, 1870).

Legs

The foot of the giraffe is highly specialized, with the first, second, and fifth metapodials usually absent. Sometimes traces of the second metatarsal can be identified in a skeleton, partly fused to the cannon bone. No evidence of lateral hooves can be seen externally. (In the okapi traces of the fifth as well as of the second metatarsal have been found; Fraser, 1951.) All of the leg bones including the scapula, the manus, and the pes are very long. The humerus of the giraffe has a double groove for the biceps muscle rather than the single groove which is usual in ruminants (Lydekker, 1891). The ulna is not well developed.

Fig. C–6   Giraffe hooves.

The hooves of the giraffe are low at the back, so that the fetlock nearly touches the ground (Fig. C–6); they are planted more flatly on the ground than are an okapi's or a deer's hooves (Putnam, 1947), no doubt partly because of the much greater weight of the giraffe that the feet must support. The forehoof is slightly wider than the hind hoof, perhaps also because of the greater weight on the forelegs.

Appendix D
Energy Relationships of the Giraffe

We are indebted to Dr. C. R. Taylor for supplying the following calculations:

Assume that the giraffe weighs 250 kg.

Then from Kleiber's (1961) equation we can determine that the giraffe has a standard metabolism of about 4,396 kcalories/day.

Assuming that the daily metabolic rate is at least twice the standard level, then a giraffe is metabolizing about 8,792 kcalories/day (an adult giraffe of 1,000 kg would metabolize about 25,000 kcalories/day; man about 3,000 kcalories/day).

Assume that giraffe are eating the leaves of

Acacia at 4.5 kcalories/gm

Balanites at 3.5 kcalories/gm

Grewia at 3.5 kcalories/gm

or an average of 3.7 kcalories/gm of dry matter eaten (ref.: Taylor and Lyman, 1967).

Assuming 50% digestibility of its food, then a 250-kg giraffe will need 8,792/3.7 = 4.76 kg dry food per day.

Assuming 60% moisture content of the leaves, then the giraffe is obtaining 7.3 liters of preformed water a day from a total of 11.89 kg fresh food per day (a 1000-kg giraffe would be eating about 33.8 kg fresh food per day or about 75 lb).

Assuming 15% crude protein and 85% carbohydrate in the food, then a 250-kg animal obtains about 1.2 liters of water a day by metabolizing this food.

Adding the preformed to the metabolic water, one gets 8.39 liters/day or 3.35 liters/100 kg body weight/day.

By comparison a Hereford steer (*Bos taurus*) requires 6.4 liters/100 kg a day, an eland (*Taurotragus oryx*) 5.5 liters/100 kg a day, a zebu steer (*B. indicus*) 3.2 liters/100 kg a day, an oryx (*Oryx beisa*) 3.0 liters/100 kg a day and a camel (*Camelus dromedarius*) about 2.0 liters/100 kg a day.

In these tests the animals were at 22°C for 12 hours and 40°C for 12 hours. Thus it would seem that the giraffe by eating succulent food need not be bound by the proximity of surface water in its search for food.

Another possibility for conservation of water is open to the giraffe by virtue of its large size. Schmidt-Nielsen et al. (1957) have shown that the body temperature of the camel falls 10°C at night and then warms during the day, thus conserving water which would otherwise be needed to control body temperature through evaporation. Taylor and Lyman (1967) have shown a similar adaptation in the eland. If one assumes that the specific heat of tissue is 0.9, then for each centigrade degree rise in body temperature a 250-kg giraffe would store 225 kcalories of heat. The 225 kcalories of heat would need 0.39 liters of water to remove it at 38°C. Therefore, about 0.39 liters of water is saved by heat storage for each centigrade degree variation of rectal temperature for a 250-kg giraffe. Assuming the same 10°C daily fluctuation in body temperature as experienced by the camel, then about 4 liters of water would be saved each day by a small giraffe. The saving would be greater for an adult giraffe.

Bibliography

Achard, P. L., and B. McCulloch. 1967. Creation of a zoo in Tanzania—Saanane Island Game Reserve. *Internat. Zoo Yearbook* **7**:235–240.

Aflalo, F. G. n.d. *A Book of the Wilderness and Jungle.* London, Partridge and Co.

Akeley, M. L. J. 1929. *Carl Akeley's Africa.* New York, Vail-Ballou Press.

Allen, G. M. 1939. A checklist of African mammals. Cambridge Mass. Mus., *Bull. Mus. Comp. Zool.* **83**:1–763.

Amoroso, E. C., O. G. Edholm, and R. E. Rewell. 1947. Venous valves in the giraffe, okapi, camel and ostrich. *Proc. Zool. Soc. London* 1947:435–440.

Angermeyer, M. 1966. Zur kenntnis der Halsmuskeln und Halsnerven von *Giraffa camelopardalis* (L.) *Zool. Anz.* **177**,3/4:188–200.

Anon. 1832. The giraffe at Paris. *Penny Magazine,* London, Nov. 3:308–309.

Anon. 1899. (Note on the broken neck of a giraffe.) *Field* 93:505.

Anon. 1902. Giraffes injured in capture. *Field* **99**:561.

Anon. 1906. Death of the giraffe Daisy. *Field* **107**:768.

Anon. 1907. Birth of a giraffe in the Zoological Gardens. *Field* **110**:594.

Anon. 1908a. George the Fourth's giraffe. *Field* **111**:748.

Anon. 1908b. The growth of giraffe. *Field* **112**:763.

Anon. 1910. Hagenbeck's giraffe. *Field* **116**:353.

Anon. 1943. The giraffe has a voice. *Anim. Kingdom* **46**,6:141.

Anon. 1951a. (Behavioral note on male giraffe—in German.) *Zool. Gart., N.F.,* **18**:75.

Anon. 1951b. (Note on death and measurements of male giraffe—in German.) *Zool. Gart., N. F.,* **18**:73.

Anon. 1951c. (Note on birth of male giraffe—in German.) *Zool. Gart., N.F.,* **18**:70.

Anon. 1960a. Breeding notes on the hippopotamus and giraffe at Cleveland Zoo. *Internat. Zoo Yearbook* 2:90–93.

Anon. 1960b. Longevity survey. Length of life of mammals in captivity at the London Zoo and Whipsnade Park. *Internat. Zoo Yearbook* **2**:288–299.

Anon. 1965. Giraffe midwives at a birth. *African Wild Life* **19**:323.

Anon. 1966. Solitary giraffe gives birth. *African Wild Life.* **20**:128.

Anon. 1968. (Picture of unspotted giraffe calf.) *Internat. Zoo Yearbook* **8**:134.

Anon. 1971. Giraffe albino. *Africana* **4,8**:39.

Anon. 1973. The wildlife veterinarians. *African Wild Life* **27**:120–123.

Ansell, W. F. H. 1960. The breeding of some large mammals in Northern Rhodesia. *Proc. Zool. Soc. London* **134**:251–274.

Ansell, W. F. H. 1968. 8. Artiodactyla (excluding the genus *Gazella*). In: *Preliminary Identification Manual for African Mammals,* J. A. J. Meester (Ed.). Smithsonian Institution, Washington, D. C.

Ansell, W. F. H. *The Mammals of Zambia.* (In press).

Ansell, W. F. H., and A. I. Dagg. 1971. The scientific name of the reticulated giraffe: proposed rejection of *Giraffa camelopardalis australis* Rhoads, 1896. *Bull. Zool. Nomenclature* **28**:100–101.

Anthony, H. E. 1928–29. Horns and antlers, their evolution, occurrence and function in the Mammalia. *Bull. New York Zool. Soc.* **31**:179–216; **32**:3–24.

Anthony, R., and F. Coupin. 1925. Recherches anatomiques sur l'okapi, *Okapia johnstoni* Scl. II. Les sinus et les cornets nasaux. *Rev. Zool. Africaine* **13**:69–96.

Apfelbach, R. 1970. Observations on the Ecology and Behavior of the East-African Giraffe *Giraffa camelopardalis* (Giraffidae). Typescript, 12 pp. Dept. of Zoology, Univ. of California, Berkeley, California.

Arambourg, C. 1963. Continental vertebrate faunas of the tertiary of North Africa. 55–64. In: *African Ecology and Human Evolution,* F. C. Howell and F. Bourlière (Eds.). Chicago, Aldine Publ. Co.

Arbuthnot, T. S. 1954. *African Hunt.* New York, Norton and Co.

Arnold, R. 1940. Eine ungefleckte Giraffe in Nord-Ost-Afrika? *Z. Säugetierk.* **15**:306–311.

Aschaffenburg, R., M. E. Gregory, S. J. Rowland, S. Y. Thompson, and V. M. Kon. 1962. The composition of the milk of the giraffe (*Giraffa camelopardalis reticulata*). *Proc. Zool. Soc. London* **139**:359–363.

Attwell, R. I. G. 1966. Oxpeckers, and their associations with mammals in Zambia. *Puku (Zambia)* **4**:17–48.

Austwick, P. K. C. 1969. Mycotic infections. 249–270. In: *Diseases in Free-living Wild Animals,* A. McDiarmid (Ed.). London, Academic Press. *Symp. Zool. Soc. London* **24.**

Babich, K. 1964. Animal behaviour with respect to tourists in the Kruger National Park. *Koedoe* **7**:124–152.

Backhaus, D. 1959. Experimentelle Prüfung des Farbsehvermögens einer Masai-Giraffe (*Giraffa camelopardalis tippelskirchi* Matschie. 1898). *Z. Tierpsychol.* **16**:468–477.

Backhaus, D. 1960. Prägung einer Tippelskirch-Giraffe, *Giraffa camelopardalis tippelskirchi* Matschie, 1898, auf den Menschen? *Säugetierk. Mitteil.* **8**:29–31.

Backhaus, D. 1961. *Beobachtungen an Giraffen in Zoologischen Gärten und freier Wildbahn.* Bruxelles, Instit. des Parcs Nat. du Congo et du Ruanda-Urundi.

Baker, J. R. 1969. Trypanosomes of wild mammals in the neighbourhood of the Serengeti National Park, 147–158. In: *Diseases in Free-living Wild Animals,* A. McDiarmid (Ed.). London, Academic Press. *Symp. Zool. Soc. London* **24.**

Baker, S. 1868. *Exploration of the Nile Tributaries of Abyssinia.* Hartford, O. D. Case and Co.

Baker, S. 1888. *Albert N'yanza—Great Basin of the Nile*. London, Macmillan.

Balch, C. C. 1955. Sleep in ruminants. *Nature* **175**,4465:940–941.

Baldwin, W. C. 1894. *African Hunting and Adventure*. London, R. Bentley and Sons.

Bannikov, A. G., and L. V. Zhirnov. 1970. (Secondary biologic productivity of semideserts in the western Pre-Caspian area—in Russian). *Ekologiya* **1**,2:33–37.

Barrow, J. 1801. An account of travels into the interior of southern Africa in the years 1797 and 1798. In: Mammals of the Uitenhage and Cradock Districts Cape Province in recent times, by C. J. Skead, 1958. *Koedoe* **1**:19–59.

Barth, H. 1858. *Travels and Discoveries in North and Central Africa*. London, Longman, Brown, Green, Longmans and Roberts.

Baudier, M. 1633. *Histoire Générale du Serrail et de la Cour du Grand Seigneur*. Guignard, Paris.

Beauford, L. F. de. 1928. On a case of correlation between blood vessels and colour pattern in a giraffe. *Tijdschr. Nederlands Dierkund. Ver.* **1**,1:31–32.

Becklund, W. W. 1968. Ticks of veterinary significance found on imports in the United States. *J. Parasitol.* **54**:622–628.

Beddard, F. 1902a. (Note on crooked neck in a giraffe.) *Proc. Zool. Soc. London* 1902:52–54.

Beddard, F. 1902b. *The Cambridge Natural History*. Vol. 10, *Mammalia*. London, Macmillan.

Beddard, F. 1906. Description of the external characters of an unborn fetus of a giraffe (*G. c. wardi*). *Proc. Zool. Soc. London* 1906:463–468.

Bego, U. 1960. Die vergleichende Anatomie der Blutgefässe und Nerven der vorderen Extremitäten bei Kamel, Lama, Giraffe und Rind. *Acta Anat.* **42**:261.

Benchley, B. J. 1946. *My Animal Babies*. London, Faber and Faber.

Ben Shaul, D. M. 1962. The composition of the milk of wild animals. *Internat. Zoo Yearbook* **4**:333–342.

Bere, R. M. 1958. The status of ungulate mammals in the Uganda National Parks. *Mammalia* **22**:418–426.

Bere, R. 1966. *Wild Animals in an African National Park*. London, André Deutsch.

Berry, P. S. M. 1973. The Luangwa Valley giraffe. *Puku (Zambia)* **7**:71–92.

Biers, M. P. M. 1923. La girafe historique du Jardin des Plantes en 1827. *Bull. Mus. Nat. d'Hist. Natur. (Paris)* **29**:278–284.

Bigalke, R. 1939. *Animals and Zoos Today*. London, Cassell.

Bigalke, R. 1951. The discovery of the giraffe in South Africa. *Fauna and Flora (Transvaal)* **2**:24–28.

Bigalke, R. 1958. On the present status of ungulate mammals in South West Africa. *Mammalia* **22**:478–497.

Binkley, K. L. 1959. Use of tranquilizer drugs on a reticulated giraffe at Woodland Park Zoo, U.S.A. *Internat. Zoo Yearbook* **1**:51–52.

Black, D. 1915a. A study of the endocranial casts of ocapia, giraffe and samotherium. *J. Comp. Neur.* **25**:329–360.

Black, D. 1915b. Notes on the endocranial casts of *Okapia Giraffa* and *Samotherium*. *Anat. Rec.* **9**:56–59.

Blancou, L. 1958a. Distribution géographique des ongulés d'Afrique Equatoriale Française en relation avec leur écologie. *Mammalia* **22**:294–316.

Blancou, L. 1958b. Note sur le statut actuel des ongulés en Afrique Equatoriale Française. *Mammalia* **22**:399–405.

Blancou, L. 1960. Destruction and protection of the fauna of French Equatorial and of French West Africa II. *African Wild Life* **14**:101–108.

Blancou, L. 1962. Mensurations et poids de quelques ongulés du Tchad et de la République Centre-Africaine. *Mammalia* **26**:84–106.

Blankenship, L. H., and C. R. Field. 1972. Factors affecting the distribution of wild ungulates on a ranch in Kenya. *Zool. Africana* **7**:281–302.

Bligh, J., and A. M. Harthoorn. 1965. Continuous radiotelemetric records of the deep body temperature of some unrestrained African mammals under near-natural conditions. *J. Physiol.* **176**:145–162.

Blum, L. 1957. (Picture of young giraffe with black band around body.) *African Wild Life* **11**:328.

Boas, J. E. V. 1934. Über die Verwandtschaftliche stellung der Gattung *Antilocapra* und der Giraffiden zu den Übrigen Wiederkäuern. *Biol. Meddel.* **11**:1–15.

Bohlin, B. 1927. Die Familie Giraffidae mit besonderer Berücksichtigung der fossilen Formen aus China. *Palaeontol. Sinica, Ser. C* **4**:1–179.

Bolton, M. 1973. Notes on the current status and distribution of some large mammals in Ethiopia (excluding Eritrea). *Mammalia* **37**:562–586.

Borelli, V., L. de Santis Prada and J. Peduti Neto. 1973. Comportaments da *ansa spiralis* do colon na girafa (*Giraffa camelopardalis*). *Rev. Fac. Med.* Vet. Zootec. Univ. S. Paulo **10**:71–74.

Boué, C. 1970. Morphologie fonctionnelle des dents labiales chez les ruminants. *Mammalia* **34**:696–711.

Bourdelle, M. E. 1934. Les allures de la girafe en particulier le galop. *Bull. Mus. Nat. d'Hist. Natur., Ser.* 2, **6**:329–339.

Bourgoin, P. 1958. Les ongulés dans les territoires de l'union française. *Mammalia* **22**:371–381.

Bourlière, F. 1961. Le sex-ratio de la girafe. *Mammalia* **25**:467–471.

Bourlière, F. 1962. Les populations d'ongulés sauvages africains: caractéristiques écologiques et implications économiques. *La Terre et La Vie* **2**:150–160.

Bourlière, F. 1963. Observations on the ecology of some large African mammals. 43–54. In: *African Ecology and Human Evolution,* F. C. Howell and F. Bourlière (Eds.). Chicago, Aldine Publ. Co.

Bourlière, F. 1965. Densities and biomasses of some ungulate populations in eastern Congo and Rwanda, with notes on population structure and lion/ungulate ratios. *Zool. Afr.* **1**:199–208.

Bourlière, F., and J. Verschuren. 1960. *Introduction à l'Ecologie des Ongulés du Parc National Albert.* Bruxelles, Instit. Parc Nat. Congo Belge. 1–158.

Brahmachary, R. L. 1969. A note on the food habits of the giraffe in East Africa. *Uganda J.* **33**:214–216.

Bridges, W. 1948. *Wild Animals of the World.* New York, Garden City Publ.

Brink, C. 1954. Hendrik Hop's expedition to Great Namaqualand (1761). In: *South African Explorers,* E. Axelson (Ed.). London, Oxford Univ. Press.

Broman, I. 1938a. Über die ersten Entwicklungsstadien der Mähne der Giraffen und der Equidae. *Anat. Anz.* **85**:241–249.

Broman, I. 1938b. Einige Erfahrungen aus einer Giraffenjagd. *Zool. Gart., N. F.,* **10**:84–94.

Bronson, E. B. 1910. *In Closed Territory.* Chicago, McClurg and Co.

Brown,————. 1947. Giraffe noise. *Field* **189**:162.

Brown, L. 1969. Wildlife, sheep and cattle in Africa. *Oryx* **10**:92–101.

Brown, W. L. 1960. Ants, acacias and browsing animals. *Ecology* **41**:587–592.

Brownlee, A. 1963. Evolution of the giraffe. *Nature* **200**,4910:1022.

Bryden, H. A. 1891. On the present distribution of the giraffe south of the Zambesi. *Proc. Zool. Soc. London* 1891:445–447.

Bryden, H. A. 1893. *Gun and Camera in Southern Africa.* London, E. Stanford.

Bryden, H. A. (Ed.). 1899. *Great and Small Game of Africa.* London, Rowland Ward.

Brynard, A. M. 1967. Game control in national parks. *African Wild Life* **21**:93–99.

Brynard, A. M., and U. de V. Pienaar. 1960. Annual report of the biologists, 1958/1959. *Koedoe* **3**:1–205.

Buchanan, A. 1926. *Sahara.* London, John Murray.

Buechner, H. K., A. M. Harthoorn, and J. A. Lock. 1960. The immobilization of African animals in the field, with special reference to their transfer to other areas. *Proc. Zool. Soc. London* **135**:261–264.

Burkitt, M. C., and P. E. Glover. 1946. *Prehistoric investigations in British Somaliland. Proc. Prehistoric Soc. (London) N. S.* **12**:49–56.

Burne, R. H. 1917. Notes on some of the viscera of the okapi (*Okapia johnstoni* Sclater). *Proc. Zool. Soc. London* 1917:187–208.

Butler, A. L. 1912a. The voice of the giraffe. *Field* **119**:49.

Butler, A. L. 1912b. A white giraffe. *Field* **119**:596.

Calcaterra, A. 1972. A giraffe is born. *Anim. Kingdom* **75**,6:15–18.

Caldwell, _____. 1923. (Note on melanism.) *Proc. Zool. Soc. London* 1923:179.

Campbell, R. 1951. *Light on a Dark Horse.* London, Hollis and Carter.

Cansdale, G. S. 1952. *Animals and Man.* London, Hutchinson.

Carrington, J. F. 1892. The scarcity of giraffes. *Field* **79**:508.

Castigli, G., and R. Sacchi. 1941. L'apparato di conduzione nel cuore della giraffa. *Riv. Biol.* **32**:71–80.

Cave, A. J. E. 1950. On the liver and gall-bladder of the giraffe. *Proc. Zool. Soc. London* **120**:381–393.

Chaffee, P. S. 1968. Report on death of a giraffe. *J. Small Anim. Practice* **9**:136–137.

Chaine, _____. 1902–3. Myologie de la région sous-hyoidienne de la girafe. *Proc. Verbaux Soc. Bordeau* 9–11.

Chapman, H. C. 1875. Notes on the great blood vessels of the giraffe. *Proc. Acad. Natur. Sci. Philadelphia* 1875:401–402.

Chapman, H. C. 1877. Note on the great blood vessels of the giraffe. *Proc. Acad. Natur. Sci. Philadelphia* 1877:37–38.

Child, G., P. Smith, and W. von Richter. 1970. Tsetse control hunting as a measure of large mammal population trends in the Okavango Delta, Botswana. *Mammalia* **34**:34–75.

Churcher, C. S. In press. "Giraffidae," Chapter 22 in: *Evolution of Mammals in Africa,* V. J. Maglio (Ed.). Princeton, New Jersey, Princeton Univ. Press.

Clarke, G. K. 1968. Large mammal building at Topeka Zoo. *Internat. Zoo Yearbook* **8**:85–89.

Clarke, G. K. 1970. The anxiety and the jubilation—our first giraffe birth. *Bear Facts (Topeka Zoological Park)* **6**,5:1–7.

Clarke, G. K. 1972. A new baby in the giraffe family. *Zoo (Topeka Zoological Park)* **8**,6:1–4.

Clerck, A. de. 1965. News from our parks. *African Wild Life* **19**:34.

Cobbold, T. S. 1854. On the anatomy of the giraffe (*Giraffa camelopardalis* Linn.). *Mag. Natur. Hist., 2nd Ser.* **13**:484–488.

Cobbold, T. S. 1855. Description of a new species of trematode worm *(Fasciola gigantica). Edinburgh New Philosophical J., N.S.* 262–267.

Cobbold, T. S. 1856. On a remarkable pouched condition of the Glandulae Peyerianae in the giraffe. *Edinburgh New Philosophical J., N.S.* 3–5.

Cobbold, T. S. 1860. Contributions to the anatomy of the giraffe. *Proc. Zool. Soc. London* 1860:99–105.

Codd, L. E. W. 1951. *Trees and Shrubs of the Kruger National Park.* Botanical Survey Memoir No. 26. Pretoria, Government Printer.

Coe, M. J. 1967. "Necking" behaviour in the giraffe. *J. Zool. (London)* **151**:313–321.

Colbert, E. H. 1935a. The classification and the phylogeny of the Giraffidae. *Amer. Mus. Nov.* **800**:1–15.

Colbert, E. H. 1935b. Siwalik mammals in the American Museum of Natural History. *Trans. Amer. Philos. Soc.* **26**:1–402. ("Giraffoidea," 323–375).

Colbert, E. H. 1936. Was the extinct giraffe *(Sivatherium)* known to the early Sumerians? *Amer. Anthrop.* **38**:605–608.

Colbert, E. H. 1938. The relationships of the okapi. *J. Mammal.* **19**:47–64.

Colbert, E. H. 1955. *Evolution of the Vertebrates.* New York, Wiley and Sons.

Colbo, M. H. 1973. Ticks of Zambian wild animals: a preliminary checklist. *Puku (Zambia)* **7**:97–105.

Cooke, H. B. S., and L. H. Wells. 1947. Fossil mammals from the Makapan Valley, Potgietersrust. III Giraffidae. *South African J. Sci.* **43**:232–235.

Cordier, _____. 1894. Recherches sur l'anatomie comparée de l'estomac des ruminants. *Ann. Sci. Natur., Zool.* 128 pp.

"Countryman." 1954. "Still hunting" for game. *African Wild Life* **8**:297–300.

Crandall, L. S. 1964. *The Management of Wild Mammals in Captivity.* Chicago and London, Univ. Chicago Press.

Cranworth, Lord. 1912. *Colony in the Making.* London, Macmillan.

Crile, G. 1941. *Intelligence, Power and Personality.* New York, McGraw-Hill.

Crisp, E. 1853. Note on the splenic vein of the giraffe. *Proc. Zool. Soc. London* 1853:99.

Crisp, E. 1864a. Contributions to the anatomy of the giraffe, with an account of the length of the alimentary canal of many other ruminants. *Proc. Zool. Soc. London* 1864:63–68.

Crisp, E. 1864b. Further contributions to the anatomy of the giraffe and the nylghau. *Proc. Zool. Soc. London* 1864:269–271.

Cully, W. 1958. *Giraffa camelopardalis. Parks and Recreation* **41**:197–198.

Cumming, R. G. 1850. *The Lion Hunter of South Africa.* London, John Murray.

Dagg, A. I. 1959. Food preferences of the giraffe. *Proc. Zool. Soc. London* **135**:640–642.

Dagg, A. I. 1960. Gaits of the giraffe and okapi. *J. Mammal.* **41**:282.

Dagg, A. I. 1962a. The distribution of the giraffe in Africa. *Mammalia* **26**:497–505.

Dagg, A. I. 1962b. The role of the neck in the movements of the giraffe. *J. Mammal.* **43**:88–97.

Dagg, A. I. 1962c. The subspeciation of the giraffe. *J. Mammal.* **43**:550–552.

Dagg, A. I. 1962d. Giraffe movement and the neck. *Natur. Hist. (New York)* **71**,7:44–51.

Dagg, A. I. 1963. A French giraffe. *Frontiers* **27**,4:115–117f.

Dagg, A. I. 1965. Sexual differences in giraffe skulls. *Mammalia* **29**:610–612.

Dagg, A. I. 1968. External features of giraffe. *Mammalia* **32**:657–669.

Dagg, A. I. 1970a. Preferred environmental temperatures of some captive mammals. *Internat. Zoo Yearbook* **10**:127–130.

Dagg, A. I. 1970b. Tactile encounters in a herd of captive giraffe. *J. Mammal.* **51**:279–287.

Dagg, A. I. 1971. *Giraffa camelopardalis.* Mammalian Species No. 5, 1–8. Published by Amer. Soc. Mammalogists.

Dagg, A. I., and A. de Vos. 1968a. The walking gaits of some species of Pecora. *J. Zool. (London)* **155**:103–110.

Dagg, A. I., and A. de Vos. 1968b. Fast gaits of pecoran species. *J. Zool. (London)* **155**:499–506.

Dagg, A. I., and A. Taub. 1971. Flehmen. *Mammalia* **34**:1–14.

Dalquest, W. W. 1965. Mammals from the Save River, Mozambique, with descriptions of two new bats. *J. Mammal.* **46**:254–264.

Darling, F. F. 1960. An ecological reconnaissance of the Mara Plains in Kenya Colony. *Wildlife Mono.* **5**:1–41.

Darwin, C. 1859. *The Origin of Species and the Descent of Man.* New York, Random House.

Dasmann, R. F., and A. S. Mossman. 1960. The economic value of Rhodesia game. *Rhodesian Farmer,* Apr. 15, 4 pp.

Dasmann, R. F., and A. S. Mossman. 1961. "Commercial Utilization of Game Mammals on a Rhodesian Range." Paper presented at meeting of Wildlife Soc., Calif. Section, Davis, California. January. 11 pp.

Dasmann, R. F., and A. S. Mossman. 1962. Reproduction in some ungulates in Southern Rhodesia. *J. Mammal.* **43**:533–537.

Davis, M. 1949. Parturition of the Nubian giraffe. *J. Mammal.* **30**:306–307.

Dawson, W. R. 1927. The earliest records of the giraffe. *Ann. and Mag. Natur. Hist., 9th Ser.,* **19**:478–485.

Debenham, F. 1953. *Kalahari Sand.* London, G. Bell and Sons.

Dembeck, H. 1965. *Animals and Men.* New York, Natur. Hist. Press.

Derscheid, J. M., and H. Neuville. 1924. Recherches anatomiques sur l'okapi, *Okapia johnstoni* Scl. I. Le caecum et la glande ileocaecale. *Rev. Zool. Afr.* **12**:499–507.

Derscheid, J. M., and H. Neuville. 1925. Recherches anatomiques sur l'okapi, *Okapia johnstoni* Scl. III. La rate. *Rev. Zool. Afr.* **13**:97–101.

Dinnik, J. A., and R. Sachs. 1968. A gigantic *Protostrongylus, P. africanus* sp. nov., and other lung nematodes of antelopes in the Serengeti, Tanzania. *Parasitology* **58**: 819–829.

Ditmars, R. L., and W. Bridges. 1937. *Wild Animal World. Behind the Scenes at the Zoo.* New York, Appleton-Century Co.

Dittrich, L. 1968. Erfahrungen bei der Gesellschaftshaltung verschiedener Huftierarten. *Zool. Gart.* **36**:95–106.

Doorn, C. 1967. Freunde des Kölner Zoo. *Jahrgang* **3,**10:79–85.

Dugmore, A. D. R. 1924. *The Vast Sudan.* London, Arrowsmith.

Dugmore, A. D. R. 1925. *The Wonderland of Big Game.* Bristol, Arrowsmith.

Duvernoy, ———. 1844. Sur une mâchoire de girafe fossile découverte à Issoudun. *Ann. Sci. Natur., 3rd Ser., Zool.* **1**:36.

England, Parliament. 1913. *Correspondence Relating to the Preservation of Wild Animals in Africa. March.* London, HMSA.

Erk, H., C. Akkayan and H. Olcay. 1967. (A case of dystocia in a giraffe in the zoological garden of Ankara, Ataturk state farm—in Turkish.) *Ankara Univ. Vet. Fak. Dergisi* **14**:541–550.

Ewert, H. O. 1965. Remedial hoof-trimming in an adult giraffe *Giraffa camelopardalis. Internat. Zoo Yearbook* **5**:197–200.

Fairall, N. 1968. The reproductive seasons of some mammals in the Kruger National Park. *Zool. Africana* **3**:189–210.

Farini, G. A. 1886. *Through the Kalahari Desert.* London, Sampson Low, Marston, Searle and Rivington.

Fiennes, R. N. 1960. Report of the Society's pathologist for the year 1958. *Proc. Zool. Soc. London* **134**:297–308.

Fife, C. W. D. 1927. *Savage Life in the Black Sudan.* London, Seeley, Service and Co.

Fitzinger, H. J. 1858. Einige Bemerkungen über die Fortpflanzung der Giraffe. *Sitzungsberichte Math. Naturw. Klasse Akad. Wiss. Wien* **31**:344–346.

FitzSimons, F. W. 1920. *The Natural History of South Africa. Mammals* Vol. 3. London and New York, Longmans, Green.

Flower, W. H. 1870. *An Introduction to the Osteology of the Mammalia.* London, Macmillan.

Foran, _____. 1946. Is the giraffe dumb? *Field* **188**:125.

Fortie, M. 1938. *Black and Beautiful.* Indianapolis and New York, Bobbs-Merrill.

Foster, J. B. 1966. The giraffe of Nairobi National Park: home range, sex ratios, the herd, and food. *East African Wildlife J.* **4**:139–148.

Foster, J. B. 1968. The biomass of game animals in Nairobi National Park, 1960–1966. *J. Zool. (London)* **155**:413–425.

Foster, J. B., and A. I. Dagg. 1972. Notes on the biology of the giraffe. *East African Wildlife J.* **10**:1–16.

Foster, J. B., and D. Kearney. 1967. Nairobi National Park Census—1966. *East African Wildlife J.* **5**:112–120.

Fox, H. 1923. *Disease in Captive Wild Animals and Birds.* Philadelphia, London and Chicago, Lippincott.

Fox, H. 1938. The giraffe, some notes upon the natural characters of this animal, its care and its misfortune. *Report Penrose Research Laboratory,* 35–67.

Frank, A. 1960. Die Glandula thyreoidea und die Glandulae thyreoideae accessoriae bei *Giraffa camelopardalis* L. *Acta Anat.* **42**:267.

Franklin, K. J., and F. Haynes. 1927. The histology of the giraffe's carotid, functionally considered. *J. Anat.* **62**:115–117.

Fraser, F. C. 1951. Vestigial metapodials in the okapi and giraffe. *Proc. Zool. Soc. London* **121**:315–317.

Frechkop, S. 1946. De l'okapi et des affinités des giraffides avec les antilopes. *Bull. Mus. R. Hist. Natur. Belgique, Bruxelles* **22**:1–28.

Freiheit, C. F. 1970. New giraffe exhibit and animal hospital at Buffalo Zoo. *Internat. Zoo Yearbook* **10**:53–54.

Friant, M. 1943. Le cerveau de l'okapi. *Comptes Rendus, Acad. Sci., Paris* **216**:81–83.

Friant, M. 1952a. Recherches sur le développement du cerveau de la girafe. *Acta Anat.* **16**:290–298.

Friant, M. 1952b. Les charactéristiques fondamentales du cerveau des Giraffidae. *Comptes Rendus, Acad. Sci., Paris* **235**:978–979.

Friant, M. 1954. Sur la morphologie du troisième sillon arqué du cerveau, chez les ongulés artiodactyles. *Acta Anat.* **22**:328–330.

Funaioli, U. 1968. (The importance of wild animals in the use of land of some arid and semi arid African countries—in Italian). *Riv. Agr. Subtrop. Trop.* **62**:400–428.

Gandal, C. P. 1961. The use of a tranquillizer and diuretic in the successful management of two "reluctant zoo mothers." *Internat. Zoo Yearbook* **3**:119–120.

Garrod, A. H. 1877. Notes on the visceral anatomy and osteology of the ruminants. *Proc. Zool. Soc. London* 1877:2–18.

Gatti, A. 1959. *Africa is Adventure.* New York, Julian Messner.

Geist, V. 1966. The evolution of horn-like organs. *Behaviour* **27**:175–214.

Gensch, W. 1969. Versuch der künstlichen Aufzucht einer Giraffe (*Giraffa camelopardalis* L.). *Zool. Gart.* **37**:231–242.

Gerhardt, U. 1905. Morphologische und biologische Studien über die Kopulationsorgane der Säugetiere. *Jenaische Z. Naturwissenschaften* **39**:43–118.

Germanos, W. 1907. Geburt einer männlichen Giraffe in Zoologischen Garten zu Athen. *Zool. Gart.* **48**:73–75.

Gijzen, A. 1958. Quelques observations concernant la naissance et la croissance des girafes (*Giraffa camelopardalis antiquorum* (Swainson)) au jardin zoologique d'Anvers. *Mammalia* **22**:112–120.

Glass, R. L., R. Jenness, and L. W. Lohse. 1969. Comparative biochemical studies of milks. V. The triglyceride composition of milk fats. *Comp. Biochem. Physiol.* **28:** 783–786.

Glover, T. D. 1973. Aspects of sperm production in some East African mammals. *J. Reprod. Fert.* **35:**45–53.

Godina, A. Y. ca.1970. (On the parallelism in the evolution of *Palaeotragus* and *Giraffa* and its importance in some evolutionary studies—in Russian.) *U.S.S.R. Acad. Sci., Paleontological Instit. Proc.* **130:**62–69.

Goetz, R. H., and O. Budtz-Olsen. 1955. Scientific safari—the circulation of the giraffe. *South African Med. J.* **29:**773–776.

Goetz, R. H., and E. N. Keen. 1957. Some aspects of the cardiovascular system in the giraffe. *Angiology* **8:**542–564.

Goetz, R. H., J. V. Warren, O. H. Gauer, J. L. Patterson, J. T. Doyle, E. N. Keen, and M. McGregor. 1960. Circulation of the giraffe. *Circulation Research* **8:**1049–1058.

Gombe, S., and F. I. B. Kayanja. 1974. Ovarian progestins in Masai giraffe (*Giraffa camelopardalis*). *J. Reprod. Fert.* **40**(1):45–50.

Goodwin, G. G. 1956. Nature's skyscrapers. *Anim. Kingdom* **59:**66–73.

Graham, P. 1967. An analysis of the numbers of game and other large mammals killed in tsetse fly control operations in northern Bechuanaland 1942 to 1963. *Mammalia* **31:**186–204.

Granvik, H. 1925. Mammals from the eastern slopes of Mount Elgon, Kenya Colony. *Acta Univ. Lundensis. N.S. Lunds Univ. Arsskrift* **21:**1–36.

Graupner, E. D. 1971. *Some Aspects of the Ecology and Management of the Sabi Sand Wildtuin.* Transvaal Natur. Conserv. Div., Pretoria.

Greed, R. E. 1960. Composition of the milk of the giraffe. *Internat. Zoo Yearbook* **2:** 106.

Gregory, W. K. 1928. *Evolution Emerging I and II.* New York, Macmillan.

Griesel, J. 1961. A new game sanctuary for the Orange Free State, the Willem Pretorius Game Reserve. *African Wild Life* **15:**121–125.

Gros Clark, W. E. Le. 1939. The brain of the okapi. *Proc. Zool. Soc. London* **109B:** 153–159.

Grzimek, B. 1956a. Schlaf von Giraffen und Okapi. *Naturwissenschaften* **43:**406.

Grzimek, B. 1956b. *No Room for Wild Animals.* London, Thames and Hudson.

Grzimek, B. 1964. *Rhinos Belong to Everyone.* London, Collins.

Grzimek, B. 1966. Apes travel from Europe to Africa. *African Wild Life* **20:**271–288.

Grzimek, B. 1972. The giraffe. *Grzimek's Animal Life Encyclopedia* **13:**255–266.

Grzimek, B. and M. 1960a. *Serengeti Shall Not Die.* London, Hamish Hamilton.

Grzimek, M. and B. 1960b. Census of plains animals in the Serengeti National Park, Tanganyika. *J. Wildlife Management* **24:**27–37.

Guggisberg, C. A. W. 1969. *Giraffes.* New York, Golden Press.

Guillaumin, A. 1946. Une médaille inconnue au sujet de la girafe. *Bull. Mus. Nat. Hist. Natur. (Paris) Ser. 2,* **18:**41–42.

Hagenbeck, C. H. 1960. Hufbehandlung einer erwachsenen Giraffe. *Zool. Gart., N. F.,* **25:**182–188.

Hall-Martin, A. J. 1974a. A note on the seasonal utilization of different vegetation types by giraffe. *South African J. Sci.* **70:**122–123.

Hall-Martin, A. J. 1974b. Food selection by Transvaal lowveld giraffe as determined by analysis of stomach contents. *J. Southern African Wildlife Manage. Assoc.* **4** (3): 191–202.

Hammond, J. A. 1972. Infections with *Fasciola* spp. in wildlife in Africa. *Trop. Anim. Health Prod.* **4:**1–13.

Hanström, B. 1953. The hypophysis in some South African Insectivora, Carnivora, Hyracoidea, Proboscidea, Artiodactyla and Primates. *Arkiv. Zool.* **4**,3:187–294.

Happold, D. C. D. 1969. The present distribution and status of the giraffe in west Africa. *Mammalia* **33**:516–521.

Harmsworth natural history. Vol. 2. 1910. London, Carmelite House.

Harper, F. 1940. The nomenclature and type localities of certain old world mammals. *J. Mammal.* **21**:322.

Hart, S. 1966. *Too Short a Day.* London, Geoffrey Bles.

Hart, S. 1972. *Listen to the Wild.* London, Collins.

Harthoorn, A. M. 1960. Methods of control of wild animals with the use of drugs. *Internat. Zoo Yearbook* **2**:302–307.

Harthoorn, A. M. 1965. Application of pharmacological and physiological principles in restraint of wild animals. *Wildlife Mono.* **14**:1–40.

Harthoorn, A. M. 1966. Restraint of undomesticated animals. *J. Amer. Vet. Med. Assoc.* **149**:875–880.

Haugen, A. O., and L. A. Davenport. 1950. Breeding records of white-tailed deer in the Upper Peninsula of Michigan. *J. Wildlife Management* **14**:290–295.

Haywood, A. H. W. 1912. *Through Timbuctu.* London, Seeley, Service and Co.

Hediger, H. 1950. *Wild Animals in Captivity.* London, Butterworths Sci. Publ.

Hediger, H. 1955. *Studies of the Psychology and Behaviour of Captive Animals in Zoos and Circuses.* London, Butterworths Sci. Publ.

Hediger, H. 1959. Wie Tiere schlafen. *Med. Klinik* **54**:938–946, 965–968.

Heinze, W. 1964. Die Muskulatur der Hintergliedmasse von *Giraffa camelopardalis angolensis.* Einige Kinweise zur Blutgefäss- und Nervenversorgung. *Anat. Anz.* **115**:476–496.

Heinze, W. 1965. Gelenke und Bänder der Hintergliedmasse der Giraffe (*Giraffa camelopardalis angolensis*). *Anat. Anz.* **116**:39–58.

Heinze, W. 1969. Das Muskeldiagramm als Methode zur Darstellung und zum Wergleich der Innenstrukturen von Muskeln am Beispiel der Kaumuskulatur, des *M. triceps surae* und des *M. flexor digitalis pedis superficialis* unserer Haussäugetiere. *Anat. Anz.* **125**:303–312.

Hesse, P. R. 1958. Identification of the spoor and dung of East African mammals. Part III. *African Wild Life* **12**:58–63.

Hett, M. L. 1928. The comparative anatomy of the palatine tonsil. *Proc. Zool. Soc. London* 1928:843–915.

Hildebrand, M. 1960. How animals run. *Sci. Amer.* **202**:148–157.

Hirst, S. M. 1966. Immobilization of the Transvaal giraffe (*Giraffa camelopardalis giraffa*) using an oripavine derivative. *J. South African Vet. Med. Assoc.* **37**:85.

Hirst, S. M. 1969a. Road-strip census techniques for wild ungulates in African woodland. *J. Wildlife Management* **33**:40–48.

Hirst, S. M. 1969b. Predation as a regulating factor of wild ungulate populations in a Transvaal lowveld nature reserve. *Zool. Afr.* **4**:199–230.

Hobley, C. W. 1929. *Kenya: from Chartered Company to Crown Colony.* London, H. F. and G. Witherby.

Hofmann, R. R. 1968a. Comparisons of the rumen and omasum structure in East African game ruminants in relation to their feeding habits. 179–194. In: *Comparative Nutrition of Wild Animals.* M. A. Crawford (Ed.). London, Academic Press. *Symp. Zool. Soc. London* **21**.

Hofmann, R. R. 1968b. (Comment.) 217–219. In: *Comparative Nutrition of Wild Animals.* M. A. Crawford (Ed.). London, Academic Press. *Symp. Zool. Soc. London* **21**.

Home, E. 1828. On the peculiarities of the tongue of the zariffa and on the muscular structure of tongues in general. *Lectures on Comp. Anat.* **5**:244.

Home, E. 1830. A report on the stomach of the zariffa. *Phil. Trans. Royal Soc. London* Pt. 1,85–86.

Hoogstraal, H. 1956. *Ticks of the Sudan. African Ixodoidea.* Vol. 1, Cairo, Egypt, U.S. Naval Medical Research Unit 3, Research Report NM 005050.29.07. 1101 pp.

Hunter, J. A. 1957. *Hunter's Tracks.* London, Hamish Hamilton.

Huxley, J. 1963. *Wild Lives of Africa.* London, Collins.

Huxley, J., and L. Koch. 1964. *Animal Language: How Animals Communicate.* New York, Grosset and Dunlap.

Iles, G. 1957. Giraffes in the Zoological Gardens Belle Vue, Manchester. *Zool. Gart., N. F.,* **23**:162–177.

Iles, G. 1960. *At Home in the Zoo.* London, W. H. Allen.

Immelmann, K. 1958. Vom Schlaf der Giraffe. *Umschau* **58**:356–357.

Immelmann, K., and H. Gebbing. 1962. *Z. Tierpsychol.* **19**:84–92.

Innis, A. C. 1958. The behaviour of the giraffe, *Giraffa camelopardalis,* in the eastern Transvaal. *Proc. Zool. Soc. London* **131**:245–278.

Jaegar, E. 1948. *Tracks and Trailcraft.* New York, Macmillan.

Jarboe, R. E. 1965. New giraffe exhibit at San Diego Zoo. *Internat. Zoo Yearbook* **5**: 86–88.

Jardine, W. 1835. *The Naturalist's Library.* Vol. 3, *Ruminantia* Pt. 1. Edinburgh, W. H. Lizars.

Jeannin, A., and M. Barthe. 1958. L'evolution africaine et la persistance de la faune sauvage. *Mammalia* **22**:328–335.

Jefferson, J. W. 1971. Electrocardiographic and phonocardiographic findings in a reticulated giraffe. *J. Amer. Vet. Med. Assoc.* **159**:602–604.

Jennison, G. 1928. *Noah's Cargo.* London, Black.

Jensen, A. S. 1934. The sacred animal of the God Set. *Biol. Meddel.* **11**:1–19.

Johnson, M. 1928. *Safari.* New York and London, Putnam and Sons.

Johnson, M. 1935. *Over African Jungles.* New York, Harcourt, Brace and Co.

Johnson, T. B. 1909. *Tramps Round the Mountains of the Moon.* Boston, Dana Estes and Co.

Johnston, H. 1902. *The Uganda Protectorate.* London, Hutchison and Co.

Joleaud, L. 1937. Remarques sur les girafidés fossiles d'Afrique. *Mammalia* **1**:85–96.

Joly, N., and A. Lavocat. 1843. Recherches historique et palaeontologiques . . . sur la girafe. *Mém. Soc. Mus. Hist. Natur. Strasbourg,* **11**, mém. 1, Paris.

Jubb, R. A. 1970. Animals killed by severe frost in Rhodesia. *African Wild Life* **24**: 241–243.

Kaliner, G., R. Sachs, L. D. Fay, and B. Schiemann. 1971. Untersuchungen über das Vorkommen von Sarcosporidien bei ostafrikanischen Wildtieren. *Z. Tropenmed. Parasitol.* **22**:156–164.

Kato, A. 1963. (A morphological study on the cerebella of *Ursus torquatus, Giraffa camelopardalis* and *Elephas maximus*—in Japanese) *J. Kyoto Prefect. Med. Univ.* **72**/7:451–470.

Kayanja, F. I. B. 1973. The ultrastructure of the mandibular and ventral buccal glands of some East African wild ungulates. *Anat. Anz.* **134**:339–350.

Kayanja, F. I. B., and L. H. Blankenship. 1973. The ovary of the giraffe, *Giraffa camelopardalis. J. Reprod. Fertil.* **34**:305–313.

Kayanja, F. I. B., and P. Scholz. 1974. The ultrastructure of the parotid gland of some East African wild ungulates. *Anat. Anz.* **135**(4):382–397.

Keen, E. N., and R. H. Goetz. 1957. Cardiovascular anatomy of a foetal giraffe. *Acta Anat.* **31**:562–571.

Kellas, L. M., E. W. van Lennep, and E. C. Amoroso. 1958. Ovaries of some foetal and prepubertal giraffes (*Giraffa camelopardalis* (Linnaeus)). *Nature* **181**,4607:487–488.

Kettlitz, W. K. 1961. Is the giraffe mute? *Fauna and Flora* (*Transvaal*) **12**:95.

Kettlitz, W. K. 1962. The capture of giraffes without immobilization. *Fauna and Flora (Transvaal)* **13**:25–27.

Kidd, W. 1900. The significance of the hair-slope in certain mammals. *Proc. Zool. Soc. London* 1900:676–686.

Kidd, W. 1903. Traces of animal habits. 234–235. In: *Hutchinson's Animal Life.* London, Hutchinson.

King, W. E. 1947. The longnecker family. *Zoonooz* **20**,1:3–4.

Kirk, H. D. 1966. Progress of Mlilwane Sanctuary, Swaziland. *African Wild Life* **20**: 313–320.

Kladetzky, J. 1954. Über Morphologie und Lage der Löwen- und Giraffenhypophyse. *Anat. Anz.* **100**:202–216.

Klasen, S. A. H. 1963. Giraffe are strictly browsers. *Black Lechwe* **3**,5:23–25.

Kleiber, M. 1961. *The Fire of Life—an Introduction to Animal Energetics.* New York, John Wiley.

Klingel, H. 1965. Notes on the biology of the plains zebra. *East African Wildlife J.* **8**: 86–88.

Kobara, J., and T. Kamiya. 1965. (On the gall-bladder of the giraffe—in Japanese.) *Acta Anat. Nippon* **40**:161–165.

Koga, T. 1939. Birth of a giraffe. *Parks and Recreation (Rockford, Ill.)* **22**:485–488.

Kollmann, M. 1920. Étude anatomique et systématique d'un spécimen remarquable de *Giraffa camelopardalis tippelskirchi* Matschie. *Soc. Zool. France, Bull.* **45**:191–204.

Koulischer, L., J. Tijskens, and J. Mortelmans. 1971. Mammalian cytogenetics: V. The chromosomes of a female giraffe. *Acta Zool. Pathol. Antverpiensia* **52**:93–95.

Krieg, H. 1944. Der Schädel einer Giraffe. *Naturwissenschaften* **32**:148–156. No. 14/26.

Krumbiegel, I. 1937. (Note on giraffe—in German.) *Zool. Gart.* **9**:53.

Krumbiegel, I. 1939. Die Giraffe. Unter besonderer Berücksichttigung der Rassen. *Monogr. Wildsäugetiere* **8**:1–98.

Krumbiegel, I. 1951. Giraffenmischlinge. *Zool. Gart.* **18**:109–114.

Krumbiegel, I. 1965. Gabelungsspuren an Giraffenhörnern. *Säugetierk. Mitteil.* **13**:107–108.

Krumbiegel, I. 1971. *Die Giraffe.* A. Ziemsen Verlag, Wittenberg, Lutherstadt.

Kruuk, H. 1972. *The Spotted Hyena.* Chicago, Univ. Chicago Press.

Kruuk, H., and M. Turner. 1967. Comparative notes on predation by lion, leopard, cheetah and wild dog in the Serengeti area, East Africa. *Mammalia* **31**:1–27.

La Monte, F. R., and M. H. Welch. 1949. *Vanishing Wilderness.* 1949. New York, Liveright Publ. Co.

Lamprey, H. F. 1964. Estimation of the large mammal densities, biomass and energy exchange in the Tarangire Game Reserve and Masai Steppe of Tanganyika. *East African Wildlife J.* **2**:1–46.

Lane, F. W. 1948. *Animal Wonderland.* London, Country Life.

Lang, E. M. 1955a. Beobachtungen während zweier Giraffengeburten. *Säugetierk. Mitteil.* **3**,1:1–5.

Lang, E. M. 1955b. Frühgeburt und künstliche Aufzucht einer Giraffe. *Schweizer Archiv. Tierheilkunde* **97:**198–205.

Langman, V. A. 1973a. Immobilization and capture of giraffe. *South African J. Sci.* **69:** 200–203.

Langman, V. A. 1973b. Radio-tracking giraffe for ecological studies. *J. Southern African Wildlife Manage. Assoc.* **3**(2):75–78.

Lankester, E. R. 1902. On *Okapia*, a new genus of Giraffidae from central Africa. *Trans. Zool. Soc. London* **16:**279–314.

Lankester, E. R. 1907. Parallel hair-fringes and colour-striping on the face of foetal and adult giraffes. *Proc. Zool. Soc. London* 1907:115–125.

Lankester, E. R. 1908. On certain points in the structure of the cervical vertebrae of the okapi and the giraffe. *Proc. Zool. Soc. London* 1908:320–334.

Lankester, E. R. 1910. *Monograph of the Okapi.* London, Trustees of British Museum.

Laufer, B. 1928. *The Giraffe in History and Art.* Chicago, Field Museum, Anthropological Leaflet 27.

Laurence, B. R. 1961. On a collection of oestrid larvae (Diptera) from East African game animals. *Proc. Zool. Soc. London* **136:**593–601.

Lavocat, R. 1958. Classification des ongulés d'après leur origine et leur evolution. *Mammalia* **22:**28–40.

Lawrence, W. E., and R. E. Rewell. 1948. The cerebral blood supply in the Giraffidae. *Proc. Zool. Soc. London* **118:**202–212.

Leakey, L. S. B. 1965. *Olduvai Gorge 1951–1961.* Cambridge, Cambridge Univ. Press.

Leakey, L. S. B., and R. J. G. Savage. 1970. *Fossil Vertebrates of Africa.* New York and London, Academic Press.

Leiper, R. T. 1935. (Notes on parasites of the okapi.) *Proc. Zool. Soc. London* 1935, 2:947–949.

Lesson, R. P. 1842. *Nouveau Tableau du Règne Animal. Mammifères.* Paris, A. Bertrand.

Leuthold, B. M., and W. Leuthold. 1971. Food habits of giraffe in Tsavo National Park, Kenya. *East African Wildlife J.* **9:**154–156.

Leuthold, B. M., and W. Leuthold. 1972. Food habits of giraffe in Tsavo National Park, Kenya. *East African Wildlife J.* **10:**129–141.

Levaillant, F. 1932. *Voyages de Levaillant dans l'Intérieur de l'Afrique 1781–1785.* Paris, Lib. Plon.

Lhote, H. 1946. Observations sur la répartition actuelle et les moeurs de quelques grands mammifères du pays Touareg. *Mammalia* **10:**26–56.

Liddell, R. 1956. *Byzantium and Istanbul.* London, J. Cape.

Linnaeus, C. 1758. *Syst. Natur.,* ed. 10,**1:**66.

Lochte, T. 1952. Das mikroskopische Bild des Giraffenhaares. *Zool. Gart.* **19:**204–206.

Lönnberg, E. 1900. On the soft anatomy of the muskox (*Ovibos moschatus*). *Proc. Zool. Soc. London* 1900:142–167.

Lönnberg, E. 1912. Mammals collected by the Swedish Zoological Expedition to British East Africa 1911. *K. Svenska Vetenskapsakademiens Handlingar. N. S.* (Ser. 4) **48,** 5:1–188.

Loomis, F. B. 1928. Phylogeny of the deer. *Amer. J. Sci.* **16:**531–542.

Loskop Dam Nature Reserve. 1962. Fieldwork section visits the Loskop Dam Nature Reserve—Transvaal. *African Wild Life* **16:**145–146.

Loveridge, A. 1945. The giraffe at home. *Frontiers (Philadelphia)* **10:**3,26–27.

Ludwig, K. S. 1962. Beitrag zum Bau der Giraffenplacenta. *Acta Anat.* **48:**206–223.

Ludwig, K. S. 1968. Zur vergleichenden Histologie des Allantochorion. *Rev. Suisse Zool.* **75:**819–832.

Lydekker, R. 1891. The giraffe and its allies. *Nature* **44:**524–526.
Lydekker, R. 1903. (Note on giraffe.) *Hutchinson's Animal Life* **2:**122. London, Hutchinson.
Lydekker, R. 1904. On the subspeciation of *Giraffa camelopardalis. Proc. Zool. Soc. London* 1904, **1:**202–227.
Lydekker, R. 1908. *The Game Animals of Africa.* London, Rowland Ward.
Lydekker, R. 1911. Two undescribed giraffe. *Nature* **87:**484.
Maberly, A. C. T. 1947. Giraffe noises. *Field* **189:**76.
Maberly, A. C. T. 1955. Some giraffe notes and problems. *African Wild Life* **9:**330–332.
MacMahon, ———. 1947. Giraffe noises. *Field* **189:**351.
MacQueen, P. 1910. *In Wildest Africa.* London, George Bell and Sons.
Madeira, P. C. 1909. *Hunting in British East Africa.* Philadelphia and London, Lippincott.
Madel, K. D. 1964. (Picture of giraffe leg bone.) *African Wild Life* **18:**66.
Mahuzier, A. 1956. *Tragic Safari.* London, Elek Books.
Major, C. I. F. 1902a. On the okapi. *Proc. Zool. Soc. London* 1902:73–79.
Major, C. I. F. 1902b. On a specimen of the okapi lately received at Brussels. *Proc. Zool. Soc. London* 1902:339–350.
Mann, W. M. 1944. *Wild Animals In and Out of the Zoo.* Vol. 6. New York, Smithsonian Institution Series Inc.
Mason, M. H. 1937. *The Paradise of Fools.* London, Hodder and Stoughton.
Matschie, P. 1898. Einige Anscheinend noch nicht beschrieben Säugetiere aus Afrika. Sitzb. Ges. Naturf. Freunde, Berlin 1898:75–81.
Matthew, W. D. 1929. Critical observations upon Siwalik mammals. *Bull. Amer. Mus. Natur. Hist.* **56:**535–554.
Matthew, W. D. 1934. A phylogenetic chart of the Artiodactyla. *J. Mammal.* **15:**207–209.
Matthews, L. H. 1962. A new development in the conservation of African animals. *Advancement of Sci.* **18,**76:581–585.
Matthews, L. H. 1964. Overt fighting in mammals. In: *The Natural History of Aggression.* London and New York, Academic Press.
McCully, R. M., M. E. Keep, and P. A. Basson. 1970. Cytauxzoonosis in a giraffe (*Giraffa camelopardalis* (Linnaeus, 1758)). *Onderstepoort J. Vet. Res.* **37:**7–9.
McDougall, D. S. A. 1939. A white giraffe. *Field* **174:**1003.
McSpadden, J. W. (Ed.). 1917. *Animals of the World.* Garden City, New York, Garden Publ. Co.
Meester, J. 1966. *Mammals of Africa, a Preliminary Identification Manual.* Smithsonian Institution, Washington, D.C.
Meinertzhagen, R. 1938. Some weights and measurements of large mammals. *Proc. Zool. Soc. London* **108A:**433–439.
Mejia, C. 1971–72. *Giraffe Behaviour.* Serengeti Research Instit. Annual Report, 39.
Mentis, M. T. 1970. Estimates of natural biomasses of large herbivores in the Umfolozi Game Reserve area. *Mammalia* **34:**363–393.
Mertens, R. 1968a. Zur Nomenklatur der Netzgiraffe, *Giraffa camelopardalis reticulata. Senckenbergiana Biol.* **49:**85–87.
Mertens, R. 1968b. *Giraffa camelopardalis reticulata* de Winton, 1899: proposed preservation under the plenary powers (Mammalia). *Bull. Zool. Nomenclature* **25:**2–3, 113.
Mitchell, P. C. 1905a. On a young female giraffe from Nigeria. *Proc. Zool. Soc. London* 1905:244–248.
Mitchell, P. C. 1905b. On the intestinal tract of mammals. *Trans. Zool. Soc. London* **17:**437–536.

Mitchell, P. C. 1908. On a young female Kordofan giraffe. *Proc. Zool. Soc. London* 1908:130–134.

Mitchell, P. C. 1911. On longevity and relative viability in mammals and birds. *Proc. Zool. Soc. London* 1911:425–548.

Mongez, M. 1827. (Mémoires sur la girafe.) *Ann. Sci. Natur. (Paris)* **11**:225–235, 444.

Monod, T. 1963. The late tertiary and Pleistocene in the Sahara. 117–229. In: *African Ecology and Human Evolution,* F. C. Howell and F. Bourlière (Eds.). Chicago, Aldine Publ. Co.

Moreau, R. E. 1966. *The Bird Faunas of Africa and its Islands.* New York, Academic Press.

Mossop, E. E. 1931. *Journals of the Expeditions of the Honourable Ensign Olof Bergh (1682 and 1683) and the Ensign Isaq Schrijver (1689).* Cape Town, Van Riebeeck Soc. No. 12.

Mossop, E. E. 1947. *The Journals of Brink and Rhenius, Being the Journal of Carel Frederik Brink of the Journey into Great Namaqualand (1761–62) Made by Captain Hendrik Hop and the Journal of Ensign Johannes Tobias Rhenius (1724).* Cape Town, Van Riebeeck Soc. No. 28.

Müller-Liebenwalde, J. 1896. Eine junge Giraffe im Berliner Zoologischen Garten. *Zool. Gart.* **37**:289–291.

Munoz, P. A. 1959. Vergleichende Untersuchungen zur endocranialen Morphologie und zur craniocerebralen Topographie von Giraffe und Okapi. *Morphol. Jahrbuch, Leipzig* **100**:213–264.

Murie, J. 1870. On the saiga antelope, *Saiga tartarica. Proc. Zool. Soc. London* 1870:451–503.

Murie, J. 1872. On the horns, viscera and muscles of the giraffe. *Ann. and Mag. Natur. Hist., 4th Ser.* **9**:177–195.

Naaktgeboren, C. 1969. Geburtskundliche Bemerkungen uber die Hörner der neugeborenen Giraffen. *Z. Säugetierk.* **34**:375–379.

Nakaegawa, R. and S. Nakagawa, 1957. (Pregnancy and birth of the giraffe—in Japanese.) *Tier and Tiergarten, Tokyo* **95**.

National Parks Board. 1970. *Annual Report of the National Parks Board of Trustees.* No. 44. Nat. Parks Board, Pretoria.

Nesbit Evans, E. M. 1970. The reaction of a group of Rothschild's giraffe to a new environment. *East African Wildlife J.* **8**:53–62.

Neuville, M. H. 1914a. Sur l'aorte antérieure des girafes. *Bull. Mus. Nat. Hist. Natur.* **20**:8–13.

Neuville, M. H. 1914b. Sur le foie des girafes. *Bull. Mus. Nat. Hist. Natur.* **20**:208–214.

Neuville, M. H. 1922. La glande iléo-caecale des girafes. *Bull. Mus. Nat. Hist. Natur.* **28**:140–144.

Neuville, M. H. 1930. Particularités dentaires des girafidés. *Bull. Nat. Mus. Hist. Natur., 2nd Ser.* **2**:604–608.

Neuville, M. H. 1931–32. Remarques odontologiques sur quelques mammifères. *Archiv. Anat. Histol. et Embryol.* **14**,1/3:125–164.

Neuville, M. H. 1935. L'urètre glandaire des girafes. *Bull. Mus. Nat. Hist. Natur., Ser. 2* **7**:333–339.

Neuville, M. H., and J. M. Derscheid. 1929. Recherches anatomiques sur l'okapi, *Okapia johnstoni* Scl. IV. L'estomac. *Rev. Zool. Bot. Afr.* **16**:373–419.

Newman, E. 1862. "Has the giraffe two horns or three?" *Zoologist* **20**:8221–8224.

Noack, T. 1908. Die Giraffe des Sambesi-Gebietes. *Zool. Anz.* **33**:354–356.

Nouvel, J. 1958. Remarques sur la fonction génitale et la naissance d'un okapi. *Mammalia* **22**:107–111.

Oates, L. G. 1970. *An Ecological Study of the Hans Merensky Nature Reserve, for the Formulation of Future Management Policy.* Ann. Rep., Transvaal Nature Conserv. Div., Pretoria.

Oboussier, H., and G. Möller. 1971. Zur Kenntnis des Gehirns der Giraffidae (Pecora, Artiodactyla, Mammalia): ein Vergleich der Neocortex-Oberflächengrösse. *Z. Säugetierk.* **36**:291–296.

Ogilby, W. 1836. Generic distinctions of Ruminantia. *Proc. Zool. Soc. London* 1836:131–139.

Ogrizek, D. (Ed.). 1954. *South and Central Africa.* New York, McGraw-Hill.

Owen, R. 1839. Notes of giraffe birth. *Proc. Zool. Soc. London* 1839:108–109.

Owen, R. 1841. Notes on the anatomy of the Nubian giraffe. *Trans. Zool. Soc. London* **2**:217–248.

Owen, R. 1849. Notes on the birth of the giraffe at the Zoological Society Gardens. *Trans. Zool. Soc. London* **3**:21–28.

Owen, R. 1868. *Anatomy of Vertebrates.* Vol. 3, *Mammalia.* London, Longmans, Green.

Pairó, M. C. 1952. Los jirafidos fosiles de España. *Memorias y Communicaciones Instit. Geol.* **8**:1–239. (Barcelona.)

Patten, R. A. 1940. Breeding the giraffe. *Australian Zool., Sydney* **9**,4:452–454.

Patterson, J. L., J. V. Warren, J. T. Doyle, O. Gauer, T. Keen, and R. H. Goetz. 1957. Circulation and respiration in the giraffe. *J. Clin. Invest.* **36**:919.

Paulus, M. 1943. Les girafes ayant vécu à Marseille. *Bull. Mus. Hist. Natur. Marseille* **3**,2–3:33–40.

Payne, H. C. 1961. Our national parks—report. *African Wild Life* **15**:181–190.

Pennycuick, C. J., and D. Western. 1972. An investigation of some sources of bias in aerial transect sampling of large mammals populations. *East African Wildlife J.* **10**: 175–191.

Percival, A. B. 1913. On *reticulata* giraffe. *J. East African and Uganda Natur. Hist. Soc.* **3**,6:55.

Percival, A. B. 1924. *A Game Ranger's Note Book.* New York, George H. Doran Co.

Petzsch, H. 1950. Zur Frage des Vorkommens ungefleckter albinotischer Giraffen. *Zool. Gart., N. F.,* **17**:44–47.

Philipps, T. 1956. Discoveries in an African nature reserve. *Country Life* **119**,3080:146.

Phipson, E. 1883. *Animal-lore of Shakespeare's Time.* London, Kegan Paul, Trench and Co.

Pienaar, U. de V. 1961. A second outbreak of anthrax amongst game animals in the Kruger National Park. *Koedoe* **4**:4–17.

Pienaar, U. de V. 1963. The large mammals of the Kruger National Park—their distribution and present-day status. *Koedoe* **6**:1–37.

Pienaar, U. de V. 1968. Recent advances in the field immobilization and restraint of wild ungulates in South African national parks. *Acta Zool. Pathol. Antverpiensia* **46**: 17–38.

Pienaar, U. de V. 1969. Predator-prey relationships amongst the larger mammals of the Kruger National Park. *Koedoe* **12**:108–176.

Pienaar, U. de V. 1970. Water resources of the Kruger Park. *African Wild life* **24**: 181–191.

Pienaar, U. de V., J. W. Van Niekerk, E. Young, P. Van Wyk, and N. Fairall. 1966. Neuroleptic narcosis of large herbivores in South African national parks with the new potent morphine analogues M99 and M183. *J. South African Vet. Med. Assoc.* **37**:277–291.

Pilgrim, G. E. 1911. The fossil Giraffidae of India. *Palaeont. Indica, N.S.* **4**:1–29.

Pillai, P. B. K. 1957. Birth of giraffe in zoological gardens. *Ceylon Vet. J.* **5**:65.

Pincher, C. 1949. (Letter on the evolution of the giraffe.) *Nature* **164,** 4157:29.

Pitman, C. R. S. 1942. *A Game Warden Takes Stock.* London, James Nisbet and Co.

Plowright, W., and D. M. Jessett. 1971. Investigations of Allerton-type herpes virus infection in East-African game animals and cattle. *J. Hyg.* **69**:209–222.

Pocock, R. I. 1910. Cutaneous scent-glands of ruminants. *Proc. Zool. Soc. London* 1910:840–986.

Pocock, R. I. 1936. Preliminary note on a new point in the structure of the feet of the okapi. *Proc. Zool. Soc. London* 1936, **1**:583–586.

Podmore, C. R. 1958. The art of C. G. Schillings. *African Wild Life* **12**:33–39.

Poglayen-Neuwall, I. 1970. Giraffe building at Louisville zoo. *Internat. Zoo Yearbook* **10**:55–58.

Pournelle, G. H. 1955. Notes on the reproduction of a Baringo giraffe. *J. Mammal.* **36**: 574.

Putnam, B. 1947. *Animal X-rays.* New York, Putnam's Sons.

Puxley, F. L. 1929. *In African Game Tracks.* London, H. F. & G. Witherby.

Rae, _____. 1952. Voice of the giraffe. *Field* **199**:909.

Rai, B. N., and K. P. Chandrasekharan. 1958. A case of tuberculosis in a giraffe (*Giraffa camelopardalis*). *Indian Vet. J.* **35**:221–224.

Rensenbrink, H. P. 1968. Geboorte van een giraffe. *Artis (Amsterdam)* **14,**3:76–81.

Retterer, E., and H. Neuville. 1914. Du pénis et du gland d'une girafe. *Soc. Biol. (Paris) Comptes Rendus* **77**:499–501.

Retterer, E., and H. Neuville. 1916. De la rate des camélidés, des girafidés et des cervidés. *Soc. Biol. (Paris) Comptes Rendus* **79**:128–131.

Reuther, R. T. 1961. Breeding notes on mammals in captivity. *J. Mammal.* **42**:427–428.

Reuther, R. T., and J. Doherty. 1968. Birth seasons of mammals at San Francisco Zoo. *Internat. Zoo Yearbook* **8**:97–101.

Reventlow, A. 1949. The growth of our giraffes and giraffe-calves. *Bijdr. Dierkd.* **28**: 394–396.

Rhumbler, L. 1932. Die Verschiedenheiten in der Stirnwaffenentwicklung bei Wiederkäuern und ihre Gründe. I. *Jenaische Z. Naturwissenschaft* **67**:310–325.

Richiardi, S. 1880. Sull'anatomia della giraffa. *Zool. Anz.,* **3**:92–93.

Ried, T. H. 1958. Giraffes. *Smithsonian Instit. Annual Report* 1958:166–167.

Riney, T., and W. L. Kettlitz. 1964. Management of large mammals in the Transvaal. *Mammalia* **28**:189–248.

Roberts, A. 1951. *The Mammals of South Africa.* New York, Hafner Publ. Co.

Roberts, G. 1969.—And giraffe. *African Wild Life.* **23**:171.

Robin, E. D., J. M. Corson, and G. J. Dammin. 1960. The respiratory dead space of the giraffe. *Nature* **186,**4718:24–26.

Robinson, H. G. N., W. D. Gribble, W. G. Page, and G. W. Jones. 1965. Notes on the birth of a reticulated giraffe, *Giraffa camelopardalis antiquorum. Internat. Zoo Yearbook* **5**:49–52.

Rogister, M. von. ca. 1957. *Momella.* London, Odhams Press.

Roosevelt, T. 1910. *African Game Trails.* New York and London, Syndicate Publ. Co.

Roosevelt, T., and E. Heller. 1914. *African Game Animals.* New York, Scribners.

Rosevear, D. R. 1953. *Checklist and Atlas of Nigerian Mammals.* Lagos, Gvmt. Printing.

Rossof, A. H. 1972. An electrocardiographic study of the giraffe. *Amer. Heart J.* **83**: 142–143.

Roth, H. H. 1966. Game utilization in Rhodesia in 1964. *Mammalia* **30**:397–424.

Rothschild, M., and H. Neuville. 1911. Recherches sur l'okapi et les girafes de l'est africain. *Ann. Sci. Natur., Zool. (Paris), 9th Ser.* **13**:1–185.

Sachs, R. 1970. Über den Befall ostafrikanischer Wildtiere mit parasitischen Fliegenlarven (Diptera, Oestridae). *Acta Trop.* **27**:281–290.

St. Hilaire, G. 1827. Quelques considérations sur la girafe. *Ann. Sci. Natur. (Paris)* **11**: 210–223.

Saito, I. 1962. (A method of preparing the skeletal specimen of giraffe, and the characteristics of teeth and bone system of the animal in comparative anatomy—in Japanese.) *Bull. Fac. Agric. Univ. Miyazaki* **7**:258–267.

Savoy, J. C. 1966. Breeding and hand-rearing of the giraffe *Giraffa camelopardalis* at Columbus Zoo. *Internat. Zoo Yearbook* **6**:202–204.

Schaller, G. B. 1967. *The Deer and the Tiger.* Chicago, Univ. Chicago Press.

Scheidegger, S., and W. Wendnagel. 1949. Eine besondere Erkrankung des Skelettsystems, Osteodystrophia deformans beim Orang. *Zool. Gart., N. F.,* **16**:66–74.

Schenkel, R. 1966. On sociology and behaviour in impala (*Aepyceros melampus* Lichtenstein.) *East African Wildlife J.* **4**:99–114.

Scherren, H. 1905. George the Fourth's Nubian giraffe. *Field* **106**:387.

Scherren, H. 1908. On certain errors with reference to George the Fourth's giraffe. *Proc. Zool. Soc. London* 1908:403–405.

Schillings, C. G. 1905. *With Flashlight and Rifle.* London, Hutchinson.

Schillings, C. G. 1907. *In Wildest Africa,* Vol. 2. London, Hutchinson.

Schlott, M. 1952. Erfahrungen bei der Giraffenzucht. *Zool. Gart., N. F.,* **19**:171–180.

Schmidt-Nielsen, B., K. Schmidt-Nielsen, T. R. Houpt, and S. A. Jarnum. Water balance of the camel. *Amer. J. Physiol.* **185**:185–194.

Schmidt-Nielsen, K., B. Schmidt-Neilsen, S. A. Jarnum, and T. R. Houpt. 1957. Body temperature of the camel and its relation to water economy. *Amer. J. Physiol.* **188**: 103–112.

Schneider, K. M. 1951. Nachrichten aus Zoologischen Garten. *Zool. Gart.* **18**:73.

Schomber, H. W. 1962. Wild life protection in the Sudan II. *African Wild Life* **16**: 205–212.

Schomber, H. W., and D. Kock. 1961. Wild life protection and hunting in Tunisia. *African Wild Life* **15**:137–150.

Schomberg, G. 1957. British zoos. London, Wingate.

Schouteden, H. 1912. Note sur la girafe du Congo. *Rev. Zool. Africaine, Bruxelles* **2**: 134–137.

Schreider, E. 1950. Geographical distribution of the body-weight/body-surface ratio. *Nature* **165**:286.

Sclater, W. L. 1900. *The Fauna of South Africa. Mammals I.* London, R. H. Porter.

Selous, F. C. 1907. *A Hunter's Wanderings in Africa.* London, Macmillan.

Selous, F. C. 1908. *African Nature Notes and Reminiscences.* London, Macmillan.

Selous, F. C. 1911. The voice of the giraffe. *Field* **118**:1289.

Setzer, H. W. 1956. Mammals of the Anglo-Egyptian Sudan. *Proc. U. S. Nat. Mus.* **106,** 3377:571–572.

Shortridge, G. C. 1934. *The Mammals of South West Africa.* Vol. 2. London, Heinemann.

Sidney, J. 1965. The past and present distribution of some African ungulates. *Trans. Zool. Soc. London* **30**,5:139–168.

Sigel, W. L. 1886. Die junge Giraffe des zoologischen Gartens in Hamburg. *Zool. Gart.* **27**:1–7.

Sigel, W. L. 1887. Die junge Giraffe des zoologischen Gartens in Hamburg. *Zool. Gart.* **28**:80–83.

Sikes, S. 1964a. A game survey of the Yankari Reserve of northern Nigeria. *Nigerian Field* **29**:54–82.

Sikes, S. 1964b. The Yankari Game Reserve, northern Nigeria. *African Wild Life* **18**: 313–323.

Sikes, S. 1969. Habitat and cardiovascular disease: observations made on elephants *(Loxodonta africana)* and other free-living animals in East Africa. *Trans. Zool. Soc. London* **32**:1–104.

Simon, N. 1962. *Between the Sunlight and the Thunder.* London, Collins.

Sinclair, A. R. E. 1972. Long term monitoring of mammal populations in the Serengeti: census of non-migratory ungulates, 1971. *East African Wildlife J.* **10**:287–297.

Singer, R., and E. Boné. 1960. Modern giraffes and the fossil giraffids of Africa. *South African Mus.* **45**:375–548.

Sitwell, O. 1954. *The Four Continents.* London, Macmillan.

Skinner, J. D. 1966. An appraisal of the eland *(Taurotragus oryx)* for diversifying and improving animal production in southern Africa. *Afr. Wild Life* **20**:29–40.

Slijper, E. J. 1946. Comparative biologic-anatomical investigations on the vertebral column and spinal musculature of mammals. *Verh. Kon. Neder. Akad. Wetens., Afd. Naturkunde* **42**:1–128.

Slijper, E. J. 1958. Birth in ungulates. *Mammalia* **22**:104–106.

Sloan, J. E. N. 1965. Helminthiasis in ungulates. *Internat. Zoo Yearbook* **5**:24–28.

Smythe, R. H. 1961. *Animal Vision.* London, Herbert Jenkins.

Sonntag, C. F. 1922. The comparative anatomy of the tongue of the Mammalia. *Proc. Zool. Soc. London* 1922:639–657.

Spinage, C. A. 1962a. Rinderpest and faunal distribution patterns. *Afr. Wild Life* **16** :55–60.

Spinage, C. A. 1962b. *Animals of East Africa.* London, Collins.

Spinage, C. A. 1968a. *The Book of the Giraffe.* London, Collins.

Spinage, C. A. 1968b. Horns and other bony structures of the skull of the giraffe, and their functional significance. *East African Wildlife J.* **6**:53–61.

Spinage, C. A. 1968c. Meanders of the giraffe through art and history. *Natur. Hist.* (April) **77**:56–61.

Spinage, C. A. 1970. Giraffid horns. *Nature* **227**:735–736.

Stanley, H. M. 1890. *How I Found Livingstone.* London, Sampson Low, Marston, Searle and Rivington.

Stanton, J. 1955. Is the giraffe mute? *Natur. Hist.* **64**:128–129.

Steinemann, P. 1963. *Cubs, Calves and Kangaroos.* London, Elek Books.

Stephan, S. A. 1925. Forty years' experience with giraffes in captivity. *Parks and Recreation* **9**:61–63.

Stevenson-Hamilton, J. 1912. *Animal Life in Africa.* New York, E. P. Dutton.

Stevenson-Hamilton, J. 1947. *Wild Life in South Africa.* London, Cassell and Co.

Stewart, D. R. M. 1968. Rinderpest among wild animals in Kenya, 1963–1966. *Bull. Epizoot. Dis. Afr.* **16**:139–140.

Stewart, D. R. M., and D. R. P. Zaphiro. 1963. Biomass and density of wild herbivores in different East African habitats. *Mammalia* **27**:483–496.

Stokes, C. S. 1942. *Sanctuary.* Cape Town, Special Committee.

Stott, K. 1950. Highboys. *Natur. Hist.* **59**:164–167.

Stott, K. 1953. The incredible giraffe. In: *Strangest Creatures on Earth.* E. M. Weyer (Ed.). New York, Sheridan House.

Stott, K. 1959. Giraffe intergradation in Kenya. *J. Mammal.* **40**:251.

Street, P. 1956. *The London Zoo.* London, Odhams Press.

Sundevall, C. J. 1842. *Kongl. Vetenskaps-Akad. Handlingar, p. 243.*

Swainson, W. 1835. A Treatise on the Geography and Classification of Animals. London.

Talbot, L. M., W. J. A. Payne, H. P. Ledger, L. D. Verdcourt, and M. H. Talbot. 1965. *The Meat Production Potential of Wild Animals in Africa.* pp. 16–42, Commonwealth Agr. Bureaux. Techn. Comm. Farnham Royal Bucks (England).

Talbot, L. M., and M. H. Talbot. 1961. How much does it weigh? *Wildlife (Nairobi)* **3:** 47–48.

Talbot, L. M., and M. H. Talbot. 1962. Flaxedil and other drugs in field immobilization and translocation of large mammals in East Africa. *J. Mammal.* **43:**76–88.

Talbot, L. M., and M. H. Talbot. 1963. The wildebeest in western Masailand, East Africa. *Wildlife Mono.* **12:**1–88. Washington.

Taylor, C. R. 1968. The minimum water requirements of some East African bovids. *Symp. Zool. Soc. London* **21:**195–206.

Taylor, C. R., and C. P. Lyman. 1967. A comparative study of East African antelope, the eland and the Hereford steer. *Physiol. Zool.* **40:**280–295.

Theiler, G. 1962. *The Ixodoidea Parasites of Vertebrates in Africa South of the Sahara (Ethiopian Region).* Report to Director of Vet. Services, Onderstepoort. Project S9958, 26 mimeo pp.

Thomas, E. M. 1959. *The Harmless People.* New York, Knopf.

Thomas, O. 1894. A giraffe from Somaliland. *Proc. Zool. Soc. London* 1894:135–136.

Thomas, O. 1898. On a new subspecies of giraffe from Nigeria. *Proc. Zool. Soc. London* 1898:39–41.

Thomas, O. 1901. On a five-horned giraffe obtained by Sir Harry Johnston near Mt. Elgon. *Proc. Zool. Soc. London* 1901:474–483.

Thomas, O. 1911. The mammals of the tenth edition of Linnaeus; an attempt to fix the types of the genera and the exact bases and localities of the species. *Proc. Zool. Soc. London 1911:120–158.*

Tjader, R. 1910. *The Big Game of Africa.* New York, D. Appleton.

Trouessart, E. 1908. La nouvelle girafe du Muséum et les différentes variétés de l'espèce. *La Nature (Paris)* **36:**339–342.

Turner, M. 1969. (Partial albino giraffe.) *Africana (Nairobi)* **3,**10:45.

Urbain, A., J. Nouvel, and P. Bullier. 1944. Neóformations cutanées et osseuses de la tête chez les girafes. *Bull. Mus. Nat. Hist. Natur., Ser. 2* **16:**91–95.

Van Citters, R. L., W. S. Kemper, and D. L. Franklin. 1966. Blood pressure responses of wild giraffes studied by radio telemetry. *Science* **152:**384–386.

Van Citters, R. L., W. S. Kemper, and D. L. Franklin. 1968. Blood flow and pressure in the giraffe carotid artery. *Comp. Biochem. Physiol.* **24:**1035–1042.

Van den Berghe, L., and G. Boné. 1944. De la parenté sérologique de l'okapi et de la girafe. *Bull. Classe Sci., 5 Ser.* **30:**239–244.

Van der Schijff, H. P. 1959. Weidingsmoontlikhede en weideingsprobleme in die Nasionale Krugerwildtuin. *Koedoe* **2:**96–127.

Van Niekerk, J. W., and U. de V. Pienaar. 1963. A report on some immobilizing drugs used in the capture of wild animals in the Kruger National Park. *Koedoe* **6:**126–133.

Van Niekerk, J. W., U. de V. Pienaar, and N. Fairall. 1963. A preliminary note on the use of quiloflex (Benzodioxane hydrochloride) in the immobilization of game. *Koedoe* **6:**109–114.

Verschuren, J. 1958a. Le statut actuel des grands ongulés du Congo Belge et du Ruanda-Urundi principalement dans les parcs nationaux du Congo belge. *Mammalia* **22:**406–417.

Verschuren, J. 1958b. Écologie et biologie des grands mammifères (Primates, Carnivores, Ongulés). Bruxelles. *Exploration du Parc National de la Garamba* **9:**167–172.

Vesey-Fitzgerald, D. F. 1960. Grazing succession among East African game animals. *J. Mammal.* **41**:161–172.

Wackernagel, H. 1960. Complete nutrition of zoo animals. *Internat. Zoo Yearbook* **2**: 95–102.

Wakuri, H., and H. Hori. 1970. (On the gall bladder of a giraffe—In Japanese.) *J. Mammal. Soc. Jap.* **5**:41–44.

Walker, J. B. 1974. *The Ixodid Ticks of Kenya.* Commonwealth Instit. Entomology.

Walker, J. B., and B. R. Laurence. 1973. *Margaropus wileyi* sp. nov. (Ixodoidea, Ixodidae), a new species of tick from the reticulated giraffe. *Onderstepoort J. Vet. Res.* **40**:13–21.

Wallace, C., and N. Fairall. 1965. Chromosome analysis in the Kruger National Park with special reference to the chromosomes of the giraffe (*Giraffa camelopardalis giraffa* (Boddaert)). *Koedoe* **8**:97–103.

Wallach, J. D. 1969. Etorphine (M-99), a new analgesic-immobilizing agent, and its antagonists. *Vet. Med. Small Anim. Clin.* **64**:53–55, 57–58.

Walther, F. 1960. "Antilopenhafte" Verhaltensweisen im Paarungszeremoniell des Okapi (*Okapia johnstoni* Sclater, 1901). *Z. Tierpsychol.* **17**:188–210.

Walther, F. 1962. Über ein Spiel bei *Okapia johnstoni. Z. Säugetierk.* **27**:245–251.

Warren, J. V. 1974. The physiology of the giraffe. *Sci. Amer.* (Nov.) **231**(5):96–105.

Watson, R. M., A. D. Graham, and I. S. C. Parker. 1969. A census of the large mammals of Loliondo controlled area. *East African Wildlife J.* **7**:43–59.

Waza National Park. 1962. The Waza National Park in northern Cameroun. *African Wild Life* **16**:293–298.

Webb, C. S. 1954. *The Odyssey of an Animal Collector.* New York, Longmans, Green.

Weidman, F. D. 1918. *Uncinaria* in the liver of a giraffe. *Proc. Pathol. Soc. Philadelphia* (1917) o.s. vol. **38**; n.s. vol. **20**:24.

Weinland, D. F. 1863. Zur Erinnerung an unsere Giraffe. *Zool. Gart.* **4**:204–207.

Weir, J. and E. Davison. 1965. Daily occurrence of African game animals at water holes during dry weather. *Zool. Africana* **1**,2:353–368.

Wells, C. 1931. *In Coldest Africa.* New York, McBride and Co.

Wendt, H. 1956. *Out of Noah's Ark.* London, Weidenfeld and Nicolson.

Western, D. 1971. Giraffe chewing a Grant's gazelle carcass. *East African Wildlife J.* **9**:156–157.

Weyrauch, D. 1974. Über das Vorkommen von Parenchymzellteilen im Sinusoidsystem, in subendothelialen und interstitiellen Raum der Nebennierenrinde der Masaigiraffe (*Giraffa camelopardalis tippelskirchii*). *Anat. Anz.* **135**(3):267–276.

White, A. C. 1948. *Call of the Bushveld.* Bloemfontein, White.

Wilkinson, J. F., and P. de Fremery. 1940. (Letter about hormones in pregnant female giraffe's urine.) *Nature* **146**:491.

Willemse, M. C. A. 1950. The shifting of the molar row with regard to the orbit in *Equus* and *Giraffa. Zool. Medelelingen* **30**:311–326.

Willemse, J. J. 1958. The innervation of the muscles of the trapezius-complex in giraffe, okapi, camel and llama. *Arch. Neerland. Zool.* **12**:532–536.

Williams, J. G. 1967. *A Field Guide to the National Parks of East Africa.* London, Collins.

Williamson, J. R., N. J. Vogler, and C. Kilo. 1971. Regional variations in the width of the basement membrane of muscle capillaries in man and giraffe. *Amer. J. Pathol.* **63**: 359–367.

Williamson, W. M., and J. D. Wallach. 1968. M.99-induced recumbency and analgesia in a giraffe. *J. Amer. Vet. Med. Assoc.* **153**:816–817.

Wilmet, M. 1913. L'okapi. *Acad. Sci. Paris, Comptes Rendus* June 30, 2006–2008.

Wilson, V. J. 1968. Weights of some mammals from eastern Zambia. *Arnoldia (Rhodesia)* **3**,32:1–20.

Wilson, V. J. 1969. The large mammals of the Matopos National Park. *Arnoldia (Rhodesia),* **4**, 13:1–18.

Winton, W. E. de. 1899. On the giraffe of Somaliland *(Giraffa camelopardalis reticulata). Ann. Mag. Natur. Hist., 7th Ser.* **4**:211–212.

Wood, C. E. W. 1894. Giraffe in Somaliland. *Field* **83**:269.

Woodhouse, C. W. 1913. Lions killing giraffe, Rombo Hill, October 1912. *J. East Africa and Uganda Natur. Hist. Soc.* **3**,6:55–56.

Wood-Jones, F. 1949. Evolution of the giraffe. *Nature* **164**,4164:323.

Wright, B. S. 1960. Predation on big game in East Africa. *J. Wildlife Management* **24**: 1–15.

Wrobel, K. H. 1965. Das Nierenbecken der Giraffe. *Z. Säugetierk.* **30**:233–241.

Wyatt, J. R. 1969. "The Feeding Ecology of Giraffe *(Giraffa camelopardalis* Linnaeus) in Nairobi National Park, and the Effect of Browsing on their Main Food Plants." M.Sc. thesis, Univ. of East Africa, Nairobi.

Wyatt, J. R. 1971. Osteophagia in Masai giraffe. *East African Wildlife J.* **9**:157.

Yeoman, G. H., and J. B. Walker. 1967. *The Ixodid Ticks of Tanzania.* London, Commonwealth Instit. Entomology.

Young, E., P. A. Basson, and K. E. Weiss. 1970. Experimental infection of game animals with lumpy skin disease virus (prototype strain Neethling). *Onderstepoort J. Vet. Res.* **37**:79–87.

Zannier-Tanner, E. 1965. Vergleichende Verhaltensuntersuchung über das Hinlegen und Aufstehen bei Huftieren. *Z. Tierpsychol.* **22**:696–723.

Zellmer, G. 1960. Hand-rearing of giraffe at Bristol Zoo. *Internat. Zoo Yearbook* **2**: 90–93.

Ziccardi, F. 1960. The unmaned zebra of Jubaland. *African Wild Life* **14**:7–12.

Zuckerman, G. S., and F. Kiss. 1932. The spinal accessory nerve of the giraffe. *Proc. Zool. Soc. London* 1932, 2:767–770.

Index